# Housing Market Dynamics in Africa

El-hadj M. Bah
Issa Faye • Zekebweliwai F. Geh

# Housing Market Dynamics in Africa

El-hadj M. Bah  
African Development Bank  
Abidjan, Côte d'Ivoire

Issa Faye  
African Development Bank  
Abidjan, Côte d'Ivoire

Zekebweliwai F. Geh  
African Development Bank  
Abidjan, Côte d'Ivoire

Disclaimer: The views expressed in this book are those of the authors only and do not necessarily represent those of the African Development Bank.

ISBN 978-1-349-95120-8     ISBN 978-1-137-59792-2   (eBook)  
https://doi.org/10.1057/978-1-137-59792-2

Library of Congress Control Number: 2017956090

© The Editor(s) (if applicable) and the Author(s) 2018, corrected publication April 2018 This book is an open access publication  
The author(s) has/have asserted their right(s) to be identified as the author(s) of this work in accordance with the Copyright, Designs and Patents Act 1988.  
**Open Access** This book is licensed under the terms of the Creative Commons Attribution 4.0 International License (http://creativecommons.org/licenses/by/4.0/), which permits use, sharing, adaptation, distribution and reproduction in any medium or format, as long as you give appropriate credit to the original author(s) and the source, provide a link to the Creative Commons license and indicate if changes were made.  
The images or other third party material in this book are included in the book's Creative Commons license, unless indicated otherwise in a credit line to the material. If material is not included in the book's Creative Commons license and your intended use is not permitted by statutory regulation or exceeds the permitted use, you will need to obtain permission directly from the copyright holder.  
The use of general descriptive names, registered names, trademarks, service marks, etc. in this publication does not imply, even in the absence of a specific statement, that such names are exempt from the relevant protective laws and regulations and therefore free for general use.  
The publisher, the authors and the editors are safe to assume that the advice and information in this book are believed to be true and accurate at the date of publication. Neither the publisher nor the authors or the editors give a warranty, express or implied, with respect to the material contained herein or for any errors or omissions that may have been made. The publisher remains neutral with regard to jurisdictional claims in published maps and institutional affiliations.

Cover illustration: Jenny Vong

Printed on acid-free paper

This Palgrave Macmillan imprint is published by Springer Nature  
The registered company is Macmillan Publishers Ltd.  
The registered company address is: The Campus, 4 Crinan Street, London, N1 9XW, United Kingdom

The original version of this book was revised: An acknowledgement has been added. An erratum to this book can be found at https://doi.org/10.1057/978-1-137-59792-2_8

# Foreword

Africa's economic growth is being driven by a burgeoning demographic shift and rapid urbanization trends. The continent's population of 1.18 billion is projected to double by 2050, with the region urbanizing faster than any other in the world. This presents both an opportunity and a challenge for the continent. In many urban areas in developed countries, the housing sector has been at the forefront of stimulating economic growth. Increased agglomeration in African cities has the potential to create economies of scale and catalyze the structural transformation of African economies. However, the benefits of urbanization will materialize only if policymakers adopt effective urban policies to address urban infrastructure and severe housing deficits. This has not been the case in the past as lack of urban planning or effective implementation of policies has resulted in the proliferation of slums. Now the opportunity is there to provide effective solutions both affordable and sustainable taking into account the potential.

*Housing Market Dynamics in Africa* provides the most comprehensive analysis on Africa's growing housing crisis due to rapid urbanization, poor urban planning, dysfunctional land markets, rising construction costs, proliferation of informal settlements and underdeveloped financial systems. The authors ably provide a data-rich analysis in their quest to catalogue new insights on the challenges and opportunities to house millions of Africans currently living in dire conditions in slums. This timely manuscript walks the reader through Africa's housing delivery value chain, which increases the ability of stakeholders to understand the fundamentals of the continent's housing market. Cognizant of the continent's rich diversity, this well-researched publication reflects such on-the-ground development realities.

As highlighted in this book, African governments alone cannot solve the continents housing crisis. The solution lies in a well-coordinated and collaborative effort among all stakeholders, including governments, multilateral institutions, nonprofit actors, and the private sector. Given Africa's housing development conundrum, solving the continent's acute affordable housing shortage should focus on four main factors.

First and perhaps most important is that focused political leadership is imperative for solving Africa's housing shortage. The complex land tenure systems in many countries, and the resentment in some quarters from those who have a vested interest in maintaining the status quo, are but a few obstacles governments of all stripes need to grapple with as they tackle our continent's housing problem. Second, inclusive housing finance including affordable mortgage facilities and housing microfinance, and micro-insurance is crucial. Third, sustainable solutions must focus on increasing access to affordable housing for the continent's poor and middle-income families. This implies improving land management practices to increase the supply of well-located affordable land through densification, lowering construction costs through local production of building materials, and increasing the availability of skilled labor. Fourth, industrializing the housing construction sector is necessary for filling the housing deficit of over 50 million units throughout the continent. Promoting technological innovation in the building and construction process, as well as using prefabricated materials, would help harness economies of scales, cut costs, and facilitate the delivery of housing at massive scale. As the authors suggest, taking a value chain approach will improve the productivity of the sector and its ability to deliver affordable housing. Fifth, the often-overlooked rental sector should be given a boost. Doing so will provide an affordable alternative for youths, young families, and families priced out of the property ladder, especially residents of informal settlements.

The authors succinctly provide a blueprint for the role of governments, private sector, nongovernmental organizations, and multilateral institutions in developing the continent's housing market. It is my hope that this book will spur further discussions on the important link between the housing sector, job creation, and economic inclusion. The African Development Bank has a critical role to play in assertively pushing this important source of growth. Doing so will contribute in industrializing Africa and improving the quality of life for the people of Africa.

Former Coordinating Minister for the Economy
and Minister of Finance, Nigeria                     Ngozi Okonjo-Iweala

# Acknowledgments

The authors wish to thank several individuals for their contribution toward the realization of this manuscript. Michael Majale, Paul Rabé, Delphine Sangodeyi, and Olivier Hassler prepared background papers that informed the discussions in this report. Special thanks to Christophe Lalande, Fernanda Lonardoni, and the UN-Habitat colleagues that meticulously reviewed the draft papers and provided comments and suggestions. We are grateful to the African Development Bank (AfDB) and UN-Habitat managements for their support and guidance.

This book draws extensively from the regional housing workshops in Casablanca (Morocco), Addis Ababa (Ethiopia), and Dakar (Senegal), which provided a unique opportunity for over 200 policymakers, private sector actors, practitioners, academics, civil society representatives, and development partners from over 40 countries to discuss on the issues impeding the continent's housing market development, as well as brainstorm on potential policy recommendations, that led to many of the ideas presented here. The authors also gratefully acknowledge the inputs by staff members of the AfDB during the bank-wide seminar and departmental consultation meetings.

External peer reviewers for the study were provided by experts gathered under a technical advisory committee composed of Kecia Rust (Director and founder of the Centre for Affordable Housing Finance in Africa (CAHF)), Britt Gwinner (Head of Housing Finance, IFC),

Alphonse N'guessan (Technical Adviser, Bureau National d'Etudes Techniques et de Développement (BNETD)), Prof. Gerald Jerry Magutu (University of Nairobi), Prof. Benoit Mougoué (University of Yaoundé), Allan Cain (Executive Director, Development Workshop), Dr. Graham Tipple (Housing Expert), Prof. Tumsifu Jonas Nnkya (Director of Housing, Ministry of Lands, Housing and Human Settlements Development, Tanzania), Dr. Hassan Radoine (Director, Ecole Nationale d'Architecture, Morocco), and Prof. Elias Alemayehu (Addis Ababa University). We remain thankful to numerous government officials, researchers, bankers, real estate developers, and members of the civil society who graciously accepted our interview request and diligently responded to our inquiries during our fact-finding missions to Angola, Cameroon, Côte d'Ivoire, Ethiopia, Kenya, and South Africa. On the basis of these interviews and other information received during these missions, we were able to construct a factual picture of the continent's housing market dynamics.

We would like to express our deepest gratitude to Rhoda Bangurah, Ines Hajri, and Eve Adjoua Kra for their administrative support, Tiguéné Nabassaga for data analysis, and Lise Lingo for editorial support. Finally, the book benefited from financial support from the South-South Cooperation Trust Fund hosted by the AfDB.

# Contents

1 The Housing Sector in Africa: Setting the Scene — 1

2 The Political Economy of Housing Development in Africa — 23

3 Housing Finance in Africa — 57

4 Unlocking Land Markets and Infrastructure Provision — 109

5 The Construction Cost Conundrum in Africa — 159

6 Slum Upgrading and Housing Alternatives for the Poor — 215

7 The Way Forward: A Stakeholder Analysis — 255

Erratum to: Housing Market Dynamics in Africa — E1

# List of Figures

| | | |
|---|---|---|
| Fig. 1.1 | Housing quality and child mortality | 12 |
| Fig. 1.2 | Malaria incidence by type of toilet facility | 13 |
| Fig. 1.3 | African bond market size, as a percentage of GDP | 16 |
| Fig. 1.4 | Average mortgage interest rates in selected countries (%) | 17 |
| Fig. 2.1 | Housing Development Pillars | 24 |
| Fig. 2.2 | Africa's divided cities | 29 |
| Fig. 2.3 | Real GDP growth by region (%) | 44 |
| Fig. 2.4 | Household Income Distribution in Africa, 2015 | 47 |
| Fig. 2.5 | National housing affordability in 2015, by region | 49 |
| Fig. 3.1 | Africa's underdeveloped mortgage market | 60 |
| Fig. 3.2 | Size of residential mortgage market (most recent data available) | 61 |
| Fig. 3.3 | Evolution of housing loans in selected francophone African countries, 2005–2013 | 62 |
| Fig. 3.4 | An illustrative REIT structure for affordable housing projects | 96 |
| Fig. 4.1 | Average residential plot size by region | 117 |
| Fig. 4.2 | Continuum of land rights | 124 |
| Fig. 4.3 | The urban tenure continuum | 127 |
| Fig. 4.4 | Land titling priorities for selected housing stakeholders | 145 |
| Fig. 5.1 | Construction investment as a share of total investment, by country | 161 |
| Fig. 5.2 | Housing spending as a share of total household spending, by country (%) | 162 |
| Fig. 5.3 | Formal housing cost structure, Kenya | 163 |

| | | |
|---|---|---|
| Fig. 5.4 | Housing delivery value chain | 167 |
| Fig. 5.5 | Imports of Lime, Cement, and Fabrication Construction Materials (Excluding Glass and Clay), 2000–2014 (*metric tons per year*) | 173 |
| Fig. 5.6 | Cement imports by source for top 20 importers, 2014 (*US$ million*) | 173 |
| Fig. 5.7 | Top 20 steel products importers, 2014 (*US$ million*) | 175 |
| Fig. 5.8 | Association between construction permits and construction costs | 192 |
| Fig. 5.9 | Imports of building materials versus price per square meter, single-story detached house | 194 |
| Fig. 6.1 | Urban development cycle in Sub-Saharan Africa: "Slum Urbanism" | 216 |
| Fig. 6.2 | Components of slum upgrading | 225 |

# List of Tables

| | | |
|---|---|---|
| Table 1.1 | Housing backlog and urbanization in Africa | 6 |
| Table 3.1 | Housing loans in WAEMU, 2013 | 64 |
| Table 3.2 | Key features of housing microfinance loans | 66 |
| Table 3.3 | Selected HMF products available in Africa | 66 |
| Table 3.4 | Monthly income threshold for housing saving plan in Ethiopia, as of November 2014 | 73 |
| Table 3.5 | House prices in Ethiopia under the government-housing program, as of December 2014 | 73 |
| Table 3.6 | Benefits of mortgage liquidity facilities for key stakeholders | 79 |
| Table 3.7 | Rental yields in selected emerging markets | 97 |
| Table 4.1 | Land reforms in selected African countries | 113 |
| Table 4.2 | Registering property: Inefficient land administration systems in Africa | 118 |
| Table 4.3 | Africa's infrastructure deficit | 131 |
| Table 4.4 | Land value capture mechanisms | 139 |
| Table 5.1 | Construction costs in Africa | 165 |
| Table 5.2 | Installed production capacity in various Sub-Saharan African countries, 2015 | 172 |
| Table 6.1 | Variations in the prevalence of slums among African Countries | 218 |

**List of Tables**

| | | |
|---|---|---|
| Table 6.2 | Cost estimates for infrastructure provision in slum upgrading | 230 |
| Table 6.3 | Examples of social housing projects in Africa | 240 |
| Table 7.1 | The role of development finance institutions | 266 |

# 1

# The Housing Sector in Africa: Setting the Scene

## 1.1 Background

The analysis presented in this book comes at a very critical time for Africa. Several countries are embarking on structural transformation processes and undergoing tremendous economic, demographic, and social change while trying to minimize the negative effects of climate change. After more than a decade of strong economic growth, declines in commodity prices and economic weaknesses in developed and emerging markets are putting downward pressures on Africa's economic growth. Major exporters of oil and minerals, which include some of the most populous countries in the continent, are facing severe budget constraints, inherently undermining growth. Whether this economic slowdown is transitory or long lasting remains to be seen. However, this phenomenon will increase the economic challenges faced by many African cities, including high unemployment rates, large housing deficits, and poor urban infrastructure. If African countries are to spur inclusive growth and reduce poverty, the way in which they respond to their demographic and urban challenges will be crucial.

This book is an attempt to respond to the urgent need for a critical assessment of Africa's housing market dynamics, opportunities, and challenges, as well as to the role that the main stakeholders—including governments, private sector, NGOs, civil society, and development finance institutions (DFIs)—can play in designing and implementing policies and programs to improve access to affordable housing products for the poor. It highlights the fact that housing construction is a source of inclusive growth, given the labor-intensive nature of the sector. Moreover, in light of the severe housing deficit, which disproportionally affects low- and middle-income households, addressing the continent's housing crisis has the potential to boost economic growth and mitigate income disparities. The extensive backward and forward linkages of housing construction also mean that growth will be broad based.

Although the housing sector varies across countries and regions, the common reality among urban developing markets has been a surge in the demand for housing, effectively driving up housing prices and pushing quality housing out of reach for the majority of those who are in need, especially poor and middle-income households. Simultaneously, slum populations have continued to grow, as social housing cannot keep up with the demand from those in the bottom half of the income distribution. Affordability issues are preventing households from getting their foot on or moving up the housing ladder. Although all these trends are known, much of the literature on housing has been anecdotal. The unique character of this book is related to its comprehensive collection and analysis of housing sector data gathered from across the continent, in order to better tell Africa's housing sector story. A substantial number of fact-finding visits and consultations have been carried out in all five regions of the continent to get first-hand data, to collect secondary data, and to meet and discuss with key stakeholders involved in the housing value chain.

The analysis presented in this book also aims to come up with good practices and approaches that have proved successful in other emerging markets that may be adaptable to the circumstances encountered in the African housing market. In so doing, the study draws from experiences, programs, and approaches in developed and emerging countries that have shown success in responding to affordable housing challenges. The fact-finding visits also provided a sizeable amount of knowledge about what works and what does not work in different parts of the continent. All in all, the book provides avenues for collaboration, peer learning, and cross-fertilization.

To better frame the discussion in this book, this chapter discusses below a few trends and patterns recently observed in Africa's development that have a bearing on housing market dynamics, with a view to establishing or reemphasizing the importance of the housing market in Africa and why special attention should be devoted to the housing sector.

## 1.2 The Roots of Africa's Housing Crisis: Demography and Urbanization

Africa's population has grown tremendously in the past decades, increasing on average by 2.53 percent annually between 1950 and 2015.[1] This rapid growth is expected to continue in the next four decades. According to the latest projections, Africa's population will grow from 1.18 billion in 2015 to 2.44 billion in 2050. Although Africa's population lives predominantly in rural areas (60 percent), the rate of rural flight to urban areas is alarming. The urbanization rate between 2000 and 2015 averaged 3.5 percent, which is the highest rate in the world. The urban share of Africa's population is expected to surpass 50 percent by 2037.[2] This trend is visible in its fast-growing cities, which are also becoming more densely populated. Africa's four largest cities, with populations greater than 10 million (Cairo, Lagos, Johannesburg, and Kinshasa) account for an average of 20 percent of their countries' populations. The top 20 most populous cities account for an average of 14 percent of their countries' populations. It is important to note that there are large regional variations. Southern Africa and Northern Africa have already reached urban-majority populations, with shares of 62 percent and 52 percent, respectively. At the other end of the spectrum, Eastern and Central Africa are the least urbanized regions, with shares of 26 percent and 44 percent, respectively. Although West Africa's urban share is still below 50 percent, it is growing rapidly and is expected to surpass 50 percent in 2023. By 2050, the urban population in sub-Saharan Africa is expected to grow by almost 800 million.

At the same time that this rapid urbanization growth is taking place, urban planning is lagging behind. In many cities, urban plans are drawn from the colonial era and are based on crude adaptations of planning polices and zoning rules existing in the United Kingdom or France in the 1940s and 1950s. Such plans are applied in a nontransparent and inconsistent manner, often to evict the poorest urban dwellers and to free land for special interests, and do not take into account the demographic, social, and economic changes that have taken place in cities over the past decades. Even new plans are often inspired by international cities in developed countries and fail to take into account local realities.

The consequence of the rapid urbanization process and inadequate urban planning are increased pressure on urban infrastructure and resources, growing housing deficits resulting in more people living in slums, urban sprawl in major agglomerations, and accelerating loss of agricultural lands.

## 1.3 Housing Deficits in Africa: A Challenge for Structural Transformation

The rapid urbanization rates and lack of urban planning have resulted in very large housing deficits, defined as the difference between the number of households and the number of permanent dwellings. The deficit can be estimated for a given period of time (flow), for example, an annual deficit, or it can be at a given date in which case it is sometimes referred to as housing backlog (stock). Without an up-to-date census of dwellings in African countries, accurate information on housing backlogs is not readily available; however, various estimates are cited by government officials and housing professionals for several countries. Following extensive research and interviews with stakeholders in several countries, we assembled the largest existing database of Africa's housing backlog, with estimates for 42 countries (Table 1.1). Although the table uses the latest information available, the estimates in some countries are a few years old. Moreover, annual shortages are often not added to the backlog; therefore, the numbers presented should be viewed as very conservative baseline estimates.

> **Box 1.1 Estimating the Housing Backlog and the Costs to Eliminate It**
>
> The data in Table 1.1 was assembled following extensive literature search and conversation with housing stakeholders. For some countries, the backlog was estimated following housing profiles conducted by UN-Habitat. In other countries, the data is from past housing censuses and household surveys. Housing ministries in most countries have backlog figures they cite often but the source of those figures and the reference dates are often unknown. Therefore, the data should be viewed with caution.
>
> The estimation of the costs to eliminate the backlog was obtained based on a few assumptions. First, we need to know what the construction costs per housing units are. As shown in Table 5.1, construction costs per square meter ($m^2$) vary by housing type. The housing backlog in the continent is mostly for low- and middle-income households. Therefore, following housing typologies for this population segments in countries visited (Angola, Cameroon, Cote d'Ivoire, Ethiopia, Kenya, and South Africa), we assumed that 40 percent of the demand is for single-story detached housing unit of 40 $m^2$, 40 percent for 60 $m^2$ single-story apartments, and 20 percent for 80 $m^2$ two-story apartments. Currently, most people prefer single-family, semi-detached housing, but shortage of land is making this housing option expensive and apartment living is gaining ground and will be the dominant housing typology in the future in most large African cities. The next assumption is about the growth in housing demand. Given that the demand for housing is far greater than the supply, we assumed that demand will grow with the average urbanization rate for Africa (3.5%). These assumptions with the estimate of housing backlog and constructions costs from Table 5.1 were then used to compute the cost of eliminating the housing backlog in Africa. This estimate also needs to be viewed with caution because of the lack of accuracy of the underlying data. However, it provides a conservative estimate on how much it will cost to eliminate Africa's housing backlog.

The current housing backlog in the continent accounts for at least 51 million units, with large variation across countries. Countries such as Tunisia, Botswana, and Mauritius do not have an overall deficit as there are more dwellings than households, but deficits exist for the lowest income categories. On the other end of the spectrum, Nigeria—the most populous country, with an urbanization rate of 4.8 percent since 2000— is estimated to have a deficit of at least 17 million. This figure has been cited since 2010. However, given the annual demand of 700,000 units and annual supply of less than 100,000, the current backlog should be at

Table 1.1 Housing backlog and urbanization in Africa

| Country | Housing backlog[a] | Urbanization rate, 2000–2015[b] | Urban share 2015 (percent) |
|---|---|---|---|
| Algeria | 1,200,000 | 2.76 | 70.7 |
| Angola | 1,900,000 | 5.34 | 44.0 |
| Benin | 50,000 | 3.90 | 44.0 |
| Botswana | 0 | 1.56 | 57.4 |
| Burkina Faso | 100,000 | 6.33 | 29.9 |
| Burundi | 30,000 | 5.75 | 12.1 |
| Cabo Verde | 82,000 | 2.29 | 65.5 |
| Cameroon | 1,200,000 | 3.74 | 54.4 |
| Central African Republic | 1,000,000 | 2.26 | 40.0 |
| Chad | 200,000 | 3.54 | 22.5 |
| Congo | 140,000 | 3.40 | 65.4 |
| Côte d'Ivoire | 600,000 | 3.31 | 54.2 |
| Democratic Republic of the Congo | 3,000,000 | 4.05 | 42.5 |
| Egypt | 3,500,000 | 1.70 | 43.1 |
| Ethiopia | 1,000,000 | 4.55 | 19.5 |
| Gabon | 200,000 | 2.94 | 87.2 |
| Ghana | 1,700,000 | 3.78 | 54.0 |
| Guinea | 140,000 | 3.51 | 37.2 |
| Kenya | 2,000,000 | 4.36 | 25.6 |
| Liberia | 200,000 | 3.72 | 49.7 |
| Libya | 350,000 | 1.52 | 78.6 |
| Madagascar | 2,000,000 | 4.60 | 35.1 |
| Malawi | 100,000 | 3.55 | 16.3 |
| Mali | 400,000 | 5.35 | 39.9 |
| Mauritania | 50,000 | 4.03 | 59.9 |
| Mauritius | 20,000 | -0.11 | 39.7 |
| Morocco | 600,000 | 1.92 | 60.2 |
| Mozambique | 2,000,000 | 3.31 | 32.2 |
| Namibia | 80,000 | 3.98 | 46.7 |
| Niger | 100,000 | 4.72 | 18.7 |
| Nigeria | 17,000,000 | 4.78 | 47.8 |
| Rwanda | 109,000 | 7.00 | 28.8 |
| Senegal | 125,000 | 3.32 | 43.7 |
| Sierra Leone | 166,000 | 3.58 | 39.9 |
| South Africa | 2,300,000 | 2.04 | 64.8 |
| Swaziland | 20,000 | 0.85 | 21.3 |
| Tanzania | 3,000,000 | 5.19 | 31.6 |
| Togo | 250,000 | 3.88 | 40.0 |
| Tunisia | 0 | 1.43 | 66.8 |

(continued)

**Table 1.1** (continued)

| Country | Housing backlog[a] | Urbanization rate, 2000–2015[b] | Urban share 2015 (percent) |
|---|---|---|---|
| Uganda | 1,600,000 | 5.27 | 16.1 |
| Zambia | 1,500,000 | 3.95 | 40.9 |
| Zimbabwe | 1,250,000 | 0.96 | 32.4 |
| Africa | 50,562,000 | 3.5 | 40.4 |

[a] Online sources, expert interviews
[b] United Nations Population Division, World Urbanization Prospects, 2014 revision

least 20 million. Whether 17 or 20 million, reducing the housing backlog in Nigeria requires a fundamental change in housing delivery. Three other countries have backlogs of at least 3 million housing units: the Democratic Republic of Congo (DRC), Egypt, and Tanzania. All three countries have large populations but different urbanization trends. Egypt is the most urbanized, with an urban share of 43.1 percent in 2015. Its urbanization rate for 2000–2015 was 1.7 percent, and that figure is expected to increase slightly to 1.8 percent in the next 15 years. The DRC, with an urban share of 42 percent in 2015, has experienced an urbanization rate of 4.0 percent since 2000. However, this trend is expected to slow down to an average of 3.6 percent in the next 15 years. Combined with an annual housing deficit of 240,000 units (mid-2000s estimate), the housing situation is expected to worsen. Tanzania started with a low urban share but has experienced one of the highest urbanization rates, at 5.2 percent, since 2000. Another group of countries, comprising Kenya, Madagascar, Mozambique, and South Africa, have housing backlogs of at least 2 million units. This figure is increasing annually, given the large supply shortfall and high urbanization rates.

Overall, 17 African countries have housing deficits of more than 1 million units. If nothing is done to dramatically change the situation, poor urban planning and inadequate housing supply will severely constrain Africa's structural transformation. The shortage of housing will lead to an increase in slums, which are associated with a number of social problems: overcrowding, poor sanitation, and high crime rates. Beyond the social consequences, housing shortages have economic consequences as they decrease labor participation in the formal sector and reduce productivity. Indeed, the economic benefits of agglomeration are realized only if people have the opportunity to fully participate in economic activities and firms can benefit from economies of scale.

## 1.4 Housing Construction as an Economic Opportunity and Source of Job Creation

The large housing backlog in Africa can be viewed as both a huge challenge and a tremendous opportunity to expand economic activity and create millions of jobs. The links between housing investments and economic development have been established for many regions at different periods of time (Chen and Zhu 2008; Terzi and Bolen 2007; Doling et al. 2013). In developed countries, the construction sector is viewed as a large contributor to economic activity and job creation. This view has led to various support measures for the housing sector that have created bubbles and are believed to be the main cause of the recent global financial crisis.

Despite losing a large share of employment and output, the construction sector continues to be important in member countries of the Organization for Economic Co-operation and Development (OECD). OECD data show that in the European Union, the sector provided 14.8 million direct jobs and contributed to 5.4 percent of GDP in 2014. In the United Kingdom, the sector employed 2.3 million people and contributed to 6.2 percent of GDP. In the United States, the sector's contribution to GDP has declined from 5.3 percent in 2006 to 3.9 percent in 2013, but it still employed nearly 10 million people in 2014. Data from the US Bureau of Economic Analysis show that residential investment and housing services accounted for 15.3 percent of US GDP in 2014. In the OECD overall, the construction sector employs 36.1 million people and contributes to 5.2 percent of GDP. The large direct effects are not limited to developed countries. In 2014, the sector accounted for 6.3 percent of GDP in Brazil, 7.9 percent in Chile, 6.9 percent in China, and 10.1 percent in Indonesia.

In addition to direct effects, there are large multiplier effects for both jobs and economic activity. Industry associations in various countries have estimated the job and economic multipliers of housing construction. The economic multiplier for construction in Australia is estimated at 2.9, which means that A$1 (US$0.76) spent in construction generates a total output of A$2.9 (US$2.2). For every A$1 million spent, the sector creates 37 jobs overall (9 direct, 7 indirect, and 21 induced) (ABS 2007). A 2009 study commissioned by the Canada Mortgage and Housing Corporation found that the construction of one single-family house generates Can$330,000 (US$254,736) in direct and indirect economic impact and creates 1.9 direct and indirect jobs with large induced effects (Altus Group Consulting 2009). In the United Kingdom, £1 (US$1.29) spent on construction generates £2.8 (US$3.62) in output (L.E.K Consulting 2009). It is estimated that 1.5 jobs are directly created for every new house built, with multipliers of about 2.51, meaning that one construction job leads to 1.51 indirect and induced jobs (Home Builders Federation and Nathaniel Litchfield & Partners 2015). Overall, estimates range between 4 and 4.6 jobs per house built in the United Kingdom (Kleinman 2014). In the United States, the National Association of Home Builders (NAHB) estimates that the construction of an average single-family home creates 2.9 direct and indirect jobs and adds US$280,433 to the economy in the form of wages and profits (Emrath 2014). It also generates US$110,957 in tax revenues to all levels of government. When induced effects are taken into account, the construction of 100 single-family homes in a typical state leads to US$30.4 million in income, US$6.1 million in taxes, and 491 jobs. In addition to the impact of the new housing construction, the annual flow of housing services generates $4.6 million in income, $1.6 million in taxes, and 78 jobs (NAHB 2015).

The large indirect economic effects of housing construction are similar in developing countries. A literature review by Katsura (1984) shows that the economic multiplier for housing investment in Columbia, Korea, Pakistan, India, and Mexico is about 2. The labor intensity of housing varies across countries but is found to be high, with higher employment creation for low-cost housing construction. A 2014 study by the National

Council of Applied Economic Research for India finds that construction and housing services contribute 19.6 percent of GDP, with employment in residential construction accounting for 6.9 percent of total employment. Among all sectors, labor intensity for residential construction is found to be the highest, with an employment to output ratio of 2.34, as compared with 2.11 for agriculture, the second highest ranked sector, and 0.42 on average for all sectors. Overall, the economic effect of residential construction is significantly high. One Indian rupee (US$0.0154) spent in residential construction creates additional income of Rs 1.54 (US$0.0237) in related industries (indirect effects) and Rs 2.84 (US$0.0438) in overall output, considering the ripple effects of spending from income earned from the construction activity. Moreover, an investment of Rs 100,000 (US$1543) in housing generates 2.69 direct and indirect jobs and 4.06 jobs overall, considering induced effects. The spending multiplier effect in the Philippines is much higher, as 1 peso (US$0.0197) spent on housing activities generates 16.61 pesos (US$0.328) in total output (Uy 2006).

Data on the impact of housing construction in Africa are scarce. However, UN-Habitat and ILO (1995) estimate that given the sector's high labor intensity, housing construction has multiplier effects on initial investment of between 2 and 3 in most developing countries. It is important to stress that the magnitude of the multiplier depends on the import content of housing construction. Viruly (2014) shows that every house built in South Africa creates 3.14 direct jobs and 2.48 indirect jobs. In Ethiopia, data from the Ministry of Urban Development, Housing, and Construction show that the government housing program generates about 2.24 direct jobs per housing unit constructed.

It is clear from the above that eliminating the housing deficit in Africa constitutes a huge economic opportunity including contribution to GDP, job creation, and tax revenues. We estimate the minimum cost to eliminate the housing backlog in 10 years at US$2.08 trillion. Although eliminating the housing backlog represents a huge investment, doing so will also generate large economic effects. It will result in a total output of US$5.07 trillion, using a conservative spending multiplier of 2.5. Using an estimate of four jobs overall per house built, eliminating the housing deficit will create 288 million full-time-equivalent jobs in 10 years, or 26 million per year on average. In the bigger picture, these projections show that embarking on massive housing programs in the continent will be important in absorbing the bulge in unemployed youth and will create a solid industrial base.

Theoretically, another important channel through which housing investment affects the economy is the development of housing finance (see Chap. 3). As housing purchases require large investments, strong housing performance is associated with the development of housing finance. The links between housing finance and financial sector development are well established (Wolswijk 1993). The first impact is increased personal savings to cover initial down payments and monthly installments. Housing loans, which in general are secured by collateral, are less risky than other types of loans; therefore, they contribute to the resiliency of the financial sector. They also give financial intermediaries a relationship with consumers for the provision of other financial products (Buckley et al. 2009). In addition, the primary mortgage market is often associated with a secondary market that increases the flow of funds in the financial sector and provides additional securities. This attracts institutional investors such as pension funds and insurance companies and leads to diversification of risks (Dubel 2007).

## 1.5 Housing Deficits in Africa: A Human Right and Social Development Issue

An adequate shelter is one of the basic needs of humans, along with food and clothing. Most of the countries in Africa have one way or the other included access to a decent shelter in their Constitution. The social development aspect of housing is recognized by Goal 11 of the 2030 agenda for sustainable development: "Make cities and human settlements inclusive, safe, resilient, and sustainable." The literature has established clear links between housing conditions and social outcomes, including health, social belonging, education outcomes, social security, and satisfaction with living conditions (Doling et al. 2013; Thomson and Pettigrew 2005).

Using data from the Demographic and Health Surveys and the Mo Ibrahim Foundation, we find a clear positive correlation (0.32) in Africa,

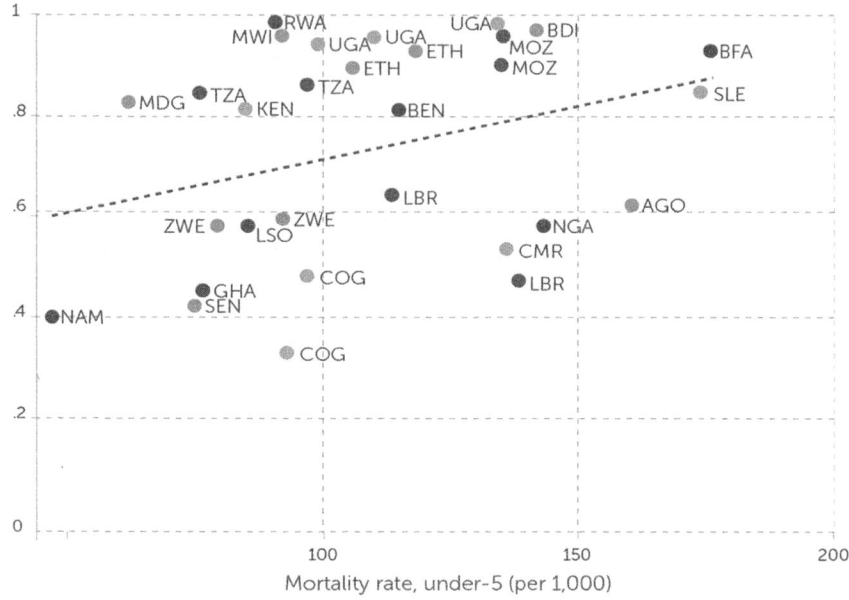

**Fig. 1.1** Housing quality and child mortality (Source: Based on demographic and health survey and Mo Ibrahim Foundation data)

between the percentage of households living in poor-quality housing and the rates of child mortality (Fig. 1.1). Poor housing conditions—sanitation and ventilation—can lead to higher child mortality through higher incidences of malaria, waterborne diseases, or respiratory issues. Data from the Demographic and Health Surveys for eight of the ten African countries with the highest incidence of malaria show a clear link with poor-quality housing (Fig. 1.2).

## 1.6 Africa's Housing Finance: A Challenging Environment

The financing of housing development, like many other development issues faced by African countries, is quite challenging. This is mainly due to the lack of adequate conditions or resources to facilitate such financing. In fact, the housing finance market in Africa is exposed to a number

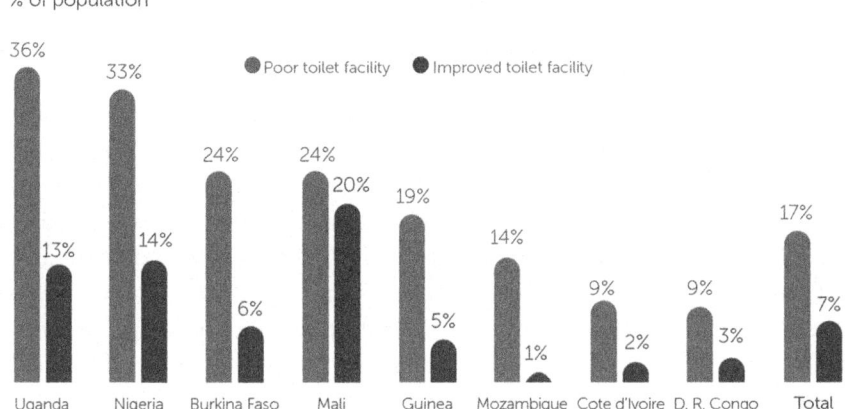

**Fig. 1.2** Malaria incidence by type of toilet facility (Source: Based on demographic and health survey data)

of risks. Diamond and Lea (1995) classify these risks under six categories: (1) credit risk arising from the fact that the borrowers may fail to pay back their loans; (2) liquidity risk stemming from maturity mismatch; (3) cash flow risk—which includes interest rate, prepayment, inflation, and exchange rate risks—which increases uncertainty about cash flows over time as the credit may be worth more or less over time; (4) agency risk or information asymmetry risk (moral hazard or adverse selection type of risks) that a divergence of interests will cause an intermediary to behave in a manner other than expected; (5) systemic risk, or the risk that a crisis at one institution or in a part of the system will affect the whole system; and (6) political risk, which refers to uncertainty about adverse government action that can trigger the other risks. In Africa, these risks are present in varying degrees. The management and mitigation of such risks are key elements that the finance system factors into the design and pricing of housing finance products, which ultimately affect the availability and supply of long-term capital for affordable housing. These risks are reflected by a very challenging environment characterized by weak legal frameworks and enforcement of property rights, by information asymmetry and credit risk, and by low levels of financial intermediation and a lack of long-term funding. These characteristics are examined in the following subsections.

## 1.6.1 Weak Legal Framework and Enforcement of Property Rights

Strong protections for privately held property are a prerequisite for attracting private capital to affordable housing. In most African countries, it is difficult to "crowd in" private investment due to weak legal and regulatory frameworks, which result in high payoffs for rent-seeking behavior. The facts that property rights are not always well defined and not strongly enforced constitute high risks that scare away scarce private investments. Reportedly, in many countries, the ability to use property—including land—as collateral to secure a loan is often constrained by legal uncertainties. Moreover, extensive foreclosure processes and related high costs are additional factors pushing away private investors. This is true in housing finance systems around the continent, where the principal asset at stake is land or a property sitting on that land, under a land tenure regime that is inadequate and does not promote strong property rights (see Chap. 4). This basically prevents the housing finance system from going "down market" and catering to low-income households, with which those risks are higher.

## 1.6.2 Information Asymmetry and Credit Risk

If one is concerned with allocating resources in an optimal fashion, information is key. Information asymmetry, or the lack of data—whether through *moral hazard, adverse selection,* or *non-verifiability*—could prevent society from achieving a first-best allocation of resources because of the additional costs that such asymmetry entails (Laffont and Martimort 2002).[3] These constitute transaction costs, which are challenging and very difficult to manage (Akerlof 1970; Spence 1974; Williamson 1975; Rothschild and Stiglitz 1976). Without adequate incentive mechanisms, investors and financial institutions cannot effectively price and manage risks. As a result, investors may have to incur some additional transaction costs due to the information gap. This risky situation is prevalent in many African countries, where information is imperfect and credit history information on individuals and firms is often not available. As a result, in Africa, as in other emerging markets, commercial banks shy away from lending to households that earn low and informal income.

What is more, this aversion of credit risk by the conventional banking sector does not seem to take into account the fact that the informal sector dominates Africa's economy. In sub-Saharan Africa, according to the African Development Bank (AfDB 2013), 55 percent of the economic output derives from the informal sector and 80 percent of the labor force is employed in it. In South Africa, for instance, the size of the informal economy is estimated to be R 157 billion (US$12.5 billion), according to the Institute of Economic Research on Innovation in South Africa. However, as a reflection of commercial banks' inexperience with putting in place the right incentive mechanisms, including underwriting processes tailored to risky clients, such banks continue to ignore this market segment while keeping lending on a tight leash. This has undoubtedly affected the development of mortgage markets in some African countries. The evidence from selected countries seems to point to an inverse relationship between the size of the informal economy and the depth of mortgage markets. In South Africa and Namibia, the countries with the most developed mortgage markets, the informal sector accounts for 33 percent and 44 percent of economic activities, respectively. Conversely, in countries where the informal economy dominates, such as Mali (82 percent), Côte d'Ivoire (78 percent), Tanzania, and Zambia (76 percent each), the mortgage market is very shallow.

## 1.6.3 Credit Markets and Macroeconomic Volatility

In many African countries, the capital markets remain shallow and are not a significant source of financing for long-term housing investments. They are dominated by bond markets (Fig. 1.3), which are highly driven by treasury bills. This reflects the share of government debt, which sometimes crowds out commercial banks, thus limiting the availability of adequate funding instruments. In addition, the contractual savings industry

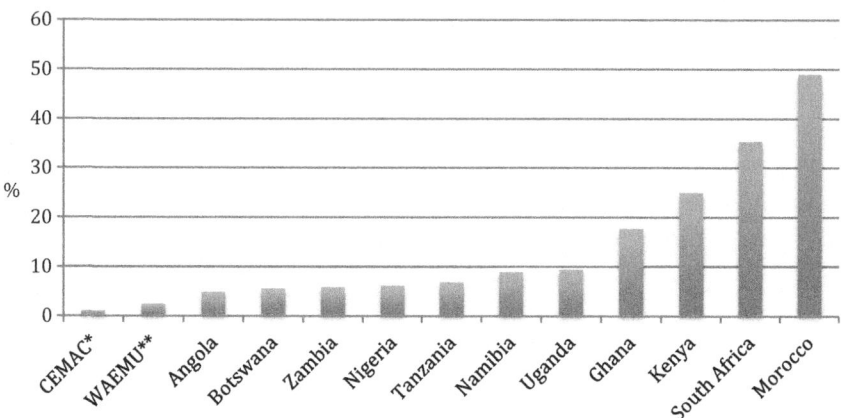

**Fig. 1.3** African bond market size, as a percentage of GDP (Sources: African Market Initiative; *CONSUMAF (cumulative issues 2007–2001); **CREPMEF (market capitalization))

(insurance companies, pension funds, etc.) is not sufficiently developed. As such, this source of long-term institutional capital remains untapped. Furthermore, the few existing financial instruments are inadequate to address the long-term housing financing need.

Consequently, most housing loans in the continent are funded through short-term deposits. This can be done up to a certain extent, depending on the stability of deposits, the existence of deposit guarantee schemes, or the degree of political and social stability. These conditions do not always exist, and in the majority of countries, the lack of long-term financing is a significant roadblock to the development of housing finance. In some countries, such as those that are members of the West Africa Economic and Monetary Union (WAEMU) and the Central African Economic and Monetary Community (CEMAC), for instance, term transformation regulations that link long-term assets to long-term resources further constrain the provision of medium- and long-term credit for housing. This phenomenon translates to short loan tenors, which increases the costs of mortgages, thereby pricing out many potential borrowers as the repayment period is spread over a shorter time period.

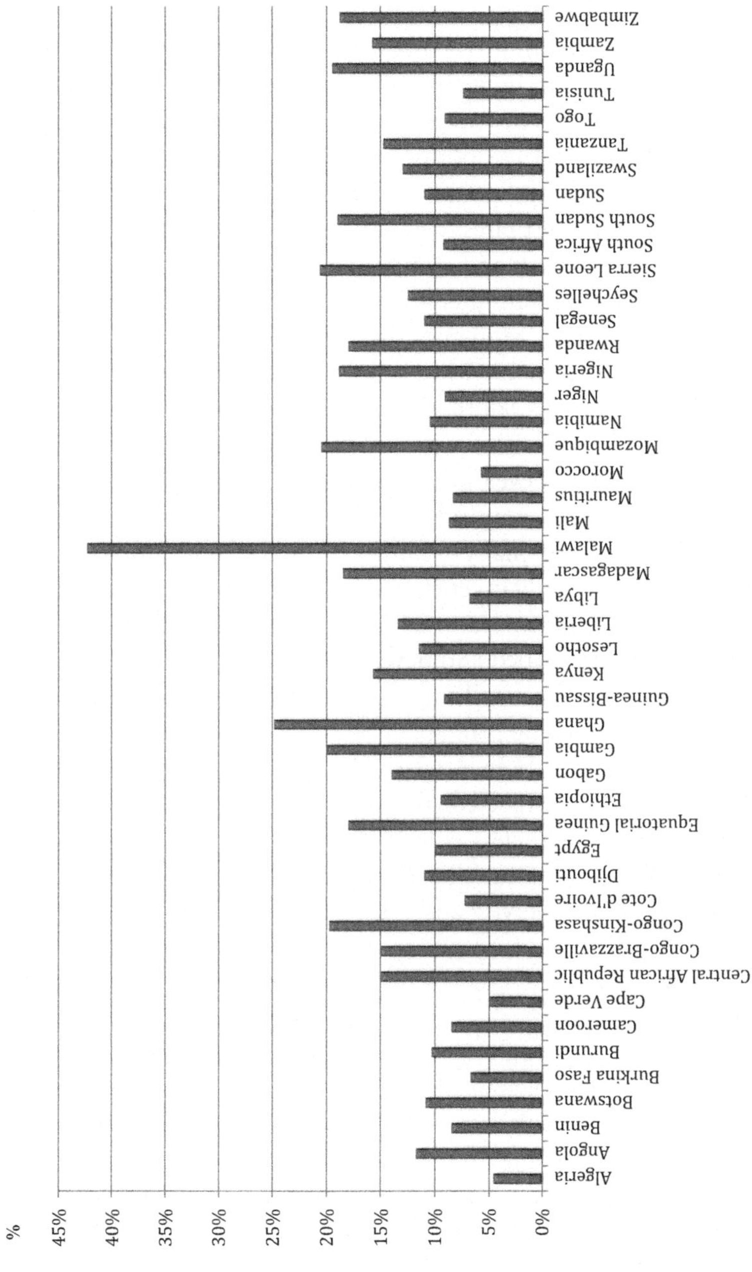

# The Housing Sector in Africa: Setting the Scene

**Fig. 1.4** Average mortgage interest rates in selected countries (%) (Sources: Author's analysis, BCEAO, CAHF, Numbeo)

Besides, in many African countries, the level of financial intermediation is reported to still be low, with the ratio of credit to the economy over GDP barely reaching 18 percent, implying limited involvement of the financial system in financing the economy. This is a reflection of the inadequate financing instruments and the weak finance markets, as explained above. Macroeconomic stability is a key feature for the development of the housing finance system and requires sound management of inflation and interest rates to avoid economic volatility. Unfortunately, both high inflation rates and rising interest rates are widespread in many African countries, which inherently affect housing affordability. Double-digit interest rates on residential mortgages and housing loans are the norm in many countries, with a few exceptions in countries such as Morocco, Tunisia, and South Africa. These high lending rates are often associated with high inflation and currency depreciation, which reflect to some extent the low development of the housing finance system on the continent. Figure 1.4 captures average interest rates for mortgages in selected countries. In many countries, interest rates are variable, with Morocco being the only exception as mortgage interest rates are fixed.

High inflation and interest rates have continuously plagued mortgage lending in both developed and developing economies. Primary mortgage lenders in Kenya, Nigeria, Tanzania, and many other countries identify high interest rates as the principal obstacle to mortgage market development efforts. In the absence of generally accepted interest rate benchmarks, rate changes are based on the internal cost of funds, a nontransparent approach that nonetheless allows for the smoothing out of ample fluctuations—to the point that loans are commonly perceived as being fixed rate (e.g., in WAEMU and CEMAC countries).

## Notes

1. UN Population Division, World Population Prospects, 2015 revision.
2. UN Population Division, World Urbanization Prospects, 2014 revision.
3. For details on the asymmetry of information problem, see Akerlof (1970), Spence (1974), Williamson (1975), Rothschild and Stiglitz (1976), or Laffont and Martimort (2002).

# Bibliography

ABS (Australian Bureau of Statistics). 2007. *The Construction Industry's Linkages with the Economy*. Belconnen, Australian Capital Territory. http://www.abs.gov.au/Ausstats/abs@.nsf/94713ad445ff1425ca25682000192af2/ed6220072793785eca256b360003228f!OpenDocument.

AfDB (African Development Bank). 2013. *Recognizing Africa's Informal Sector*. Abidjan. http://www.afdb.org/en/blogs/afdb-championing-inclusive-growth-across-africa/post/recognizing-africas-informal-sector-11645/.

Akerlof, G. 1970. The Market for 'Lemons': Quality Uncertainty and the Market Mechanism. *Quarterly Journal of Economics* 84: 488–500.

Altus Group Economic Consulting. 2009. *Economic Impacts of Residential Construction*. Report for the Canada Mortgage and Housing Corporation, Ottawa. http://www2.hamilton.ca/NR/rdonlyres/1F84E3C3-009A-46AF-B95E-7F6D3F05D697/0/Jun17Item88iieconomicimpact.pdf.

Ball, Michael. 2015. *The Labor Needs of Extra Housing Output: Can the Housebuilding Industry Cope*, Report for the Home Builders Federation, London. http://www.hbf.co.uk/?eID=dam_frontend_push&docID=20266&filename=CITB_REPORT.pdf.

Buckley, R., L. Chiquier, and M. Lea. 2009. Housing Finance and the Economy. In *Housing Finance Policy in Emerging Markets*, ed. L. Chiquier and M. Lea. Washington, DC: World Bank.

Chen, Jie, and Aiyong Zhu. 2008. *The Relationship Between Housing Investment and Economic Growth in China: A Panel Analysis Using Quarterly Provincial Data*, Uppsala University Working Paper, Sweden. http://www.diva-portal.org/smash/get/diva2:128349/FULLTEXT01.pdf.

Diamond, D., and M. Lea. 1995. *Sustainable Financing for Housing: A Contribution to Habitat II*. Fannie Mae, Office of Housing Research Working Paper, Washington, DC.

Doling, John, Paul Vandenberg, and Jade Tolentino. 2013. *Housing and Housing Finance—A Review of the Links to Economic Development and Poverty Reduction*, ADB Economics Working Paper Series No. 362. Asian Development Bank, Manila. http://www.adb.org/publications/housing-and-housing-finance-review-links-economic-development-and-poverty-reduction.

Dubel, H. 2007. *Does Housing Finance Promote Economic and Social Development in Emerging Markets?* Study commissioned by the International Finance Corporation, Washington, DC. http://www.hofinet.org/documents/doc.aspx?id=260.

Emrath, Paul. 2014. *Impact of Home Building and Remodeling on the U.S. Economy*, Report for the National Association of Home Builders, Washington, DC. https://www.nahb.org/en/research/housing-economics/housings-economic-impact/impact-of-home-building-and-remodeling-on-the-u-s--economy.aspx.

Home Builders Federation and Nathaniel Litchfield & Partners. 2015. *The Economic Footprint of UK House Building*. London. http://www.hbf.co.uk/?eID=dam_frontend_push&docID=24568&filename=Economic_Fotprint_BPF_Report_March_2015_WEB_01.pdf.

Katsura, Harold M. 1984. *Economic Effects of Housing Investment*, Report for USAID Office of Housing and Urban Programs, Washington, DC. http://pdf.usaid.gov/pdf_docs/PNAAU426.pdf.

Kleinman, Mark. 2014. *Measuring Jobs from the Housing Programme*, Appendix 3 of Progress Report. London City Government. https://www.london.gov.uk/moderngov/documents/s38594/Measuring%20Jobs_Appendix%203.pdf.

L.E.K Consulting. 2009. *Construction in the U.K Economy—The Benefits of Investment*, Summary of a report commissioned by the UK Contractors Group, London. http://www.wates.co.uk/sites/all/modules/filemanager/files/PDF/L.E.K._Construction_in_the_UK_Economy.pdf.

Laffont, J.-J., and D. Martimort. 2002. *The Theory of Incentives: The Principal-Agent Model*. Princeton: Princeton University Press.

NAHB (National Association of Home Builders). 2015. *The Economic Impact of Home Building in a Typical State: Income, Jobs, and Taxes Generated*. Washington, DC. https://www.nahb.org/~/media/Sites/NAHB/Economic%20studies/1-REPORT_local_20150318115955.ashx?la=en.

National Council of Applied Economic Research. 2014. *Impact of Investments in the Housing Sector on GDP and Employment in the Indian Economy*. New Delhi. http://mhupa.gov.in/writereaddata/UploadFile/Impact_of_Housing_on_GDP_Employment_FULL_REPORT.pdf.

Rothschild, M., and J. Stiglitz. 1976. Equilibrium in Competitive Insurance Markets. *Quarterly Journal of Economics* 93: 541–562.

Spence, M. 1974. *Market Signaling: Informational Transfer in Hiring and Related Processes*. Cambridge, MA: Harvard University Press.

Terzi, Fatiha, and Fulin Bolen. 2007. *The Impacts of Housing on Economic Development*, Presented at the 14th Annual European Real Estate Society Conference, London, June 27–30.

Thomson, H., and M. Pettigrew. 2005. *Is Housing Improvement a Potential Health Improvement Strategy?* Health Evidence Network Report, World Health Organization Regional Office for Europe, Copenhagen.

UN-Habitat and ILO. 1995. *Shelter Provision and Employment Generation*. United Nations Human Settlements Programme and International Labor Organization, Nairobi and Geneva.

Uy, Willie J. 2006. *Medium-Rise Housing: The Philippines Experience*, Presentation at the 5th Asian Forum, Tokyo, Japan.

Viruly, Francois. 2014. *What Are the Derived Social Benefits of Occupying Affordable Housing in South Africa? A Social Audit Conducted on Residential Units Built by International Housing Solutions*, Study commissioned by International Housing Solutions, Gauteng, South Africa. http://www.ihsinvestments.co.za/wp-content/uploads/2015/07/2012_IHS-Final-Report-1.pdf.

Williamson, O. 1975. *Markets and Hierarchies*. New York: The Free Press.

Wolswijk, Guido. 1993. *Housing: Enabling Markets to Work*. Washington, DC: World Bank.

**Open Access**  This chapter is licensed under the terms of the Creative Commons Attribution 4.0 International License (http://creativecommons.org/licenses/by/4.0/), which permits use, sharing, adaptation, distribution and reproduction in any medium or format, as long as you give appropriate credit to the original author(s) and the source, provide a link to the Creative Commons license and indicate if changes were made.

The images or other third party material in this chapter are included in the chapter's Creative Commons license, unless indicated otherwise in a credit line to the material. If material is not included in the chapter's Creative Commons license and your intended use is not permitted by statutory regulation or exceeds the permitted use, you will need to obtain permission directly from the copyright holder.

# 2

# The Political Economy of Housing Development in Africa

Housing market dynamics in Africa cannot be understood without a comprehensive grasp of the political economy of the housing sector. In fact, it is important to understand the interactions between the main stakeholders that have shaped the housing production and delivery value chain, as well as what is at stake at each of the critical stages throughout the value chain. In so doing, it is crucial to explore the incentive mechanisms facing the main stakeholders in the housing value chain as well as the induced outcomes in terms of the provision of decent and affordable housing for everyone. In this chapter, we examine the incentive mechanisms with regards to the five main pillars that are crucial to building a sound housing sector and delivering decent and affordable housing for all African households (Fig. 2.1). These five pillars are (1) urbanization and infrastructure, (2) land, (3) construction, (4) informal settlements, and (5) housing finance.

© The Author(s) 2018
El-hadj M. Bah et al., *Housing Market Dynamics in Africa*,
https://doi.org/10.1057/978-1-137-59792-2_2

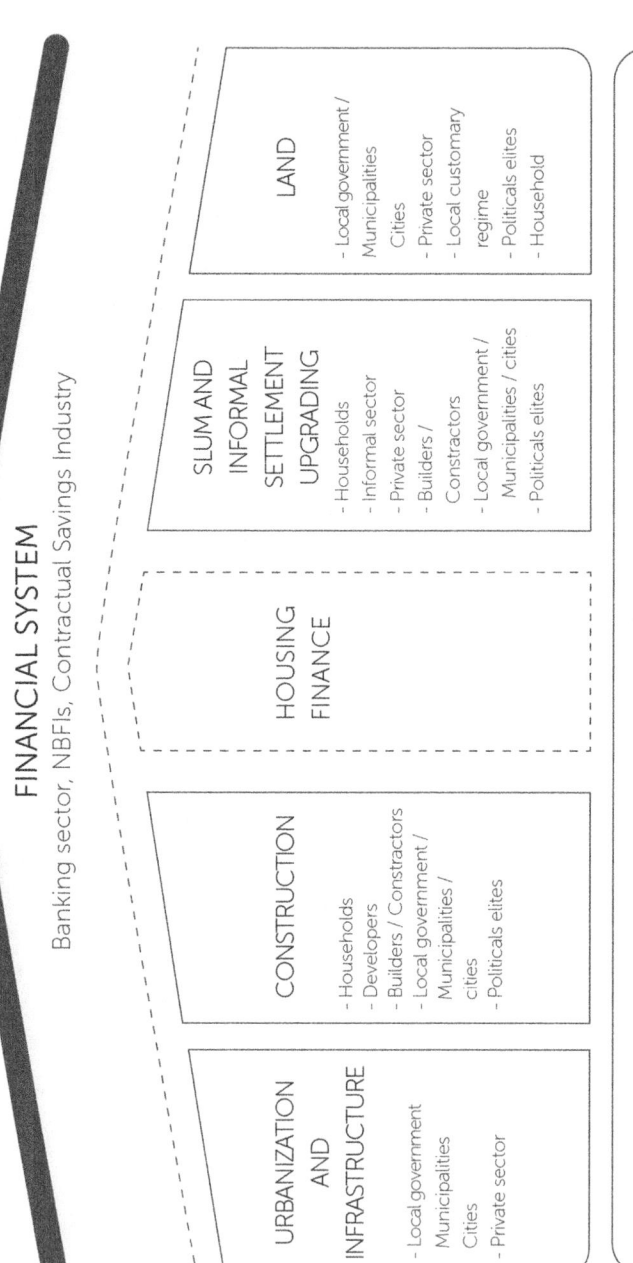

**Fig. 2.1** Housing development pillars (Source: Author)

## 2.1 Lack of Urban Planning and Strategies: Inadequate Housing Policies and Poor Infrastructure Development

The current urbanization dynamics, if not controlled, could be a roadblock to the development of the housing sector. This could prevent the achievement of Sustainable Development Goals (SDGs) 11, which seek to ensure access for all to adequate, safe, and affordable housing and basic services and to upgrade slums, as well as the achievement of the SDGs related to poverty and inequality. The rapid growth and changes in population structure discussed in Chap. 1 are both due to natural population growth and migration flows, resulting from attraction to economic opportunities and from conflicts in some countries. The urban population growth rate has been higher than the rate of economic growth, resulting in an increase in urban poverty and inequality in many countries. For instance, urban poverty rates are high in Eritrea (62 percent), Angola (62.3 percent), the DRC (61.5 percent), Liberia (55 percent), and Madagascar (52 percent). Urban inequality in Africa is the second highest in the world: the Gini index is at 0.54, well above the international alert line of 0.40.[1] Moreover, there is also a gender dimension to urban Africa's slums. According to UN-Habitat, female-headed households account for over 30 percent of slums in urban Africa, compared to 26.8 percent in the developing world. These female-led households usually suffer disproportionately from poverty, have lower average earnings than men, and so on (Buvinić and Gupta 1997; Cohre 2008; EC 2008; UN-Habitat 2003).

Urban dynamics in Africa have led to cities being built back to front—buildings first and services afterward. Many African cities lack basic infrastructure and social services such as quality housing; reliable electricity, water, and sanitation services; and efficient transport systems. Addis Ababa has the least-developed urban infrastructure, with an index of 0.521, followed by Lagos at 0.576. At the other extreme, cities such as Durban are performing better; it has the highest infrastructure development index, at 0.996. Moreover, poor drainage systems make African cities prone to flooding during raining seasons. In 2014, heavy rainfall in

Abidjan clogged drainage systems, damaged roads, and killed 23 people living in the city's slums. There is therefore a need to redesign city sewerage and drainage systems to meet current rising demand. This is essential to improving the livability of Africa's cities.

Limited transportation infrastructure has made many cities heavily congested, lowering the quality of life of urban dwellers and the ease of doing business, thereby reducing productivity. Similarly, low urban electrification rates in Africa, ranging from 4 percent in South Sudan to 100 percent in Mauritius with a continental average of 68 percent is also a serious threat to African firms' productivity and competitiveness (IEA 2015). Moreover, it is well known that the unreliable power supply affects the delivery of quality health care services and people's well-being.

Therefore, it is clear that the current urbanization processes around the continent have generated dysfunctional cities with poor service delivery, notably with respect to decent and affordable housing and infrastructure. Such unsatisfactory outcomes reflect the lack of adequate incentives and mechanisms to enable relevant stakeholders, particularly governments which are responsible for urban planning and strategies, to take appropriate measures to ensure that the urbanization process, in tandem with the housing sector development, can be harnessed for Africa's structural transformation.

The current inadequate incentive system could be characterized as follows:

- *Cost to remedy inadequate urban planning and strategies is very high and potential benefits uncertain.* In fact, in most African countries, the urbanization plans and strategies were conceived following independence but with a strong influence and inheritance from colonial times (see Chaps. 1 and 4). It is also important to note that, as reported by Parnell and Simon (2011), some African countries do not even have an urbanization strategy. Although some countries are now trying to update their urban plans and strategies, the process in most countries has been very slow. This is due to the fact that most cities were built from back to front, which has generated numerous problems or deleterious outcomes that are difficult to reconcile in one policy or strategy and, most importantly, are very costly for governments. Those deleterious outcomes include huge housing deficits, high costs to retrofit infrastructure, inefficient transportation networks and services, urban sprawl, and related threat for food security.

- *Sound housing policies have been neglected.* Rather than leading the way with a clear and coherent vision, governments are acting as followers and implementing only minimal policy changes. Oftentimes, they underestimate the potential of the housing sector, consider it as very risky and challenging, and have neglected the fact that a dynamic housing sector and sound housing policy are needed for successful urbanization planning and strategies. In fact, the tendency to overlook the close interrelationship between urbanization processes and housing market dynamics has generated situations in which housing policies have until recently been ignored in urban planning and strategies on the continent. This has resulted in widespread shortages of affordable housing supply in Africa, especially in cities.
- *Incomplete decentralization processes and weak institutions.* In many African countries, there is a disconnect between urban planning strategies and decentralization processes. Very often, urbanization strategies and plans are not consistent with the decentralization processes, which are a more recent phenomenon for several African countries. In addition, in most countries, the decentralization process has not been designed to enable municipalities to develop their own development strategies and address issues related to urbanization plans and housing developments. Most decentralization processes have also failed to empower local governments to mobilize financial resources independently from central governments. This is a huge impediment to the financing and development of infrastructure in most cities. Moreover, even in some countries where the decentralization process is fairly advanced, the central government still does not really enforce decentralization laws and is reluctant to provide the necessary conditions for local governments and municipalities to thrive. This is in most cases a translation of unnecessary political tensions that often exist between the ruling party and the opposition, which generate frustrations and conflicts. The other challenge facing municipalities and cities as well as central governments is the lack of capacity (institutional and technical) to deliver on their mandates related to urbanization and housing development.

- *Diverging interests, lack of coordination, and conflicts:* In most African countries, different ministries (Finance, Urbanization, Housing, Decentralization, Infrastructure, etc.) as well as different spheres of government are involved in the urbanization and housing development process. Most often, the roles of these institutions are not clearly defined. As a result, these institutions tend to work in silos focusing on the same issues, while using different teams, agencies, resources, and approaches. This, together with the fact that they have unaligned interests and incentives, has generated a lot of frustrations, conflicts, redundancies and lack of coordination. This is the case when the decentralization process is not complete and the appropriate mechanisms for transparency and accountability are lacking, thereby allowing the central government through national fiscal administration to undermine local governments' capacity to play their roles (UN-Habitat 2009). In such an environment, which is plagued by inefficiencies, redundancies, and political tensions, it is difficult to implement any housing development plan or strategy.

Therefore, it appears that the incentive systems related to the urbanization process is not adequate for governments to take necessary policies and actions. It is also not conducive to attract the participation of the private sector, which faces high-perceived and real risks, and is discouraged by high cost of doing business. This has resulted in a worsening of the housing infrastructure financing gap (see Chap. 3) and constitutes a serious disadvantage in a context where housing infrastructure must compete against other types of public infrastructure (energy, roads, information and communication technologies [ICT], etc.) for scarce long-term financing. Moreover, as discussed in Chap. 1, this situation undermines private firms' productivity and their ability to take advantage of the economies of scale associated with large agglomerations.

## 2.2 Poor Land Governance and Administration

Land is one of the most important pillars of the housing value chain and can account for a sizeable share of housing cost (see Chaps. 4 and 5). The cost can even be prohibitive, when one takes into account all the transaction costs and time required to secure land tenure. The political economy of land in Africa is complex, as it involves not only economic, financial, and institutional factors, but also has emotional and cultural underpinnings. In fact, the land issue has been exacerbated by inadequate urban planning and strategy, which has disrupted the urban-rural balance and landscape. Most of the urban expansion in Africa is occurring through rapid, unplanned, and low-density occupation of peri-urban and rural land. This urban sprawl reflects governments' (at both central and local levels) failures to drive the urbanization process and shape urban expansion according to its vision and strategy. This approach has also generated divided cities, resulting from a twin development process—formal and informal settlements developing in parallel as discussed in Chap. 6 (Fig. 2.2).

## 2.2.1 Complex and Unclear Incentive Systems Based on Multiple Land Tenure Regimes

A majority of urban residents are unable to access or afford land or housing in the formal sector and are stuck in "informal" settlements. The twin development process in land occupancy is a consequence of a complex and unclear incentive systems based on multiple land tenure regimes, of

**Fig. 2.2** Africa's divided cities

which the most popular are the formal land right regime and the customary or informal land right regime (see Chap. 4 for more detailed discussions on land issues). Even though in most countries land belongs to the state by law (under constitutional arrangements), in the face of governments' failures and weak capacity, local chiefs and communities have managed to enforce customary land rights that allow them to claim ownership of land. This has exacerbated the difficulties of accessing land in some countries, such as Côte d'Ivoire, where a formal transaction on land in the Abidjan area involving land administration officials cannot be considered as settled as long as the local chiefs and communities have not been compensated through the "land purging" system agreement with the government as discussed in Chap. 4.

According to Kakai (2012), in Benin, the dual land tenure regime also exists, and in practice, the impreciseness of these two types of rights leads to land insecurity, with probably greater recourse to the customary land right, "which makes the land vulnerable and subject to all sorts of misappropriation (pp. 2)." This multiplicity of land tenure regimes and its corollaries in terms of lack of efficiency and security constitute a set of incentives that enable counterproductive and deleterious behaviors such as speculation, corruption, and rent-seeking actions. This to some extent explains the low level of housing development and the difficulties of providing decent and affordable housing, given that the uncertainty and insecurity of land rights makes it difficult to enforce property rights on acquired land for new construction. This system of inadequate incentives, therefore, crowds out private investors from the housing sector, complicates land assembly for new housing projects, and contributes in making housing prices out of reach of the majority, as the formal land supply is constrained.

## 2.2.2 No Incentives for Governments to Harness the Potential Benefits from Land Value Capture

Government failures related to urban planning and strategy as well as land tenure discussed above suggest that the incentive systems in place in most African countries are not sufficient for governments to be cognizant of opportunities related to land value capture, which will eventually enable them to put in place the necessary measures to harness them (see Faye et al. 2013). The limited capacity available in both central and local governments—including weak land administration systems, dysfunctional cadaster systems, outdated equipment to map available land for urban development and housing, out-of-date land registries, and lack of computerized land titling systems—prevents governments from having a good idea and measurement of the amount of land available for different purposes and its value in light of factors such as geography (spatial location, population density), agro-ecology (arable land or not), and economy (distance to central business district, proximity to markets, major infrastructure, and connection to electricity). Even if these information and data exist, it is not comprehensive and not available to government officials. Moreover, these officials do not have the required skills to analyze the available information most of the time. This situation tends to distort government officials' views regarding the positive incentives inherent to harnessing land value capture.

The lack of capacity in governments to assess the fair value of land has been a huge impediment to governments' ability to capture the significant potential for domestic resource mobilization related to land value capture, through land and property taxation, for instance. Moreover, the capacity dearth associated with the above-mentioned failures has undermined governments' efforts to harness the potential related to land value capture. Consequently, governments have until recently neglected the required land reforms, particularly in urban areas. Given the inadequacy of incentives in place, governments are more or less taking a *laissez-faire* approach when it comes to implementing land reforms. This is often guided by the misleading view that they have nothing to lose in the short term, whereas they are in fact missing an opportunity to mobilize a substantial amount of resources that could help build urban infrastructure.

### 2.2.3 The Incentive Mechanisms in Place Facilitate Speculation and Poor Governance

The failure to get the land tenure system right not only constitutes an opportunity cost with respect to the land value capture, but also has generated situations wherein the poor governance mechanisms encourage speculation and wrongdoings (e.g., corruption and money laundering). Across the continent it is common to hear the story of landowners or impostors who have managed to sell the same piece of land to several buyers. Anecdotal evidence paint pictures of people carrying bags full of cash in order to purchase large tracts of land that is worth several hundreds of thousands of US dollars. These wrongdoings are possible only because the incentive system in place does not work and the required capacities, checks and balances, including an appropriate land governance system, are missing.

Among those taking advantage of weak governance systems are bureaucrats and government officials who are aware of the weaknesses and the possibilities of cheating the system. Kakai (2012) demonstrates that in Benin, "in the absence of a rigorous legal framework for land appropriation, land rights implicitly give rise to the monopolizing of land by politico-administrative players and citizens who have a fixed position in the administration and in other spheres of activity." The author also demonstrates that the land governance issue can take several forms through rent-seeking activities and corruption of urban elites, policymakers, and, more generally, players in the political arena. In Kenya, Transparency International found that the likelihood that people visiting the Ministry of Lands might be asked to pay a bribe was 65.7 percent, with 36.3 percent of those who declined to pay a bribe refused service (TI 2005). Molen and Tuladhar (2006) assert that "the [then] Minister of Lands and Settlements of Kenya [stated] that since independence land has been used as a payback system for political supporters, though limited to certain groups of people."

## 2.2.4 Shady Private Investors Are on the Lookout for Speculative and Rent-Seeking Opportunities in Countries Where the Land Governance System Is Weak

While such a system poses serious obstacles to doing business and the effective participation of the private sector—including banks, which consider land and housing development risky—speculators from the private sector in collusion with corrupt bureaucrats or government officials remain highly involved in such activities, to the detriment of the end buyer. Owing to ignorance about the fair value of land, the complicity of some government officials or politicians, and the absence of proper land governance systems, some private companies (both foreign and national) involved in agribusiness, housing development, and construction are acquiring large pieces of land at ridiculously low prices (e.g., reportedly, prices as low as US$0.04/hectare in one African country) for speculative purposes and realizing disproportionate capital gains, to the detriment of local communities (see Faye et al. 2013). Such economic agents would be opposed to land reforms and would associate with corrupt politicians to ensure they continue their illegal activities. Findings by Transparency International show that one in five people globally reported paying a bribe for land services (TI 2013). In Kenya for instance, the average bribe paid for land services is US$100 (TI 2012). It is important to note that according to Transparency International (2011 and 2015), some land developers and speculators specifically target countries with weak governance and collide with local elites to perpetrate corruption and rent-seeking activities to the detriment of the poor in these countries. In the same vein, the 2004 Ndungu Report by Southall (2005) provides a detailed overview about land and graft in Kenya. It talks about the "unbridled plunder" of urban, state, and ministerial lands; of settlement schemes and trust lands; and of forestlands, national parks, game reserves, wetlands, riparian reserves, and protected areas—all facilitated by the extensive complicity of professionals (lawyers, surveyors, land valuers, land registrars, etc.).

## 2.2.5 Poor Governance Incentive Mechanisms Translate into Conflicts, Civil Unrest, Political Instability and Promote Informal Settlements

At the household or individual level, this generates frustrations, discontent, and resentments. It is well known that most Africans have a special attachment to their land. Ownership of land gives a sense of belonging to a certain community and, most of the time, confers respect from other members of the community. As discussed in Chaps. 3 and 4, the majority of potential land buyers are unable to afford a mortgage from the formal banking sector or to get a loan without collateral based on a formal titled and registered land. Therefore, people are denied one of the basic rights granted by their fundamental laws, which is a right to decent shelter. Still the majority in need keep trying to fulfill their aspiration for a decent housing of their own. Yet if they are not cautious, many households or individuals may lose their meager resources and savings while trying to acquire a piece of land from impostors operating within a customary land regime. Besides, such discontent and frustration could also incite violence. In Mali, for instance, weak land delivery systems and poor land governance have contributed to social unrest and political instability, which precipitated the ousting of President Amadou Toumani Touré in 2012 (Durand-Lasserve et al. 2015).

Besides failing to take appropriate measures to resolve frustrations and discontents through a profound overhaul of the land governance systems, politically connected individuals usually leverage their personal relationships and networks to secure protection from some politicians, bureaucrats, or power brokers (such as traditional authorities, politicians, bureaucrats, and the police) to occupy land in the public domain and manage to acquire a degree of tenure security. This also explains the proliferation of informal settlements (see Chap. 6). These individuals could also become rent seekers or informal land brokers and speculate on the basis of fake land titles and still be protected by those to whom they offer bribes, political support, or some sort of obligation in return for protection against legal action. These informal land brokers—called "coxers" in Mali—are defined by Durand-Lasserve et al. (2015: 46) as individuals involved in customary land sales "to whom many buyers and sellers resort to transact land. They have informers in peri-urban villages to identify land that can be transacted and negotiate with village authorities; therefore, they are key players in the rural to urban conversion process. They are also aware of the 'tricks' that can be used to circumvent regular procedures and deal with the administration to make sales effective. They are often found in publicly visible places, including on the side of roads not far from plots that are for sale." Box 2.1 provides an analysis of the role that politics and social connections play in the allocation of public land in Mali.[2]

> **Box 2.1 The Role of Political and Social Connections in the Public Allocation of Land: Evidence from Mali**
>
> A list of households entitled to resettlement following a tenure regularization project that took place in a commune of Bamako District had been set up by the town council. People whose names were on the list had priority access to the land in the resettlement area. A decision allocating a parcel of land for housing was made for the benefit of Mr. X, who had recently been evicted from his plot following a tenure regularization project. His name was on a list with many other beneficiary households. Less than a week later, another decision made by the same commune modified the list of beneficiaries. The land originally allocated to Mr. X was then reallocated to Mr. Y, a high-ranking ministerial officer. Officially, Mr. X had sold the land that had been allocated to him shortly after the allocation. The justification given by the land administration was that Mr. X sold his land either because he did not need it anymore or because he was unable to pay the administrative costs and fees associated with the allocation of the plot. Many other beneficiaries of the same resettlement scheme also "resold" their plots right after allocation. Mr. X. may have been duped out of his plot, but he may also have been part of a concerted plan.
> Source: Durand-Lasserve et al. (2015: 53).

## 2.3 A Construction Sector Plagued by Rent-Seeking Behaviors, Compliance Issues, Resistance to Technology, and Lack of Capacity

The construction sector is one of the pillars of the housing sector that is worth exploring if one is concerned with the political economy of the housing sector and how it affects the market's ability to deliver decent and affordable housing units. It is noticeable in this sector that the main stakeholder incentives are inadequate and most of the time misaligned.

### 2.3.1 Rent-Seeking Behaviors and Lack of Compliance to Norms and Standards

It is noted that one of the main aspirations of individuals and households in African societies is to become homeowners. This provides a sense of accomplishment for most households and reflects their attachment to their native land. However, construction costs are very high on the continent, owing to several factors that go beyond the control of households (see Chap. 5).[3] Consequently, a dominant feature of the housing market is the adoption by households of self-built housing, whereby they build their houses incrementally, using resources at their disposal, from land acquisition to finishing. The danger in this process is that some households may be tempted to cut corners to reduce costs and not comply with the building code standards, which they may consider as onerous and not conducive to affordable housing construction.

Very often, the lack of adherence to regulations and norms stipulated in the country's building codes is prevalent in many countries across the continent. However, this is more acute in countries with poor governance systems where some individuals can get construction permits without following normal procedures or, worse still, build houses without construction permits with the complicity of inspection agents or leveraging their relationships with decision-makers, politicians, and bureaucrats who will protect them from penalties for violation. Bribery or relationships with political elites and high-ranking public officials are used to ensure that laws are not enforced. This has resulted in the construction of poor-quality housing and frequent accidents such as collapsing of two- and three-story buildings and other catastrophic events related to ill-designed construction that did not meet building codes.

## 2.3.2 Resistance to Technology Change

Another element worth mentioning under the political economy analysis is that households have a certain perception of quality housing and their preferences. More often, individuals associate quality housing to the regular "brick-and-mortar" housing structure. Most households are not open to adopting alternative building techniques and materials which in general are not considered as good as the traditional building techniques. There is a general belief that the "brick-and-mortar" type of housing is a must-have and that decent housing should not be constructed using alternative building techniques and materials including prefabricated material, timber, and so on. Although these alternative building materials and techniques could go a long way toward cutting costs, it remains that the incentive mechanisms in place—including cost and taxes related to acquiring these materials, as well as their reliability and quality of provision—are not adequate to promote the uptake of such techniques and materials (see Chap. 5).

### 2.3.3 In the Absence of a Strong Political Will, Countervailing Incentives Inhibits Governments' Actions

The implementation of the required policy efforts with regards to issues discussed above is not as straightforward as it seems, given that most governments face countervailing incentives. On one hand, most governments are facing huge housing deficits, which is a time bomb waiting to explode. There is a need to provide housing at scale and in a sustainable manner. On the other hand, it is not clear that a radical reform of the construction sector will be beneficial from a government's standpoint, given the competing and entrenched interests of various stakeholders. Moreover, it may appear quite risky for governments to implement widespread reforms in the current construction sector, which has so far played a vital role in the strong economic growth achieved in the continent over the last decade. Furthermore, it is important to note that such efforts will have significant economic, policy, and legislative implications. It may entail a drastic shift in industrial and sectorial policies so as to facilitate the move from imported to locally produced building materials. This could have some economic and social consequences, including restructuring of the construction industry, layoff of some workers, and social tensions (workers on strike) that a populist government may not want to encounter. This may also involve the need to go through tedious and often lengthy legislative processes to amend building codes and adjust the legal and regulatory frameworks in the sector so as to facilitate the uptake and use of alternative local building materials.

Such legislative processes can prove to be very cumbersome with several impediments coming from pressure groups or lobbyists defending some vested interests in the construction industry. The process of amending building codes could be a case in point. As discussed in Chap. 5, building codes in a number of African countries were inherited from colonial times, often reflecting the building codes of France and Great

Britain in the 1960s regardless of local realities and affordability. As such, these codes have been serving the interests of some foreign construction companies and their representatives in the construction industry. Amending them will require going through a long and tedious process with little certainty about the outcome. In fact, it has been noticed that in some countries, lobbyists and pressure groups have representatives in parliaments which are eager to advance their interests. Moreover, some members of parliaments also have vested interests in the construction sector that would lead them to block any amendments of existing building codes.

Overall, in the absence of a strong political will, the countervailing incentives faced by governments are not conducive to implementing measures geared toward bringing down costs, at least in the short run.

### 2.3.4 Lack of Capacity for Developers and Weak Competition

When it comes to builders and developers, they find themselves between a rock and a hard place. On the one hand, they are called upon to produce at scale in order to fill the immense housing deficit. On the other hand, the predominance of self-built housing across the continent suggests that there may not be a sizeable market for developers. Most developers are unable to adequately respond to housing development challenges due mainly to the lack of capacity in terms of equity, human resources, and equipment to produce cost-efficient housing units at scale. African developers that can deliver sizeable housing projects of at least 10,000 housing units are practically nonexistent. As a result, developers are confined to delivering relatively small housing projects and are not able to harness economies of scale. Their limitations in terms of resources also prevent them from investing in innovative techniques and materials in order to cut costs. This has serious implications in terms of competition, which is weak, and in terms of affordability as the houses delivered are not cost efficient. This is the case in several African countries such as DRC and Zambia.

Another point to add to this situation is that developers, given their limited capacity and the lack of appropriate incentives, do not take much risk. Although off-plan sales are a means for developers to raise financing required for their projects, they limit affordability and expose the buyer to high risks if the project does not materialize. This explains to some extent why most of the large housing construction projects on the continent are handled by foreign construction companies such as the Chinese CITIC, and so on. Until fairly recently, the construction industry in Africa was characterized by the dominance of oligopolistic or monopolistic conglomerates, especially in the cement industry. This has been the case in Ethiopia, Sénégal, and other countries, which has contributed in maintaining the *status quo*, while undermining affordability. Recent privatization and the liberalization of the cement market in different countries have triggered competition with private companies entering these markets. Dangote Cement, with operations in 10 Africa countries, illustrates this point.

## 2.4 Lack of Adequate Incentive Mechanisms to Handle Slum Proliferation

Slum proliferation is a salient feature of Africa's dysfunctional urbanization process (see Chap. 1). This has brought about the twin development process referred to earlier—formal and informal settlements developing in parallel and generating the proliferation of slums in Africa (see Chap. 6) with their related socioeconomic and environmental problems (e.g., high rates of crime, public health issues, unemployment, and environmental degradation). With an average annual increase in the slum and squatter population of about 4.5 percent, sub-Saharan Africa has the highest rate in the world. Over 200 million Africans live in slums, and cities accommodate 72 percent of all slum dwellers in the continent. More specifically, in the Central African Republic, 82 percent of households in the capital and large cities live in slums, whereas in Chad virtually all households live in slums, in both large and small cities. It is noted that the bulk of the countries in sub-Saharan Africa display significant levels of slum prevalence in capital and large cities as well as small cities (30 percent and 41 percent, respectively, in Ghana) and (23 percent and 47 percent, respectively, in South Africa). The number of countries experiencing low or moderate concentrations of slums in capitals and large cities, as well as in small cities and towns, is limited (e.g., Zimbabwe [7 percent and 4 percent, respectively] and Morocco [12 percent and 14 percent, respectively]).

### 2.4.1 Slums as a Source of Political and Economic Benefits

The persistence and proliferation of slums, despite their large negative socioeconomic impacts, is related to the inadequacy of the incentive systems in place. Underinvestment and ineffective legislative and regulatory control in urban areas continue to foster favorable and profitable conditions for political and economic opportunists in slum areas. For example, it is noted that squatters on public land can in some countries acquire a degree of tenure security by offering money or political support to local decision-makers and power brokers (such as traditional authorities, politicians, bureaucrats, and the police) in return for protection against eviction. According to UN-Habitat, in informal settlements with inadequate water infrastructure, informal service providers make inordinate profits selling water at inflated prices. Deficiencies in public transport systems have also given rise to a multibillion-dollar informal transport industry, which, in many African cities, is controlled by politicians and senior police officers. Hence, poor urban management, resource deficiencies, underinvestment in infrastructure, and the absence of effective urban governance all combine to perpetuate informality and slum development, and enable powerful and influential groups to benefit from the status quo (UN-Habitat 2014).

In fact, some of the key stakeholders involved (e.g., slum dwellers, public authorities, private entrepreneurs, and even NGOs) have a vested interest in keeping the *status quo*. This echoes the idea according to which "urban underdevelopment—including slum proliferation—has proven politically and economically beneficial to a wide range of actors in African cities" (Fox 2013: 3).

Given the configuration of the housing sector, the high level of housing deficits, and the affordability issues observed in African cities (see Chap. 5), slums or informal settlements are the only reasonable option for the poorest of the poor. They pay an unduly high price for very low-quality rental housing. According to UN-Habitat (2003), "The majority of slum dwellers earn their living from informal sector activities located either within or outside slum areas, and many informal entrepreneurs [operating from slums] have clienteles extending to the rest of the city." Most slum dwellers are people struggling to make a living, within the context of extensive urban poverty and formal unemployment. The fact that their working places are within the slum or well connected to the slum makes it difficult for them to move out of the slum. This explains why it is very common that slum dwellers displaced to some remote areas without economic opportunities tend to come back to their original settlements (see Chap. 6).

It is noted that the inefficiency of the governance and spatial planning systems as well as the infrastructure inequalities inherited from colonial administrations created slums together with opportunities for postcolonial political and economic entrepreneurs to develop power and patronage networks, and take advantage of rent-seeking opportunities (Fox 2013). This situation exposes slum dwellers to rent seekers including the landlords or economic entrepreneurs who own the land and are renting it out to slum dwellers. During our field visits in different countries,[4] it was evident in our discussions that the owners of land where Kibera, the largest slum in Africa, is sitting include medical doctors, some civil servants, political elites, and some other wealthy individuals who have their housing elsewhere in town and use that piece of land as a source of additional revenues.

Besides, it is important to note that the political and economic elite taking advantage of those at the bottom of the pyramid do not have incentives to stop slum development, knowing that there is little chance that they will get back their land and put it to productive use. They are aware of the fact that for political reasons, the unpopularity and costs related to taking displacement measures, and the resistance of slum dwellers to moving out of slums, it will be very difficult and costly in terms of timing and procedures to get back that piece of land and put it to a use that will generate the same kind of revenues. The trade-off for those landlords is therefore straightforward: they would keep the slum dwellers as tenants and pocket their rents, rather than embark on tedious and lengthy procedures of eviction that will only generate costs to bear without any assurance that they will reap some benefits in the near term.

In general, public authorities from the central government as well as many city authorities turn a blind eye to urban sprawl and to the proliferation and expansion of slums and informal settlements for pragmatic reasons and self-interest—slums are a source of low-cost labor for businesses and middle-class households. The vast majority of semiskilled and unskilled workers in the construction, manufacturing, and service sectors live in slums, as do most of the domestic workers in middle-class households. Moreover, public authorities from both central and local governments have a vested interest in slum proliferation. They have failed to put in place the required urbanization strategies, so they have no credible means to guide their urban investments and mobilize the resources required for proper urban development, free of slums. In addition, most African governments do not have the fiscal space or the capacity to embark on a vast eradication of slums, due to the heavy costs involved (e.g., compensation packages and relocation costs) in the provision of infrastructure and adequate housing. They also do not have the institutions and capacity required to successfully roll out vast relocation programs.

Political elites are also among the slums' rent seekers. In addition to being a source of cheap labor, slums and informal settlements are seen as a source of easily "bought" urban votes by both incumbent governments and opposition movements in many African countries. This is partly due to the fact that democratization has not advanced enough to provide mechanisms geared toward ensuring transparency, accountability, and responsiveness of political leaders with respect to their constituencies. These politicians enjoy and maintain a political clientele composed of a small network of people, including representatives of some communities or religious groups. They often promise slum dwellers security of tenure and/or better living conditions, through upgrading interventions, in return for their vote. However, these electoral promises are rarely realized.

Even nongovernmental organizations (NGOs) do not always have the adequate incentives geared toward eradicating slums. They most often plead for slum upgrading and rehabilitation, which in turn contribute to the proliferation of slums. This is related to the very fact that several efforts and programs geared toward moving slum dwellers out of slums and informal settlements have not been quite successful. As discussed above, the slum dwellers usually sell or rent out their new houses in relocated neighborhoods and then move back to slums. Those who decide to stay in their new houses either do not find in the new neighborhood similar work opportunities or are not well connected to city business districts or the wealthy areas where they make their living, posing the risk that they will frequently be late for work and the possibility of losing their jobs. Both outcomes could push these displaced slum dwellers, who are already at the bottom of the pyramid, into extreme poverty. This is simply not an acceptable outcome for most NGOs working in the slums, which thus prefer to promote slum upgrading rather than displacements and eradication of slums. However, due to NGOs' limited resources, their efforts do not always generate substantial outcomes at scale and they have difficulties preventing slums from growing.

## 2.5 Macroeconomic Environment and Affordability Issues

In order to have a comprehensive view of the political economy of the housing sector, it is necessary that the analysis covers the macroeconomic context in which African countries are operating so as to understand how the economic dynamics and constraints are shaping incentives and opportunities in the sector. It is also of utmost importance to discuss affordability issues that are vital for any housing finance policy geared toward catering for poor and low-income households.

### 2.5.1 A Conducive Macroeconomic Environment, But Almost No Sound Housing Finance Policies

Over the last decade, Africa has been one of the fastest-growing regions in the world (Fig. 2.3). The continent's economic outlook remains strong, with the economy projected to rebound in 2017 following the slowdown in 2016. In 2016, East Africa and North Africa maintained their lead in

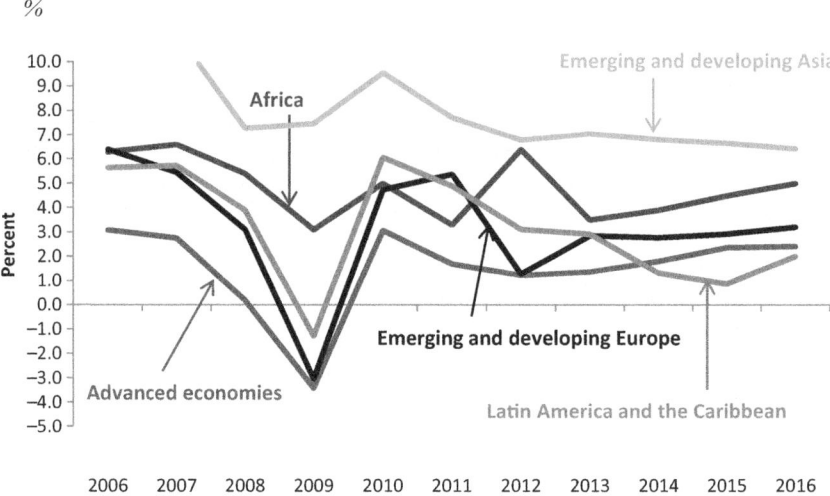

**Fig. 2.3** Real GDP growth by region (%) (Sources: AfDB, IMF)

regional growth with a real gross domestic product (GDP) growth of 5.3 percent and 3 percent, respectively. Increasing infrastructure investments, structural reforms in a number of countries, and sustained domestic consumption continue to drive the continent's growth. This strong growth will continue to reduce poverty in Africa and progressively enlarge the vast swath of middle-class households which have the ability to finance housing investments.

It is important to underscore the fact that the successes achieved by African governments over the last decade in terms of macroeconomic stability and in sustaining high growth performance have laid foundations that are conducive to developing sound housing development policies in accordance with their aspirations of economic structural transformation. That macroeconomic stability and performance is an opportunity to leverage, as it provides the right incentives for investors and the development community to get more involved in the housing sector.

Most importantly, until very recently, several African governments have neither elaborated their financial sector development policies and strategies in general nor developed financial inclusion policies to ensure that the financial systems are designed to contribute to an inclusive model of growth. As a result, given the lack of explicit policy measures and incentives for financial institutions to support the financial inclusion agenda of governments, some financial institutions, particularly foreign-owned institutions, have made little progress in adapting their processes and risk management frameworks as well as in terms of innovation to contribute to that objective.

Similarly, most African governments do not have detailed and explicit policies and strategies to support inclusion in housing finance. In the majority of countries, there are no specific measures or incentives for financial institutions to get more involved in housing finance and adapt their underwriting procedures, for instance, to cater for people with low or irregular income. Financial institutions—particularly foreign banks, whose domination has been stronger, as has their share in the financial system assets in most African countries (Beck et al. 2011)—perceive the housing sector as risky, and, by and large, they consider that there are no incentives to attract them to this segment of the finance market. As a consequence, these banks remain in their comfort zones and niches (which consist mostly of foreign and multinational companies and some large local businesses) and concentrate their portfolios on governments' papers and international assets. These patterns can also be observed among African domestic banks (Beck et al. 2011).

## 2.5.2 A Segmented Market and the Housing Affordability Challenge

The major challenge facing households is the issue of housing affordability. Defining affordable housing is a difficult task, given the large and heterogeneous market dynamics within and across African countries. However, a commonly accepted definition for affordable housing in developed countries such as the United States is that the cost of housing should not exceed 30 percent of a household's gross income. The following discussion further explores the concept of affordable housing in Africa and some techniques used to measure affordability.

Two significant components of housing affordability are household income and housing costs. Using data from EIU Canback, an analysis of Africa's 233 million households shows that 35 percent of households, or 81.5 million families, earned less than US$1500 in 2015, while just 24 percent of households earned over US$5500. As Africa's economic growth accelerates, we project the number of households earning over US$5500 per year to reach 90.5 million households in 2020 equivalent to 31 percent of all households. During the same period, we expect the number of households earning less than US$1500 per year to decrease by 10 percent. These projections include income earned in the informal economy, which employs the majority of African families.

The housing affordability rule of thumb for some lenders is that home prices should not exceed 2.5 times a household's annual income. Using this approach, a substantial number of African families cannot afford an entry-level home supplied by the market. This translates to 81.5 million African households that can only afford a house that costs US$3000 or less. Another 39.1 million households can afford homes that cost between US$3000 and US$5000, while only a meager 15.7 million households—6.7 percent of all African households—can afford homes supplied by the market, at an average starting price of US$28,000.

Across Africa, households in the lowest income quartile are severely overburdened by high housing costs (see Chap. 5). In 2014, Kenyan mortgage lenders cited the high cost of housing as the main obstacle to mortgage market development. The combination of high property costs and low household income suggests that a majority of African households cannot afford to purchase an entry-level home supplied by the market (see Chap. 5). When we include the affordability-killing effect of high interest rates and the transaction costs of obtaining mortgage loans, housing becomes virtually out of reach for low-income African households. Overall, it comes out fairly clearly that the housing finance market is segmented into three major groups: (1) the top-tier and higher-middle-income group, which can cater for itself; (2) the low-middle-income group, which still faces challenges to access decent housing (e.g., the "gap market" in South Africa); and (3) the low- and irregular-income group, which is excluded from the system and contains the majority of slum dwellers (Fig. 2.4).

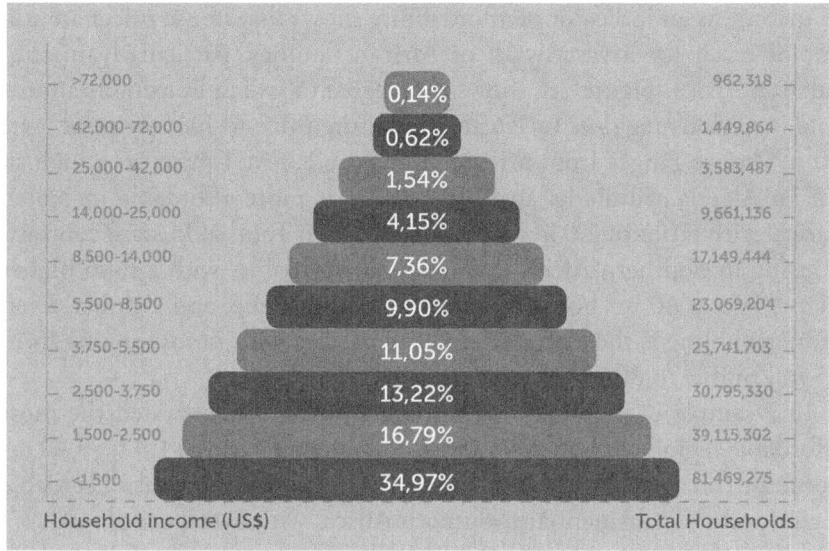

**Fig. 2.4** Household Income Distribution in Africa, 2015 (Source: Author's analysis using Canback Global Income Distribution Database)

The maximum house value that the various income segments in Africa can afford varies widely across regions. Although there are many underwriting standards and qualifying ratios to measure housing affordability, we use a conservative approach in estimating the home prices that should comfortably fit the household incomes of most Africans. Given the low-income levels of many families, we assume a housing expense ratio of 0.28 for our analysis, meaning that mortgage payments should not exceed 28 percent of gross annual income. We use a debt-to-income ratio of 36 percent of household income. This means that the total debt payment of households should not exceed 36 percent of their gross income. Finally, to arrive at the affordable home price, we assume a 15-year mortgage at current interest rates (see Fig. 1.4 in Chap. 1). Note that our working assumption is that the home values do not include a down payment, property tax, home insurance, or any other fees that lenders may charge.

The house-price-to-income ratio is another common metric used to assess housing affordability. The ratio is calculated by dividing the house price by the median income of a country.[5] Using the ratio of house price to income as an indicator of affordability shows that house prices are still out of reach for a vast swath of African families, particularly in sub-Saharan Africa. Figure 2.5 shows the degree to which housing is affordable in various regions. In North Africa, the price-to-income ratio for a 40 m$^2$ house ranges from a regional low of 1.0 in Tunisia to a high of 2.7 in Algeria. Similarly, an 80 m$^2$ home is more affordable in North Africa, with ratios of 2.0 in Morocco and 2.4 in Tunisia. In stark contrast, housing in Southern Africa is severely unaffordable, with a ratio higher than 15 for a 40 m$^2$ house in Malawi, Mozambique, and Zambia. Even more troubling is the price for an 80 m$^2$ home, with ratios ranging from 35 in Zambia to 80 in Mozambique.

In a sample of 27 African countries, North Africa is rated the most affordable region with an average price-to-income ratio of 1.9 for a 40 m$^2$ home and an average ratio of 3.3 for an 80 m$^2$ house. The least-affordable regions on the continent are Southern Africa, with average ratios of 17.7 and 55.7 for a 40 m$^2$ and an 80 m$^2$ home, respectively, followed by Central Africa (11.3 and 24.5), East Africa (9.3 and 22.3), and West Africa (8.2 and 21.6).

## 2.6 Conclusion

This chapter describes the main incentive mechanisms that are offered to the main stakeholders throughout the housing delivery value chain. According to the discussions above, inadequate incentive mechanisms are part of the root causes of the deleterious outcomes generated in terms of housing development. However, this situation also provides an opportunity for the main stakeholders to take necessary actions to reverse the patterns. This would require strong commitment of the major stakeholders and actions to be taken on several fronts. This section will discuss briefly some of the recommendations geared toward getting the incentive mechanisms right. More substantive and detailed discussions on the critical issues are provided in each of the subsequent chapters of this book.

As per urban planning and strategies, a well-planned urbanization strategy with sound housing policies would require putting in place adequate incentives to enable the main stakeholders such as governments

# The Political Economy of Housing Development in Africa 49

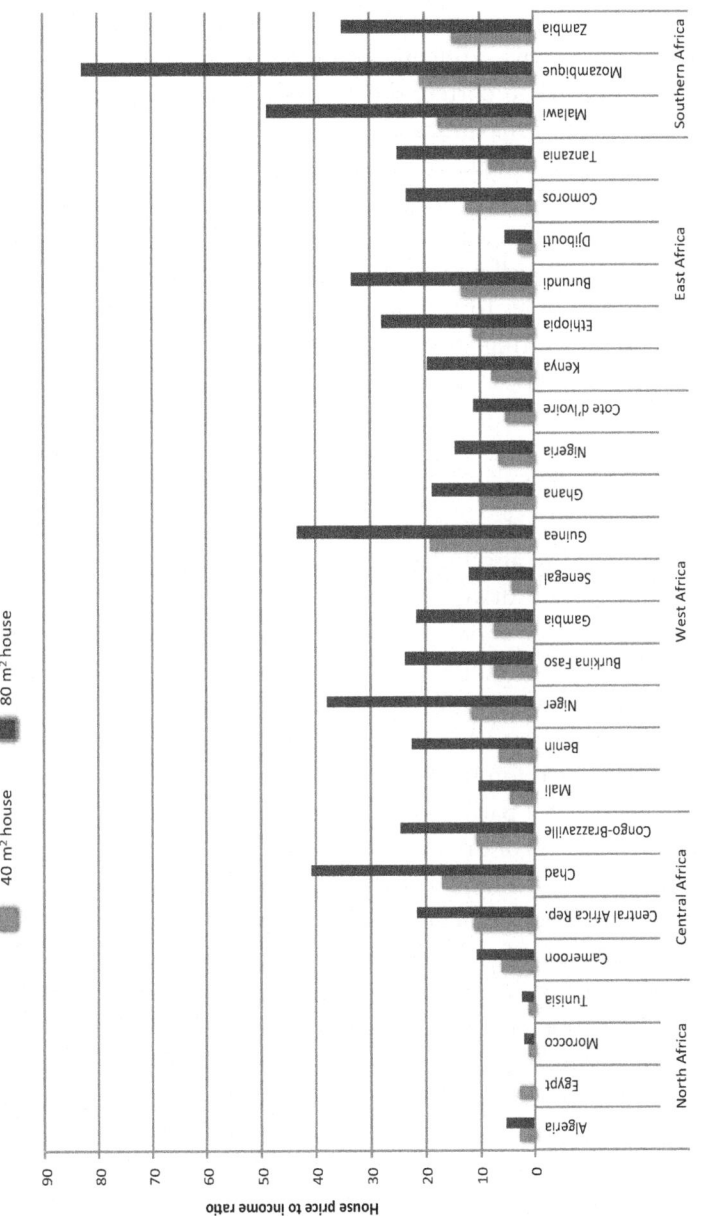

Fig. 2.5 National housing affordability in 2015, by region (Source: Author's analysis)

and private sector to be in a position to harness some of the potential benefits that urbanization and housing development offer. This would require making necessary adjustments in the urban planning and strategies in order not only to correct the mistakes from the past, but also to enable stakeholders to maximize and reap the potential economic benefits of housing development. These include:

- *Economies of scales and positive externalities related to cities.* Africa's urban dynamics, if well managed, could be designed in such a way that cities provide facilities to promote efficient and productive economic activities, while putting in place the necessary infrastructure, service delivery mechanisms, and well-functioning institutions to allow the flow of capital, skilled labor, and technology. These conditions, together with the effects induced by agglomeration dynamics and infrastructure spillovers, will generate not only economies of scale through larger markets, with growing spending power, and a sizeable number of jobs, but also linkage effects (both backward and forward), which are important drivers of structural transformation.
- *Urban middle class, a big asset:* Cities should invest in basic infrastructure and in human capital in order to meet the increasing social demand fueled by a growing middle class. In Africa, it is reported that consumer spending is expected to increase from US$680 billion in 2008 to US$2.2 trillion by 2030, spurred by the increase in size of the middle class. Such a pattern suggests that the urban middle class can be one of the drivers of urban renewal. Harnessing such an asset could go a long way toward reducing the share of Africans living below the poverty line to (33 percent) by 2060.
- *Cities as champions for promoting clean energy and environmentally friendly construction.* In African countries, a great proportion of households use kerosene, charcoal, or wood for cooking. This suggests that there is room to bring in innovative, environment-friendly solutions to bridge the energy gap while substantially contributing to the dynamic development and transformation of African cities. Smart investments in clean energy could help Africa's transformation leapfrog the energy deficit. Similarly, given the high cost of current construction materials, there is also a need for cities and municipalities to

revisit their legal and regulatory frameworks for the construction sector to promote and advocate for the local production of alternative construction materials that are cheaper and environment friendly (see Chap. 5). Moreover, wastewater and storm water management systems can be used to provide solutions to climate-related challenges faced by cities, and especially affecting the urban poor.

When it comes to land policies and governance issues, it is obvious from the discussions above that there is a long way to go to get the incentives right. The complex and unclear incentive systems based on multiple land tenure regimes have provided room for speculation and wrongdoings (e.g., rent seeking and corruption). This does not provide any incentives for governments to harness the potential benefits from Land Value Capture, but, most importantly, this entails frustrations and discontents from the majority which translate into conflicts, civil unrest, and political instability and promote informal settlements. Curtailing such deleterious outcomes would require profound land policy reforms, including revisions of regulatory and legal frameworks, with a view to reconcile the multiplicity of tenure regimes and strengthening land governance and administration systems (see Chap. 4 for more detailed discussions). The land reforms should also provide the right incentives that outweigh the potential benefits that could derive from political instability, social tensions, and civil unrest. This would require a significant amount of political will as land policy reforms can tend to be very costly in terms of social and political capitals. In other words, this will generate a lot of resistance from politicians, elites, and businesspeople who may have a vested interest in keeping the situation unchanged.

On the side of the construction sector, the need for a strong political will is even more acute, given the countervailing incentives faced by governments. Solving the construction cost conundrum requires putting in place the right policy measures and actions. A benevolent and proactive government could try to maximize the well-being of its population while putting in place the conditions for the provision of decent and affordable housing. In so doing, government could adopt measures to enforce construction standards, cut construction materials' import bill, and promote import substitution while providing the right incentives for the use of alternative techniques based on local building materials. Another possible policy measure could be for government to ban anticompetitive and rent-seeking behaviors, if any, and support private-sector engagement in the construction sector. It is also expected that governments together with some partners from civil society and NGOs would play an important role not only in raising awareness and educating the general public on new building techniques and materials, but also in supporting research and development focusing on building materials and techniques. This could bring about mentality changes, which, combined with efforts to strengthen technical, managerial (through education and Technical and Vocational Education and Training [TVET]), and financial capacity for developers, would definitely provide better incentives for stakeholders to engage and deliver positive outcomes from the construction sector (see more discussions in Chap. 5).

The political economy of slums is very complex, and all boils down to how to reconcile the divergent interests from different stakeholders while ensuring that their expected political and economic benefits are secured. Political will is key. Governments should take bold and decisive actions, but one should not underestimate the power of local networks and stakeholders who have vested interests in maintaining the status quo. Chapter 5 provides some recommendations on how to change the incentive mechanisms and curb slum proliferations on the continent.

It is noted that the macroeconomic stability and performance recorded over the last decade constitutes a great opportunity to get stakeholders, particularly investors involved in the housing sector. In so doing, policymakers, in particular monetary authorities and central banks, should continue to maintain inflation at manageable levels to ensure that financing can flow in and support the development of the housing sector. However, while trying to keep inflation at a relatively low level, they should not overlook the fact that they also need to manage the interest rates. In other words, the objective of setting targets for inflation should not be the only objective, if policy makers are concerned with supporting structural transformation and the development of investments in the productive sector, including construction and housing. The interest rate is an instrument that central banks can use to directly affect the credit market in general and indirectly affect the housing finance market through housing loans. Besides, it is noted that a fundamental element of political economy of housing development is the affordability issue. Regardless of the definition one may adopt, it turns out that housing is out of reach for the majority of households in the continent. Therefore, more efforts will be needed from financial authorities and governments to devise the appropriate financial sector policies that support housing finance and affordability while incentivizing banks and nonbank financial systems to promote financial inclusion schemes that bring housing finance down-market and accessible to the majority of people in need.

## Notes

1. As defined by UN-Habitat, the International alert line denotes the Gini coefficient value above which inequalities have negative social, political, and economic consequences.
2. Box 2.1 is entirely quoted from Durand-Lasserve et al. (2015).
3. Chapter 5 provides detailed discussions on construction cost and its main driving forces.
4. This is anecdotal but depicts faithfully the stories heard during our fact-finding missions, particularly in Kenya.
5. We use the following affordability rating scale in our analysis: 3.0 and under—affordable; 3.1–4.0—moderately affordable; 4.1–5.0—unaffordable; 5.1 and above—severely unaffordable.

## Bibliography

Beck, T., M. Munzele, I. Faye, and T. Triki. 2011. *Financing Africa: Through the Crisis and Beyond*. Washington, DC: World Bank Publications.

Buckley, R., L. Chiquier, and M. Lea. 2009. Housing Finance and the Economy. In *Housing Finance Policy in Emerging Markets*, ed. L. Chiquier and M. Lea. Washington, DC: World Bank.

Buvinić, M., and G. Gupta. 1997. Female-Headed Households and Female-Maintained Families: Are They Worth Targeting to Reduce Poverty in Developing Countries? *Economic Development and Cultural Change* 45 (2): 259–280. Retrieved from http://www.jstor.org/stable/1154535.

Centre on Housing Rights and Evictions (COHRE). 2008. *Women, Slums and Urbanization: Examining the Causes and Consequences*. Geneva: COHRE.

Durand-Lasserve, Alain, Maÿlis Durand-Lasserve, and Harris Selod. 2015. *Land Delivery Systems in West African Cities: The Example of Bamako, Mali*, Africa Development Forum Series. Washington, DC: World Bank. doi:https://doi.org/10.1596/978-1-4648-0433-5. License: Creative Commons Attribution CC BY 3.0 IGO.

EC. 2008. *Manual for Gender Mainstreaming, Social Inclusion and Social Protection Policies*, Employment, Social Affairs and Equal Opportunities Directorate. European Commission. http://ec.europa.eu.

Faye, Issa, Ousman Gajigo, and Emelly Mutambatsere. 2013. *Large Scale Agribusiness Investments and Implications in Africa: Development Finance Institutions' Perspectives*, Working Paper Series N° 193. African Development Bank, Tunis, Tunisia, December.

Fox, S., 2013. *The Political Economy of Slums: Theory and Evidence from Sub-Saharan Africa*, International Development Working Paper No. 13-146. London School of Economics and Political Science, London.

International Energy Agency (IEA). 2015. *World Energy Outlook 2015*. Paris: International Energy Agency (IEA).

Kakai, Sèdagban Hygin F. 2012. *Government and Land Corruption in Benin*, LDPI Working Paper 12. http://www.plaas.org.za/sites/default/files/publications-pdf/LDPI12Kakai.pdf

Kayizzi-Mugerwa, S., A. Shimeles, and N. Yameogo, eds. 2014. *Urbanisation and Socio-Economic Development in Africa: Challenges and Opportunities*. London: Routledge.

Parnell, Susan, and Ruwani Walawege. 2011. Sub-Saharan African Urbanisation and Global Environmental Change. *Global Environmental Change* 21 (Supplement 1): S12–S20. http://www.sciencedirect.com/science/journal/09593780/21/suppl/S1.

Southall, R. 2005. The Ndungu Report: Land and Graft in Kenya. *Review of African Political Economy* 32: 142–151.

TI (Transparency International). 2005. *The Kenya Bribery Index 2005, Transparency International Kenya*. https://tikenya.org/wp-content/uploads/2017/08/TI-Kenya_The-East-African-Bribery-Trends-Analysis_2005.pdf

———. 2012. *East Africa Bribery Index 2012, Transparency International Kenya*. www.tikenya.org/index.php?option=com_docman&task=doc_download&gid=134&Itemid=146.

———. 2013. *Global Corruption Barometer, Transparency International*. https://www.transparency.org/gcb2013/report

TI and FAO. 2011. *Corruption in the Land Sector*, Working Paper #04/2011. Transparency International and the Food and Agriculture Organization, Berlin.

UN-Habitat (United Nations Human Settlements Program). 2003. *The Challenge of Slums. Global Report on Human Settlements 2003*. Nairobi: United Nations Human Settlements Program.

UN-Habitat. 2009. *Global Report on Human Settlements 2009: Planning Sustainable Cities*. Nairobi: United Nations Human Settlements Program.

UN-Habitat. 2014. *The State of African Cities 2014: Re-Imagining Sustainable Urban Transitions*. Nairobi: United Nations Human Settlements Program.

Van der Molen, P., and A.M. Tuladhar. 2006. Corruption and Land Administration. In FIG 2006: *Proceedings of the Conference: Shaping the Change, XXIII FIG Congress*, München, Germany, October 8–13. Frederiksberg: International Federation of Surveyors (FIG).

**Open Access** This chapter is licensed under the terms of the Creative Commons Attribution 4.0 International License (http://creativecommons.org/licenses/by/4.0/), which permits use, sharing, adaptation, distribution and reproduction in any medium or format, as long as you give appropriate credit to the original author(s) and the source, provide a link to the Creative Commons license and indicate if changes were made.

The images or other third party material in this chapter are included in the chapter's Creative Commons license, unless indicated otherwise in a credit line to the material. If material is not included in the chapter's Creative Commons license and your intended use is not permitted by statutory regulation or exceeds the permitted use, you will need to obtain permission directly from the copyright holder.

# 3

# Housing Finance in Africa

## 3.1 Introduction

Housing finance plays a vital role in the housing delivery value chain. This is due to the fact that finance is needed for both the demand and the supply of housing. On the demand side, the availability of and access to housing finance is a significant determinant in a household's decision to acquire, build, or rent a house. Similarly, on the supply side, developers need financing to build the mass housing projects that are needed to address the continent's housing deficit.

Housing finance, being an essential part of financial systems, contributes to the development and deepening of financial markets and has some potential impact on the financial and economic stability of a country. Therefore, it contributes to deepening and broadening the financial sector, increasing financial access, and promoting financial inclusion. However, the development of housing finance on the continent has not kept pace with the backlog in housing demand.

Africa's rapid urbanization and economic growth have led to an increasing demand for housing finance. The dearth of long-term finance, weak credit markets, an unstable macroeconomic environment, and limited or inexistent housing finance systems are major obstacles to the continent's housing market development. Moreover, the housing deficit and the lack of adequate housing finance instruments are even more acute for lower-income groups, who by definition are the majority excluded from formal financial systems. Therefore, it is important not only to focus on how to develop housing finance systems, but also to focus on how to leverage financial systems to go "down market" in order to ensure that low-income groups have access to decent housing. There is a general belief that only government-related financing schemes could contribute to serving low-income households. This explains the numerous government-sponsored social housing schemes that have been widespread across the continent (Table 6.3). However, given the magnitude of the housing deficit, initiatives that involve private sector stakeholders are vital in addressing Africa's housing shortage.

This chapter aims to provide an overview of the housing finance market in Africa, while highlighting its challenges and opportunities. The analysis investigates the underlying fundamentals driving Africa's housing finance market and is based on primary and secondary information collected during fact-finding missions in selected countries, which is complemented with a thorough literature review. Beyond the analysis of the housing finance market (on both the supply and demand sides), this chapter aims to provide a better understanding of the challenges in financing low-income households and to shed light on what it would take to serve this income segment. It also discusses how the private sector can be "crowded in" so as to ensure increased availability of and access to housing finance services. It is targeted to the myriad of all stakeholders involved in the housing finance market: lenders, policymakers, regulators, developers, and development finance institutions (DFIs), among others.

## 3.2 An Overview of Africa's Housing Finance Market

Housing finance markets across Africa have grown in recent years as the number of financial institutions providing housing finance products have increased from the state-owned bank model in the 1980s, to now include private commercial banks. Nonetheless, the depth of the mortgage finance markets across the continent is low with the exception of a few countries such as Morocco, Namibia, and South Africa. This section provides a snapshot of the continent's housing finance market, details characteristics of housing finance products, and features prospects for developing housing finance markets that cater for the needs of low- and middle-income households.

## 3.2.1 A Nascent Housing Finance Market

The landscape of the African housing finance system is quite diverse. It involves both public and private entities offering different types of products geared toward responding to the unmet housing finance needs.

State-owned housing finance institutions have dominated housing finance in many African countries. The state housing bank model is widespread across the continent from Cameroon to Gabon in Central Africa, Ethiopia to Rwanda in East Africa, Algeria to Tunisia in North Africa, Lesotho to Namibia in Southern Africa, and Burkina Faso to Senegal in West Africa. During the 1980s, most of these banks, which largely relied on public budgets for financial support, collapsed in the economic downturn. Moreover, the fact that most of these state housing banks were not deposit-taking financial institutions created a severe asset-liability mismatch. A lax credit risk policy, poor corporate governance, and weak operational teams have also precipitated the failure of many state-run housing banks, resulting in government bailouts.

Although these banks were created with the goal of expanding the housing finance market, they have had the unintended consequence of distorting the market in some cases (Beck et al. 2011). Interest rate ceilings, credit quotas, and a lengthy foreclosure process have had the effect of further restricting lending toward low- and moderate-income households. Consequently, the continent's housing finance market is small and primarily caters to the needs of upper-middle- and high-income households, to the detriment of low- and middle-income families.

With the exception of South Africa, Namibia, Morocco, and Tunisia, housing finance markets in the continent are small and underdeveloped compared with those of other emerging economies, as reflected by the outstanding mortgage loans to GDP (Fig. 3.1). In Nigeria, Cameroon,

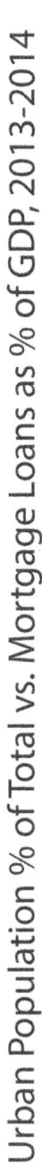

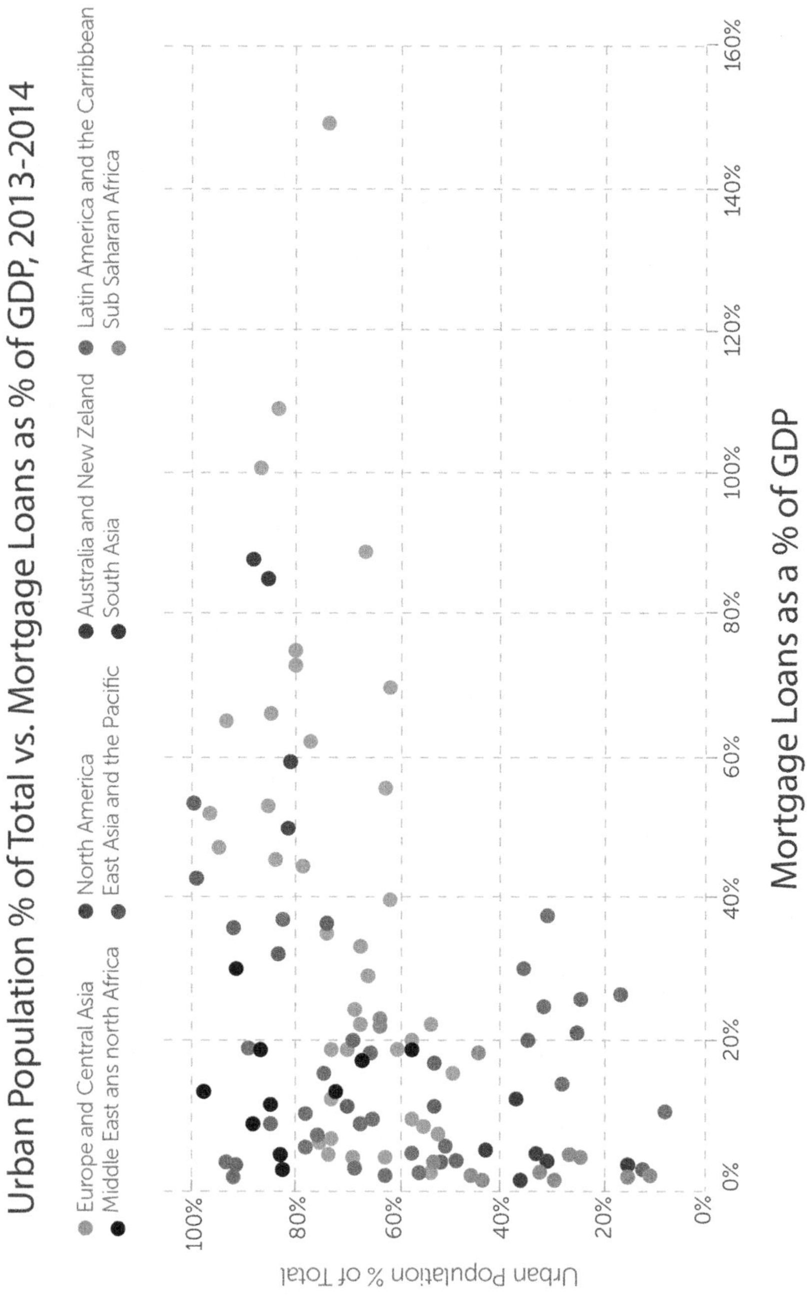

**Fig. 3.1** Africa's underdeveloped mortgage market (Source: Hofinet)

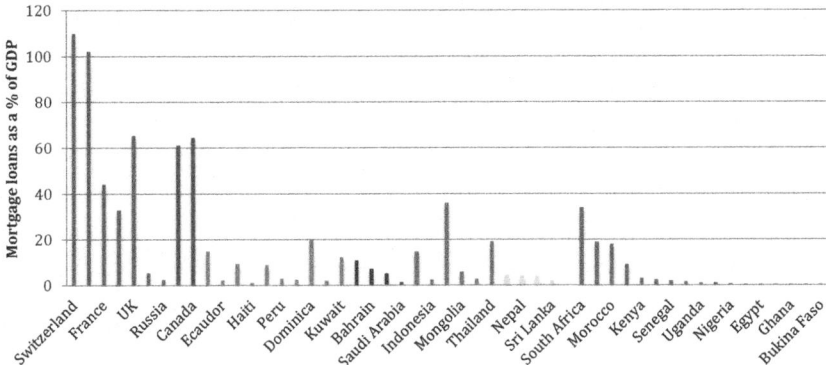

**Fig. 3.2** Size of residential mortgage market (most recent data available) (Source: World Bank, Hofinet, authors' calculations)

Egypt, Côte d'Ivoire, Ghana, Tanzania, and Burkina Faso, housing finance amounts to less than 1 percent of GDP, which is dwarfed in comparison with Chile, Costa Rica, Malaysia, and Thailand, where outstanding mortgage loans to GDP varies between 15 and 36 percent (Fig. 3.2).

Governments in many countries are beginning to adopt policies that encourage private lending while maintaining a level playing field for all lenders. In recent years, state interventions have been opened to private lenders in South Africa, Côte d'Ivoire, Morocco, Egypt, and Algeria, among others. In South Africa, the Finance-Linked Individual Subsidy Program (FLISP), a government partnership with the private sector to make housing finance accessible and affordable to low-income households, is accessible to all mortgage lenders. In Morocco, both public and private mortgage lenders also have access to Fonds de Garantie pour Populations à Revenus Irréguliers Modestes (FOGARIM), a credit-enhancement program that facilitates lending to low-income and informal-sector workers.

The financial liberalization of government assistance in many countries has partially contributed to growing the housing finance market over the past years. In South Africa, the mortgage market grew by 10.3 percent from R 124.38 billion (US$8.2 billion) in 2013 to R 137.19 billion (US$9.1 billion) in 2014. However, the number of mortgage loans approved in the affordable housing segment grew by only 4.5 percent during the same period. In Kenya, the value of outstanding mortgage loan assets has steadily increased since 2012 when the central bank started collecting data on residential mortgages. The value of outstanding mortgage loans in Kenya increased from K Sh 119.6 billion (US$1.2 billion) in December 2012 to K Sh 164 billion (US$1.6 billion) in 2014, representing a growth of K Sh 44.4 billion (US$438.7 million) or 37 percent.

In the West African Economic and Monetary Union (WAEMU) countries—Benin, Burkina Faso, Côte d'Ivoire, Guinea-Bissau, Mali, Niger, Sénégal, and Togo—the size of the housing finance market has also grown considerably over the last decades. Annual lending volumes in WAEMU increased from an average of CFAF 80 billion (US$160 million) between 2005 and 2011 to CFAF 203.7 billion (US$407.4 million) in 2013, which is a reflection of better credit conditions and improving housing market dynamics in the region (Fig. 3.3). In Morocco, the total amount

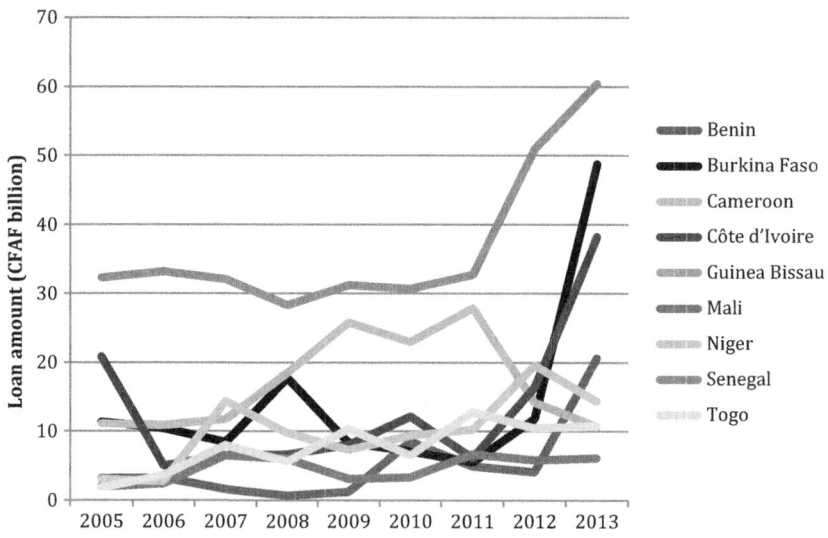

**Fig. 3.3** Evolution of housing loans in selected francophone African countries, 2005–2013 (Source: BCEAO; for Cameroon, from one leading financial institution only.)

of outstanding mortgage loans increased from US$15.99 billion to US$19.64 billion between 2011 and 2013. In Nigeria, the size of the mortgage market has grown from ₦54 billion (US$342 million) in 2006 to an estimated ₦224 billion (US$1.42 billion) in 2011. Figure 3.3 provides the evolution of housing loans in selected francophone African countries.

Notwithstanding the appreciable growth in housing finance, bank lending toward the sector has been very conservative. For the most part, beneficiaries of housing loans in Africa are wealthy individuals.

In South Africa, for instance, the number of mortgage loans approved within the affordable housing segment between 2013 and 2014 dropped significantly, by 20.4 percent, with an estimated 9 of every 10 mortgage loan applications being denied. Likewise, in Angola, the formal banking sector accounts for less than 2 percent of housing loans, with banks rejecting an estimated 82 percent of housing loan applications. As of October 2014, just 8960 mortgage accounts existed in the country. In Cameroon, the leading mortgage institution, which is undergoing restructuring, approved a paltry 262 housing loans in 2014 to serve an urban population of 12 million. In Kenya, a country of 45 million people, just 60,479 mortgage loans were outstanding between December 2012 and December 2014.

Similarly, less than 2 percent of the populations in Botswana, Malawi, Tanzania, and Zambia use mortgages to acquire their houses. In Nigeria, the housing finance market has not fared any better. Mortgage loans account for less than 1 percent of the loan portfolio of commercial banks. Only about 5 percent, or 685,000 of the 13.7 million housing units in Nigeria are financed using mortgages, owing to the fact that Nigeria's Federal Mortgage Bank (FMBN) has failed to meet expectations: as of August 2012, only about 13,000 mortgages had been provided for a total of 3.8 million eligible contributors to the National Housing Fund managed by FMBN. Today, Nigeria's mortgage deficit is estimated at ₦20–30 trillion (US$100–151 billion), according to the Mortgage Bankers' Association of Nigeria.

The figures in the WAEMU subregion have been disappointing as well. In 2013, WAEMU banks approved a meager 15,328 housing loans to serve a total population of 105 million, of which 36.3 million live in

Table 3.1 Housing loans in WAEMU, 2013

| Country | Number of housing loans approved | Amount (CFAF million) | Average amount of housing loans (CFAF million) | Average amount for households[a] (CFAF million) | Proportion (%) Loans approved | Amount |
|---|---|---|---|---|---|---|
| Benin | 539 | 20,613 | 38.5 | 5.0 | 3.5 | 10.1 |
| Burkina Faso | 1491 | 48,745 | 32.7 | 13.8 | 9.7 | 23.9 |
| Côte d'Ivoire | 696 | 38,137 | 54.8 | 15.0 | 4.5 | 18.7 |
| Guinea-Bissau | 112 | 4587 | 40.9 | 8.7 | 0.7 | 2.3 |
| Mali | 452 | 6106 | 13.3 | 11.4 | 2.9 | 3.0 |
| Niger | 1439 | 14,285 | 9.7 | 7.6 | 9.4 | 7.0 |
| Senegal | 7676 | 60,419 | 7.9 | 4.2 | 50.1 | 29.7 |
| Togo | 2923 | 10,783 | 3.8 | 2.9 | 19.1 | 5.3 |
| WAEMU | 15,328 | 203,675 | 29.7 | 9.8 | 100 | 100 |

Source: BCEAO
[a]Excluding bank staff

urban areas. The percentage of housing loans approved in the WAEMU region varies from a low of 0.7 percent in Guinea-Bissau to a high of 50.1 percent in Sénégal (Table 3.1).

If this dismal housing finance trend continues, it is obvious that the continent's housing crisis will explode in the coming years. From the foregoing discussion, it is clear that mortgage finance alone will not deliver housing to the vast majority of African households. With an average annual income of US$470 for each person, many African households cannot afford the cost of a mortgage. Recognizing the high level of informal employment in urban Africa, housing microfinance (HMF) promises to be a viable alternative to mortgage finance.

### 3.2.2 An Emerging Housing Micofinance Market

Microfinance institutions (MFIs) continue to play a vital role in Africa's financial landscape. The demand for HMF is strong. It is estimated that between 15 and 40 percent of microfinance loans are diverted toward housing purposes (Kihato 2013; HfH 2011). During our fact-finding missions across the continent, MFIs indicated a strong interest in developing specific housing finance products. In Cameroon, for instance, about 600 MFIs operate in the economy with average annual deposits of CFAF 500 billion (US$848.76 million). In Kenya, MFIs also play an important role in the financial sector. Between 2012 and 2013, Kenya's microfinance sector registered strong growth of 27.8 percent, as the total assets of microfinance banks increased from K Sh 32.4 billion (US$333.85 million) to K Sh 41.4 billion (US$426.58 million). In 2013, the gross loan portfolio of African MFIs reporting to the Microfinance Information Exchange (MIX) stood at over US$7 billion, with an average loan balance per borrower of US$478. These small loan amounts can be crucial in financing income-generating activities for low-income families. This strong market growth is being driven by improvements in market infrastructure, stronger governance, and an improving regulatory environment on the continent.

As the microfinance industry matures, product diversification becomes increasingly important to satisfy diverse client needs. HMF is one such product that needs to be expanded. HMF is well suited to the incremental housing development approach that is characteristic of Africa's housing market. It is reported that the great majority of houses on the continent are self-built. They account for over 70 percent of new housing supply in most countries. HMF consists of financial services and loans to low-income households for home construction, home improvements, home expansion, and land acquisition. A characteristic feature of HMF loans is their short maturity, usually ranging from three months to three years (Table 3.2). However, interest rates are high, sometimes above 30 percent on borrowed capital. In some countries, interest rates are capped by usury laws.

On the basis of evidence from Latin America and other regions, MFIs that add HMF to their suite of products could (1) increase their scale of operations and profitability, (2) reduce client dropout rates and decrease the overall risk portfolio, as housing loans tend to outperform other loans, (3) provide additional repayment incentives and resources to proven clients, and (4) gain access to affordable government funds that have been earmarked for housing (Goldberg and Motta 2003). Table 3.3 provides a sample of HMF products in selected African countries.

**Table 3.2** Key features of housing microfinance loans

| | |
|---|---|
| Loan amount | Amounts ranging from US$100 to US$10,000 |
| Term | Usually ranges between 3 and 36 months (3 months to 3 years) |
| Interest rate | Varies between 1 and 2 percent per month; however, it can be substantially higher (e.g., 30 percent) |
| Collateral | One or two cosigners; savings may also be required; some form of title maybe required |
| Target clients | Low- and moderate-income households |
| Technical assistance | Provided in some cases |

Source: Author

**Table 3.3** Selected HMF products available in Africa

| Country | Lender | Product/Use | Loan terms and conditions |
|---|---|---|---|
| Angola | Kixi-Credito | Land purchase<br>Incremental construction | Amount: Kz 100,000–1 million (US$914–9137)<br>Term: Up to 36 months<br>Interest: 2% per month on declining balance<br>Other: Between the ages of 18 and 60 years; proof of income |
| Cameroon | BICEC | Land purchase<br>Home construction/acquisition | Amount: Credit granted in proportion to the amount of savings<br>Term: Up to 84 months (7 years)<br>Interest: 7%<br>Other: Open savings account with a minimum savings of CFAF 20,000 (US$33) for a minimum of 1 year and a maximum of 7 years; age between 18 and 55 years |
| South Africa | Real People | Home construction<br>Home improvement | Amount: R 1000–100000 (US$83–8307)<br>Term: Up to 48 months<br>Interest rate: 20–30%<br>Other: Be employed and earn a minimum of R 2000 (US$166) per month; between the ages of 18 and 64 years old |

*(continued)*

**Table 3.3** (continued)

| Country | Lender | Product/Use | Loan terms and conditions |
|---|---|---|---|
| Kenya | KUSSCO | Home construction/ acquisition | Amount: K Sh 450,000–7 million (US$4579–71,231)<br>Term: 3–15 years<br>Interest rate: 14% on declining balance<br>Other: Savings equivalent to 20% of loan amount; land title; life insurance policy; applicant's current age plus repayment period should not exceed 65 years |
| Tanzania | Akiba Commercial Bank | Home improvement | Amount: T Sh 500,000–20 million (US$24 –9709)<br>Term: 3–12 months<br>Interest rate: 19.5–40% fees inclusive |
| Nigeria | LAPO Microfinance Bank | Home construction<br>Home improvement | Amount: Up to ₦1 million (US$5024)<br>Term: Up to 24 months; grace period of 1 month<br>Interest rate: Initial rate of 1.6% per month<br>Other: Open a savings account with a minimum of ₦1000 (US$5); this is a partnership between the French Development Agency, or AFD; LAPO; and Lafarge |
| South Africa | Rural Housing Finance Fund | Lending to financial intermediaries for on-lending to low-income households | Maximum borrower income of R 15,000 (US$1242)<br>Home improvement and construction loans, land purchase<br>Average interest on loans granted for on-lending: 10.7%<br>Focus on non-metropolitan areas |

(*continued*)

Table 3.3 (continued)

| Country | Lender | Product/Use | Loan terms and conditions |
|---|---|---|---|
| Uganda | UGAFODE Microfinance Limited | Flexible housing loan | Amount: US$80–120<br>Term: Up to 2 years; one-month principal grace period; client pays only interest in first month<br>Interest rate: 3% per month, discounted to 2% if after the first month customer uses loan for intended housing purpose<br>Other: Loans provided for different construction phases, e.g. flooring, roofing, electricity, shuttering, etc. |
| | | Micro mortgage loan | Amount: US$200–10,000<br>Term: Up to 3 years; 6 months principal grace period; client pays only interest during grace period<br>Interest rate: 2% per month<br>Other: Property to be constructed acts as collateral |

Source: Author

Despite the growing demand and promise of HMF, this financial product is relatively new in Africa compared with market developments in South-East Asia and Latin America. Although still at a limited scale, HMF is sporadically offered in Angola, Cameroon, Côte d'Ivoire, Ghana, Kenya, Nigeria, Tanzania, and Uganda, among others. Main product development constraints identified by stakeholders during our on-the-ground interviews include (1) limited in-house capacity to develop products and manage risks, (2) lack of a dedicated pool of capital to fund housing loans, and (3) lack of quantifiable data on market demand.

Savings and credit cooperatives (SACCOs) also play an active role in Africa's finance market and have two distinct strengths. First, these are community-based entities with deep outreach among informal-sector households in particular, and lower-income groups in general. Second, these institutions are large savings collectors, typically organized as networks of local institutions, with stable internal resource bases, usually consisting of thousands of depositors. Such networks are particularly strong in Mali (Nyesigiso and Kafo Jiginew credit union networks), Burkina Faso (Caisses Populaires), Rwanda (Banques Populaires), Kenya (Kenya Union of Savings and Credit Cooperatives—KUSCCO), and Cameroon (Cameroon Cooperative Credit Union League—CamCCUL). Box 3.1 provides some details on the KUSCCO Housing Fund.

> **Box 3.1 KUSCCO Housing Fund**
> 
> The KUSCCO Ltd., the umbrella organization of all savings and credit cooperatives in Kenya, was founded in 1973. Today, KUSCCO counts over 3000 SACCOs as members, with total deposits of K Sh 6.2 billion (US$63.63 million) as of June 2015. In 1996, the KUSCCO Housing Fund was created with a mandate to mobilize funds from member cooperatives in order to finance mortgages, equity release, construction, and land purchase loans.
> 
> The fund provides housing loans ranging from US$5,000 to US$77,778 to low- and middle-income SACCO members, with loan repayment periods of up to 15 years. This compares with member cooperatives, which extend housing credits only for up to US$10,000, with a five-year repayment timeline.
> 
> In order to qualify for a loan, applicants need to meet a handful of criteria: (1) pay a membership fee of US$17 upon admission to the fund; (2) save continually for at least six months prior to obtaining a loan, with a minimum monthly saving of US$56; and (3) have a title deed on a property. Although KUSCCO's housing loans are exclusively funded through short-term savings deposits, their interest rates are fixed at 14 percent, on a declining loan balance, throughout the repayment period. The majority of borrowers, most of whom are employed in the informal sector, repay their loans on time. As of December 2014, over 5,000 housing loans had been granted by KUSCCO, with a fairly good performance—the nonperforming loan rate is below 5 percent, which is comparable with that of other products offered by the institution.
> 
> Source: Author based on information obtained from KUSCCO during fact-finding mission in Kenya, October 2014.

### 3.2.3 Contractual Savings for Housing Schemes in Africa

A contractual savings for housing (CSH) plan is a contractual agreement between a financial institution and a customer that grants the customer the right to obtain a preferential mortgage after a minimal saving period. CSH has been successfully used in Europe, with the "open" French Compte Épargne Logement, or Plan Épargne Logement, and the "closed" German Bauspar system being the most prominent. In a closed system, housing loans are funded exclusively with savings pooled together by the institution under the CSH scheme, whereas in an open system, a lender is permitted to access other funding sources (such as capital markets) if the inflow of savings is not enough to meet loan demands. Housing savings loans are often restricted for housing investments. Depending on the contractual agreement, these loans can be used for land acquisition, housing construction, home improvement, or to purchase a new home. There have been increasing interest and use of housing savings contracts in Asian countries such as India, Indonesia, and China.

Mobilizing private savings for housing purposes has several benefits for lenders, customers, and the government. From a lender's perspective, this helps to mitigate credit risks in an environment characterized by information asymmetries (see Chap. 1). To a large extent, CSH minimizes credit risk, as subscribers demonstrate their ability to make timely payments by saving a portion of their income throughout an extended period of time. As a result, lending to a CSH subscriber is often less risky than lending to other borrowers. Studies have shown default rates under contractual savings schemes are usually low (Lea and Renaud 1995; Taffin 1998; United Nations 2005). In Addis Ababa, Ethiopia, for example, there have been zero nonperforming loans (NPLs) under the CSH plan as of November 2014, according to Commercial Bank of Ethiopia (CBE) officials. Given the substantial down payments made by subscribers through their contracted savings, the loan-to-value (LTV) ratio is often significantly lower, which reduces the probability of defaults and delinquency. Households also find CSH products attractive, especially in a low-interest-rate environment, where the premiums accorded to induce savings are not eroded by high inflation rates. Moreover, the accumulation of savings and the prospects of a comparative lower interest rate on housing loans is attractive to households, particularly low- and middle-income families. Contractual savings programs can also help governments mobilize long-term financing dedicated for housing construction and increase access to financial service for youth and low-income individuals.

In Africa, countries that have adopted variants of CSH schemes include Cameroon, Côte d'Ivoire, Ethiopia, Nigeria, Tunisia, and Morocco. For illustrative purposes, the discussion that follows will investigate some of the schemes developed in some of these countries.

In Nigeria, potential borrowers are required to save for a minimum of six months before they can access a loan from the National Housing Fund. In Morocco, the government introduced provisions to encourage long-term savings in its 2011 Finance Law, which provides tax exemptions on savings plans for housing. In Morocco, banks are permitted to administer contractual savings plans, while in other countries such as Tunisia only specialized financial institutions are responsible for managing the scheme. In Morocco, subscribers are required to pay an initial deposit of at least DH 500 (US$50) upon opening a housing savings account. During the savings phase, subscribers are required to contribute a minimum of DH 3000 (US$300) annually, while the cumulative amount that can be contributed under the scheme by law cannot exceed DH 400,000 (US$40,000). At the end of the required savings period, a subscriber can obtain a loan of at least three times the cumulative regular savings amount. The interest rate charged on these loans is 50 basis points lower than the interest rate applied to housing loans with the same characteristics. In order to benefit from the tax exemptions provided by law, a subscriber must also provide a certificate issued by tax officials stating that they do not own any home.

Neighboring Tunisia operates a semi-open CSH system that most sub-Saharan Africa countries have replicated with varying degrees of success. In Tunisia, the CSH system is dominated by Banque de l'Habitat (BH), a specialized housing institution, which operates two housing schemes: a conventional housing savings plan, or Plan Epargne Logement (PEL) classique and the El Jedid housing savings plan, or PEL El Jedid (El Jedid). Subscribers to BH's PEL plan—which is open to first-time home buyers only—have the option of saving at least TD 54 (US$28) and a maximum of TD 500 (US$258) per month, which is remunerated at 3.5 percent per year net of taxes. Depending on their needs and resources, subscribers can select from a four-, five-, or six-year savings plan, after which they are entitled to a housing loan to (1) purchase a new home from an approved real estate developer, (2) construct a new home, or (3) extend the first housing to the tune of at least a third of the existing living space. PEL loans have a repayment term of up to 25 years, and the interest rate is equivalent to the average money market rate plus 2.5 percent. If the loan amount is insufficient to meet the home cost, customers can obtain additional credit of between US$4,463 and US$42,250 (corresponding to their savings plan) with a repayment period of up to 25 years, and a fixed interest rate plus 0.75 percent, which is currently 5.75 percent. The El Jedid savings plan entitles subscribers to a housing loan, which can be used to (1) purchase a new home from an approved developer, (2) purchase land for residential use, (3) buy a resale home, (4) construct a new home, and (5) refurbish or extend an existing home. Under this plan, subscribers are required to save a minimum of US$54 to a maximum of US$1,298 per month.

In Ethiopia, the government launched a housing savings plan with two main objectives: provide housing for low- and middle-income families, and promote a culture of savings among Ethiopians. Unlike the Tunisian housing savings plan, subscribers to Ethiopia's CSH scheme can only purchase a house constructed under the government's Integrated Urban Housing Development Program (IUHDP). Subscribers who default on savings for six months become ineligible to participate in this program. In order to increase home affordability for target groups, the government supplies the required land and bulk infrastructure for free, as well as the requisite technical assistance (house designs, construction supervision, and project management). Proceeds from the sale of government bonds and the deposits mobilized under the CSH scheme are the primary sources of finance for the housing project. IUHDP consists of three main housing saving schemes—10/90, 20/80, and 40/60—all managed by the state-owned CBE. Table 3.4 shows the minimum monthly income requirements for participating in the various CSH plans.

**Table 3.4** Monthly income threshold for housing saving plan in Ethiopia, as of November 2014

| US$ | | | | |
|---|---|---|---|---|
| Plan | Studio | One-Bedroom | Two-Bedroom | Three-Bedroom |
| 10/90 | 37 | – | – | – |
| 20/80 | 30 | 55 | 112 | 136 |
| 40/60 | – | 171 | 266 | 424 |

Source: Ministry of Urban Development, Housing and Construction, Ethiopia

**Table 3.5** House prices in Ethiopia under the government-housing program, as of December 2014

| Program | Unit type (Bedroom) | Floor area (m²) | Sale price (US$) | Minimum monthly saving (US$) | Minimum saving period (years) | Loan period (years) |
|---|---|---|---|---|---|---|
| 10/90 | Studio | 29 | 3980 | 9 | 3 | 25 |
| 20/80 (old) | Studio | 32 | 3038 | 8 | 5 | 20 |
| | 1 | 50 | 6304 | 14 | | |
| | 2 | 65 | 11,144 | 28 | | |
| | 3 | 85 | 15,135 | 34 | | |
| 20/80 (new) | 1 | 50 | 6305 | 10 | 7 | 20 |
| | 2 | 65 | 11,144 | 20 | | |
| | 3 | 85 | 15,135 | 24 | | |
| 40/60 | 1 | 55 | 8091 | 51 | 5 | 17 |
| | 2 | 75 | 12,438 | 78 | | |
| | 3 | 100 | 19,224 | 122 | | |
| Housing Cooperatives | 2 | 60 | 10,448 | 50% at the time the cooperative is established, and the remaining 50% when they are granted the construction license | | |
| | 3 | 80 | 13,390 | | | |
| | 4 | 110 | 19,154 | | | |

Source: Ministry of Urban Development, Housing and Construction, Ethiopia
Note: US$ conversion as of November 2014

The 10/90 plan targets low-income households earning under Br 1200 (US$60) a month (Table 3.5). The 10/90 plan requires individuals to save 10 percent of the home price over a consecutive period of three years. Subscribers are required to save at least Br 187 (US$10) per month, which is remunerated at 6 percent (5 percent base rate plus 1 percent savings premium). After the three-year saving period, savers are granted a loan from the CBE for the remaining 90 percent at an interest rate of 8.5 percent—compared with over 18 percent at other financial institutions—and a 25-year repayment period. These 10/90 homes are cross-subsidized by the other CSH schemes.

The 20/80 plan, in contrast, targets lower-middle and middle-middle-income households. The 20/80 subscribers are required to save 20 percent of the total house price over a consecutive period of up to seven years, after which they are eligible for a loan amounting to 80 percent of the house cost. This loan, which carries an interest rate of 9.5 percent, has to be repaid over 20 years.

According to the CBE, 862,216 Addis Ababa residents opened CSH accounts for the 10/90 and 20/80 housing programs during the registration window, which was closed in June 2013. The savings of CSH subscribers will be used as down payment, while financing for the remaining total housing cost will be provided by the CBE.

Unlike the 10/90 and 20/80 plans, the 40/60 plan is a partnership between the CBE and the Addis Ababa Housing Development Enterprise. Subscribers under the 40/60 plan are required to save at least 40 percent of the total housing cost over five years before they are eligible for a CBE loan to cover the remaining house value, at an interest rate of 7.5 percent, with a 17-year repayment period. Over the course of five years, subscribers are requested to save on a monthly basis at least Br 1,033 (US$51) for a one-bedroom house, Br 1,575 (US$78) for a two-bedroom house, and a minimum of Br 2,453 (US$122) for a three-bedroom home. However, the CBE encourages subscribers who have the ability to contribute more to do so, or better still, to pay the total housing costs up front. In return, housing allocations will be prioritized on the basis of the amount contributed per subscriber, unlike the 10/90 and 20/80 housing savings plans under which home transfers or allocations are conducted through random draws. As of November 2014, 20,000 subscribers had paid the full house costs under the 40/60 plan, of which 8,000 were Ethiopians living abroad. These individuals will be given priority in the housing allocation process.

Building houses through housing cooperatives is another saving scheme supported by the Ethiopian government, as long as the cooperative has at least 24 members. Housing cooperatives can be organized at workplaces, by residency area, or by the Ethiopian diaspora community.

Under the housing cooperative saving scheme, houses can be constructed either by the government-owned Housing Development Enterprise—at a cost of Br 210,000 (US$10,173) for a one-bedroom home, Br 280,000 (US$13,563) for a two-bedroom home, and Br 385,000 (US$18,650) for a three-bedroom home—or by a contractor of the cooperative's choosing. Cooperative members are expected to save the estimated full cost of the housing project: 50 percent at the time of registration, and the remaining 50 percent when they are granted the construction license. Land for the construction of cooperative houses is provided for free by the government. In addition, if the government Housing Development Enterprise is contracted to construct cooperative housing developments, taxes on construction materials are also waived.

Despite the numerous advantages of CSH schemes, there are also some drawbacks. The principal limitation of the Ethiopian CSH system, for instance, is the likelihood of an increase in home prices as a result of rising construction costs. Consequently, savers would be required to increase the minimum savings amount, which may be unaffordable for many households. Another limitation of the Ethiopian CSH scheme, given the slow pace of construction, is the long queue of subscribers waiting for their turn to be allocated a house. As of December 2013, over 900,000 people had registered for the CSH plan and were in the housing queue. Opening the construction process to private and foreign investors through public-private partnerships will help reduce the construction backlog under the government-coordinated housing program (see more in Chap. 5).

Liquidity and interest rate risks are other challenges that may affect the viability of CSH systems. Under a closed contractual savings system, liquidity risk may arise when new savings and existing loan repayments are insufficient to fund loan demands from subscribers who have completed the savings phase. Interest rate risk is also predominant in a closed system where rates on savings and loans are fixed, irrespective of changing market conditions. In many African countries where the interest rate environment is volatile, a fixed interest rate may not be optimal.

Inasmuch as contractual savings plans contribute to plugging the housing finance deficit, it remains that a big chunk of the housing finance needs is unmet. In response to that need, some efforts geared toward tapping into the bond markets have been made.

### 3.2.4 The Emergence of Housing Bonds

Housing bonds are another approach used by some governments and institutions to raise funds for affordable housing development projects. Kenya provides a good example of how financial institutions and property developers can raise funds through housing bonds. Shelter Afrique, the Nairobi-based pan-Africa housing finance institution, has successfully issued five housing bonds between 2005 and 2014, with amounts varying from K Sh 500 million (US$5.2 million) to K Sh 5 billion (US$51.62 million). The tenors of these issues have ranged between three and five years, with coupon rates of between 12.5 and 12.75 percent. Kenya's favorable regulatory environment has precipitated the growth of this asset class.

Given its mandate to facilitate access to financial services through effective regulation and innovation, Kenya's Capital Markets Authority (CMA) approved Housing Finance's (HF) issue and listing of a seven-year, K Sh 10 billion (US$103.24 million) housing bond. The first tranche of this bond, which was issued in October 2010, was oversubscribed by 41 percent. During its second tranche issued in October 2012, HF raised K Sh 5.2 billion (US$53.68 million), which represented an oversubscription of 76 percent above its K Sh 2.9 billion (US$29.94 million) target. The ability of these institutions to raise funds in domestic capital markets enables them to offer local currency lending to their clients under better terms.

---

**Box 3.2 Morocco Looks to Covered Bonds to Support Housing Finance**

Based on the success story of the European covered bond industry, in the second half of 2010 the Moroccan Ministry of Economy and Finance launched a project for establishing a legal and regulatory framework for covered bonds with the main objectives of (1) allowing banks to offer mortgage loans at affordable rates; (2) reducing banks' maturity mismatch and interest rate risks; and (3) providing institutional investors, notably insurance companies and pension funds, with a new class of long-term, high-quality private debt to reduce their term gaps. Covered bonds also have a positive collateral impact in promoting sound loan origination, given that the loans that are eligible as cover assets must meet high-quality eligibility criteria on an ongoing basis.

Morocco's covered bond project was part of a broader financial sector reform supported by the World Bank. It has benefited during its different stages from specific technical assistance funded by the First Initiative trust fund. This technical assistance allowed the mobilizing of high-level experts to assess the prerequisites and rationales for introducing covered bonds in Morocco and to comment on the draft law. The most significant characteristics of the Moroccan covered bonds draft law may be summarized as follows:

- *Issuance structure*. Bonds will be issued directly by banks, which is the most common structure internationally, as it seemed the simplest and most appropriate to the nature of the bonds as senior bonds and the ongoing flows between the cover pool assets and the other bank assets.
- *Issuer and supervisory system*. On the basis of international benchmarks, the issuers will be banks that have received a specific license granted by the Central Bank on the basis of their capacities and the specific covered bond management system put in place. The draft law provides for specific supervision of the covered bonds activity by the Central Bank, monitoring of the cover pool by an independent comptroller, and implementation of specific prudential regulations on the cover pool (internal audit, risk management, liquidity obligations, etc.).
- *Eligible assets*. Eligible assets for mortgage-covered bonds are primary mortgage loans with an LTV ratio of less than 80 percent for residential loans and 60 percent for commercial loans. Eligible assets for public-covered bonds are loans to local governments that meet certain financial conditions and loans to public corporations guaranteed by the government. The inclusion of public-covered bonds is aimed at allowing a new class of assets for investors and is expected to gain importance in the medium to long term, thanks notably to the regionalization process currently ongoing in Morocco.
- *Cover pool*. The law provides that the bank has the ongoing obligation to maintain sufficient eligible assets in the cover pool to allow coverage of issued covered bonds both in stocks and in flows. To this end, the Central Bank enacts specific and prudent valuation techniques for the cover pool assets. Any asset that loses quality criteria or is prepaid must be replaced by other eligible assets. There is also a minimum legal overcollateralization of at least 5 percent that can be set to a higher level in the regulatory framework, by using substitute high-quality assets listed in the law, notably government bonds. Specifically for mortgage-covered bonds, mortgage commercial loans cannot exceed a small percentage of the cover pool (10 percent).

> - *Customer deposits protection.* In Morocco, the risk of depositors was not deemed to be a major issue in an emerging market. Yet, it was judged prudent to include in the law the provision that the issuance is limited to a share of the issuer's total assets to be set in the regulatory framework (at present, 20 percent) and more stringent limits can be set by the Central Bank, notably in the case of banks with a specific risk profile.
> - *Bankruptcy remoteness.* The law states that a specific cover pool manager will be designated in case of bankruptcy and given sufficient power and tools to continue the management of the cover pool or to transfer it to another bank. It is also important to underline that the law explicitly enacts the principle of asset continuation in case of bankruptcy.
>
> It is important to note that prerequisites for implementing covered bonds are the existence of a comprehensive financial infrastructure and of a strong financial supervisory framework, especially in the banking sector (the central bank). Establishing the covered bonds legal framework is a long and complex process that has to be managed efficiently. It is important to this end to follow a structured process involving all market participants and to benefit from international experience and expertise.
>
> Source: Based on Al Aissami and Talby 2013.

However, not all housing bond issues have been successful. In 2014, Home Afrika, the only listed property developer in Kenya, had to seek more expensive commercial loans from banks after its maiden bond issuance failed to raise the minimum required amount of K Sh 500 million (US$5.2 million). Despite offering investors an attractive return of 13.5 percent, a 2.63 percent premium over similar government paper, Home Afrika's attempt to raise K Sh 900 million (US$9.29 million) through corporate bonds was unsuccessful. Given the oversubscription of government and corporate bonds in the past, liquidity in the market was certainly not the issue. Home Afrika's bond flop can be attributed to the institution's weak performance and declining profitability. The failed launch of Home Afrika's bond sales should serve as a note of caution to institutions eager to float housing bonds in the market. Success will be restricted to those that are well respected, credible, and well managed; have a healthy balance sheet; and can fulfill all stringent requirements to be listed on the capital market and still offer attractive returns. This situation mirrors the one in the corporate bond market, which is not developed enough to solve the housing finance issues. There is a serious need to mobilize and channel long-term financing toward institutions involved with housing finance. In so doing, given the shallowness of capital markets, some intermediary financial schemes have been developed to make the link between primary mortgage banks and the bond market.

## 3.2.5 Mortgage Liquidity Facilities to Support Market Development

A mortgage liquidity facility (MLF) is a specialized financial institution that provides long-term funds to mortgage lenders. MLFs play a vital role in building domestic capital markets, especially in developing countries where mortgage markets are still small. MLFs serve as intermediaries between primary mortgage banks and the bond market. They have the capability and financial strength to raise medium- and long-term funds in capital markets through the issuance of securities such as bonds. Due to their healthy balance sheets, MLFs can raise more funds under favorable conditions than mortgage banks can provide if acting alone. Table 3.6 summarizes the key benefits of MLFs to governments, lenders, and homebuyers.

Table 3.6 Benefits of mortgage liquidity facilities for key stakeholders

| Government | Lenders | Homebuyers |
| --- | --- | --- |
| Can serve as a tool in achieving policy objectives such as increasing home ownership and affordability | Reduces maturity mismatch of financing long-term assets (houses) with short-term liabilities (deposits) | Increased access to housing loans as a result of higher competition |
| Supports financial market deepening as it contributes in developing private debt securities market | A source of affordable long-term finance for on-lending | Benefit from affordable mortgages stemming from longer maturities and lower interest rates |
| Ensures harmonization of mortgage processes, documentation, risk management, etc. | Helps in hedging interest rate risk, especially in Africa where interest rates are volatile | |
| Can be a source of liquidity in times of crisis | Promotes competition in the mortgage market | |

Source: Author

Seizing this opportunity, several African countries have established MLFs in order to address the lack of long-term capital for mortgage financing. Egypt, Nigeria, Tanzania, and WAEMU member states have all created mortgage refinancing companies in a bid to increase mortgage affordability, reduce the cost of funds, and promote the development of secondary mortgage markets (Box 3.3). Proceeds from the sale of bond securities issued by these facilities are channeled to member mortgage lenders, often at lower interest rates and longer tenor. In Tanzania, for instance, the establishment of the Tanzania Mortgage Refinance Company (TMRC) in 2010 has been critical in promoting the growth of mortgage finance. The TMRC catalyzed the entry of new banks into the mortgage financing market. Following the creation of the TMRC, the number of banks offering mortgages has increased from three 3 in 2010 when TMRC was created to 19 as of December 2014.

---

**Box 3.3 Mortgage Refinancing Companies as a Tool for Achieving Policy Objectives**

**Example 1: Nigeria Mortgage Refinancing Company—Increasing access to long-term funds**

The Nigeria Mortgage Refinancing Company (NMRC) was launched in January 2014 with the dual objective of providing long-term funds to mortgage lenders and creating a new high-quality asset class for long-term investors such as pension funds and insurance companies. An initial loan of US$250 million was negotiated under the World Bank's concessional lending window, the International Development Association (IDA), to help achieve these objectives.

Shareholders of the NMRC include the Nigerian government and the Nigerian Sovereign Investment Agency (i.e., the Nigerian sovereign wealth fund), and DFIs (such as the IFC and Shelter Afrique), as well as various primary mortgage banks and commercial banks in Nigeria. As of February 2014, the NMRC has raised ₦7.05 billion (US$35.45 million) in Tier 1 capital from its shareholders. In addition to the US$250 million IDA debt, the NMRC is expected to raise capital in the bond market. Government-guaranteed bonds in the amount of ₦50 billion (US$251.45 million) will be issued to institutional investors, with an overall target of ₦10 billion (US$50.3 million) to be issued in the medium term.

At the time of creating the NMRC, the government also initiated a parallel process to simplify land titling and reduce land registration cost. To date,

18 of the 36 Nigerian states have joined the scheme to fast-track land registration procedures and reduce associated costs. The Lagos state government, for example, has reduced land charges from a high of 15 percent to 3 percent. The NMRC is also promoting legislative reforms to standardize mortgage and foreclosure laws. Twenty-one of Nigeria's 36 states have signed onto these standardize foreclosure laws, which will ensure the timely resolution of mortgage disputes and create an efficient foreclosure process as states have agreed to an arbitration process, thereby eliminating lengthy judicial processes. The NMRC plans to refinance 400,000 mortgage loans in the next five years.

**Example 2: Caisse Regional de Refinancement Hypothecaire-UEMOA—Promoting a Regional Mortgage Market**

The West Africa regional mortgage refinance fund, known in French as Caisse Regional de Refinancement Hypothecaire-UEMOA (CRRH-UEMOA), was created in 2012 with the West African Development Bank, ECOWAS Bank for Investment and Development, Shelter Afrique, and 48 regional commercial banks as shareholders. As of June 2014, CRRH-UEMOA's capital stood at CFAF 5.632 billion (US$9.63 million).

As of February 2014, CRRH-UEMOA had mobilized CFAF 51.9 billion (US$88.85 million) through the issuance of 10-year tax-free bonds for the benefit of 23 commercial banks in seven WAEMU countries, at an average rate of 6 percent. Bond proceeds will be used to refinance fixed-rate mortgages up to CFAF 100 million (US$171,176). The impact of CRRH-UEMOA is already visible as longer-maturity loans—with a tenor of 15–20 years, and lower interest rates—are now being offered in a number of countries.

On the basis of its mandate to deepen regional financial markets and contribute to standardizing mortgage loan portfolios, documentation, and risk management, CRRH-UEMOA plans to gradually extend the maturity of future bond issuance in order to strengthen its capacity to finance low- and moderate-income housing. The listing of CRRH-UEMOA securities in the regional stock market (BRVM) serves a dual purpose of increasing the liquidity of its bonds and debt securities while deepening regional financial markets.

Source: Based on company documents and interviews with stakeholders.

Besides deepening financial markets and mobilizing long-term resources for housing, MLFs can act as a means to promote standardization in the market. Before refinancing the mortgage portfolios of banks, MLFs ensure lending banks adhere to a list of best practice standards including harmonizing mortgage documentation, processes, LTV limits, and so on. Such practices can go a long way to improve market transparency, which is presently a challenge in the continent's housing market. Through mortgage refinancing and bond floatation, MLFs serve a dual purpose of supporting the growth of the mortgage market, while at the same time developing domestic capital markets.

The discussions above provide a snapshot of Africa's housing finance landscape. The subsequent sections further examine the issues hindering the development of housing finance on the continent, and explore ways to expand access to housing finance.

### 3.2.5.1 Expanding Access to Housing Finance

Mainstream financial institutions have generally shied away from offering housing loans or mortgages to low and lower middle-income groups. In contrast, institutions that focus on these groups, such as financial cooperatives, often do not have the capacity to offer long-term, low-cost housing loans. Overall, the issue underlying the exclusion of a large part of the African population from housing finance revolves around risk. Housing finance transactions involving low- and irregular-income groups are considered risky. This prevents the conventional financial system from going down market. As a result, over 50 percent of African households do not have access to housing finance products that meet their needs. Expanding access to housing finance while going down market thus requires reducing the risk of housing finance transactions.

Most government support in sub-Saharan African countries is done through the supply side: provision of serviced land (e.g., sites and services; see Chap. 4), construction of social housing, the sale or rent of housing at below-market rates, and, in some cases, the free provision of housing units, as in South Africa. Many countries have initiated programs to provide affordable housing and its financing, sometimes through very ambitious programs that are often difficult to achieve such as Ethiopia's IUHDP, or more realistic ones (such as the ongoing program of 10,000 units and 50,000 individual plots in Cameroon, which is handicapped by the lack of developer and consumer finance). It is also noted that around presidential elections, political leaders in different countries put their ingenuity to work to devise very ambitious special housing programs, which most of time do not deliver and fade away like most of the electoral promises (see Table 6.3). In sharp contrast to the situation in many countries in Latin America or Asia, in most parts of sub-Saharan Africa there is hardly any demand subsidy system supported by governments. The absence of or limited number of credit-linked demand subsidies means that resources from the financial sector are not leveraged. The impact of government spending would be multiplied if it was combined with private resources.

These forms of government assistance have an economic or opportunity cost, whose magnitude cannot be clearly assessed, as the costs are associated with the provision of free or cheap land, or below-market interest rates that do not explicitly appear in public budgets. The cost-efficiency of such government interventions needs to be considered in policy analyses. Lately, we have seen several attempts combining governments and private sector efforts to reduce risk in housing finance transactions in order to ensure the housing finance system goes down market to include those in need. Some of those schemes are discussed in the following subsections.

### 3.2.5.2 Intermediate Housing Loans: A Top-Down Approach

Over the last few years, much consideration has been given to the concept of intermediate housing loans. These loans, also known as "micromortgages," are smaller than regular mortgages, but larger than microcredits and have longer maturities. Such products have started emerging in Africa, with some financial institutions broadening their product offerings to cater for the housing needs of the poor and of middle-income households. These are clear efforts, made to ensure that financial institutions go down market. On the one hand, they can do so following a "top-down" approach wherein appropriate incentive mechanisms are put in place in the financial system's legal and regulatory framework to bring mainstream financial institutions to cater to the poor and to middle-income households. This is the case of South Africa's Financial Sector Charter signed in 2003, which aims to expand housing finance to low- and moderate-income South African households.[1] The FLISP was designed in accordance with that charter in 2012. The FLISP enables qualifying households to acquire a first-time home by providing a one-off subsidy amount between R 10,000 and R 87,000 (US$917 and US$7980), depending on the individual's monthly income. This amount is paid directly to the bank after the borrower has secured mortgage finance. The program's objective is to enable first-time homeownership opportunities to South African citizens earning between R 3501 and R 15,000 (US$321–1376) per month. However, there has been slow progress in the implementation of the FLISP. This is largely due to the shortage of housing supply, as well as the high level of indebtedness and the poor credit of potential FLISP applicants. South Africa's Department of Human Settlements cited overdue procurement procedures, lack of financial resources, and inadequate capacity as other major obstacles to the FLISP program. As of June 2014, just 3,522 mortgage loans had been granted to individuals earning less than R 15,000 (US$1,376) per month, according to the National Credit Regulator.

### 3.2.5.3 Intermediate Housing Loans: A Bottom-Up Approach

"Bottom-up" approaches, in contrast, have mostly been led by community-based organizations or MFIs expanding their product range to be able to cater for the poor and for low-income groups. This is the case of Kenya's National Cooperative Housing Union (NACHU), Capitec Bank in South Africa, which offers unsecured housing loans up to US$25,000, and Cameroon's La Régionale d'Epargne et de Crédit, which provides unsecured loans to salaried customers with maturities of up to five years at conditions close to traditional mortgages—that is, much cheaper than microcredit. The approach used by the Community Organizations Development Institute (CODI) in Thailand is a good example from which African community-based schemes could learn (see Box 3.4).

> **Box 3.4 Example of CODI in Thailand**
>
> CODI is a government body created in 2000 to support the development of community organizations to deal with various social problems such as affordable housing, particularly among urban slum dwellers. CODI organizes communities through the successive stages of their development: the identification of individual members, the formation of cooperatives, the registration of the land, the setting up of community funds which will be the recipient of below-market-rate CODI loans, and, finally, technical assistance in the design and execution of housing developments. CODI provides long-term loans to cooperatives, after cooperatives have saved at least 10 percent of the total project. In 2007, the Government Housing Bank (GHB) agreed to finance certain projects from CODI, thus allowing slum dwellers to access funding from a financial institution. In return, CODI placed a fixed deposit of B 100 million (about US$2.8 million) with the GHB as a guarantee to cover possible losses from default repayment. Moreover, since the loans to CODI carry a below-market interest rate at 4 percent, CODI deposited part of its capital in low-interest-bearing accounts with the GHB. CODI also receives annual subsidies from the government. Since inception, CODI has sponsored the construction of over 100,000 houses in 300 cities.
> Source: Author; based on company documents.

### 3.2.5.4 Integrated Partnerships

Banque de l'Habitat du Sénégal (BHS) has a very innovative and successful scheme based on an integrated tripartite partnership between housing cooperatives, developers, and the BHS that has been established to help close the housing finance gap. In fact, BHS has formed strategic partnerships with housing cooperatives, which are represented by the National Union of Housing Cooperatives (UNACOOP-Habitat), wherein member savings are deposited at BHS, in return for preferred-rate loans (7 percent compared with 8–10 percent at commercial banks and up to 14 percent at MFIs). The BHS prequalifies cooperative members for future loans and helps arrange "wholesale" agreements between the cooperatives and land or housing developers, including price discounts. BHS offers loans for the purchase or construction of new units, as well as for the purchase of the land by the cooperatives, the repayment being secured by the accumulated savings of cooperative members. In order to encourage this partnership, the government provides the cooperatives with (1) free land as well as priority access to land developments based on public-private partnerships, (2) annual tax exemptions on profits, and (3) a reduction in registration charges for land plots (1 percent instead of 10 percent).

### 3.2.5.5 Innovative Solutions to Increase Access to Housing Finance

Expanding access to housing finance for low- and middle-income households requires innovative solutions in cutting transaction and information costs, reducing risk of the low-income housing market segment, and the provision of technical assistance. Some additional innovative housing finance models that have been designed to increase access to housing finance for low- and middle-income families are discussed below.

### A) Combining HMF with Technical Assistance

In order to help minimize risk and maximize the impact of housing investments, most lenders have identified the need to combine finance with housing support services (HSS). HSS includes construction technical assistance, capacity building, training, architectural designs, among others. In Kenya, for instance, the NACHU's staff and consultants are the primary HSS providers to NACHU member cooperatives. The housing cooperatives that are affiliated with NACHU use the organization almost exclusively to address their housing needs, relying on NACHU for various technical support services as sourcing them elsewhere is substantially costly and thus unaffordable (Houston 2010). LafargeHolcim's affordable housing program in 16 countries, 6 of which are in Africa—Algeria, Cameroon, Kenya, Morocco, Nigeria, and Zambia—provides an illustrative example of HSS. In 2012, LafargeHolcim, a cement manufacturer, launched a program for affordable housing in emerging economies. The objective of this program is to contribute in improving the housing conditions of 2 million people by 2020, while building new markets for LafargeHolcim.

LafargeHolcim works in partnership with MFIs, NGOs, and building material retailers to assess market needs and identify opportunities in affordable housing. This is an integrated solution approach, which puts the borrower together with building material retailers, MFIs, and NGOs that could provide technical assistance. It partners with MFIs to grant housing loans of an average of US$2,500 with a term of two to three years. Participating MFIs benefit from LafargeHolcim's market assessment surveys, which help them assess the size of HMF markets and better understand client needs (Box 3.5).

> **Box 3.5 Key Findings of the 2014 LafargeHolcim Survey in Cameroon**
>
> One such survey conducted by LafargeHolcim in Cameroon enabled a financial institution to have a better grasp of its housing loan applicants, including their needs and expectations. Key findings from this 2014 survey included the following:
> - The monthly income of loan applicants ranges between CFAF 200,000 and CFAF 400,000 (US$340–680) with an estimated monthly savings of CFAF 120,000 (US$204); the age of applicants varied between 25 and 45 years.
> - Some 28 percent of housing loan applicants identified interest rates as the main factor influencing their selection of a financial institution. Other key selection criteria include the reputation of the financial institution (17 percent), the quality of service (16 percent), and the proximity of the financial institution (13 percent).
> - Credit applicants were mainly interested in medium- to long-term loans: 1–5 years (27 percent), 5–10 years (32 percent), and 10–15 years (16 percent).
> - Some 86 percent of credit applicants intended to use the loan for home construction, while the remaining 14 percent intended to use the loan for home improvements.
> - Some 76 percent of loan applicants are interested in receiving free technical assistance services such as bills of quantities (22 percent), advice on type of building materials (20 percent), advice on building material use (14 percent), and design specifications (13 percent).
> - There is a strong preference for two bedrooms (BR)/1 living room (LR)/1 kitchen (KT)/1 bathroom (BA) and 3 BR/1 LR/1 KT/2 BA bungalows or duplexes, on a land size ranging from 150 m² to 400 m².
>
> Source: Author; based on information obtained during fact-finding mission in October 2014.

In addition to market surveys, LafargeHolcim has developed a toolkit to train MFI loan officers on construction basics, as well as provide them with an IT tool to facilitate the processing of housing loan applications. This has contributed to building and strengthening staff capacity in LafargeHolcim's partner MFIs. Plus, borrowers are provided with free architectural designs and construction technical assistants who help loan applicants prepare bills of quantities. Some 70 percent of the loan amount is disbursed directly to LafargeHolcim's network of building material retailers, which helps to prevent leakages and ensure the loan is used for housing construction purposes.

Although it is still early to see the impact of LafargeHolcim's value-added approach on the HMF portfolio performance of partner MFIs, evidence from CEMEX's Patrimonio Hoy in Mexico shows that direct payment mechanisms can be an important safeguard against risks associated with clients' willingness to pay (Box 3.6).

---

**Box 3.6 From Cement Sales to Integrated Solutions: Cemex Patrimonio Hoy, Mexico**

CEMEX, a multinational Mexican-based cement producer, retains a close relationship with customers by thoroughly assessing needs and supplying holistic solutions through its subsidiary Patrimonio Hoy. CEMEX has been working with integral housing solutions and affordable building materials for more than 16 years and has refined its business model for cement sales through Patrimonio Hoy. The overall goal of Patrimonio Hoy is to offer a market-based solution to the housing needs of low-income families in urban marginalized areas in order to improve their quality of life and empower them. For CEMEX Patrimonio Hoy, the initial learning curve was steep. CEMEX knew that about 30–40 percent of bagged cement was consumed in the low-income segment, but CEMEX didn't know how people built, what their problems were, and so on. To acknowledge this, CEMEX made an internal Declaration of Ignorance.

To gain knowledge and get the model right, CEMEX launched an extensive hands-on market study in Guadalajara and was open to disregarding traditional business approaches and considering new ways to reach low-income customers. The key insight was that to build a 10 m² house, families on average spend four to five years on construction due to significant market failures, including (1) lack of access to credit and/or financing; (2) lack of

> competency (people are self-builders but lack construction knowledge and often get cheated); and (3) lack of storage opportunities, which leads to long building time.
> 
> As a result of these findings, CEMEX decided to rethink its customer relations by launching Patrimonio Hoy—an inclusive business, which offers integral housing solutions, covering not only construction, but also financing, expert advice, and the like. To ensure the development of valuable costumer relations, customers enter into a microlending model, where families sign up without any requirement beyond personal identification. The customer is responsible for committing to a 70-week project and remitting a modest weekly installment of US$21, which is held as credit toward future building material. The model functions as a saving and credit scheme where customers can choose between a schedule with multiple deliveries of building materials, depending on their needs and the desired timeline for building the construction.
> 
> Patrimonio Hoy retains a membership fee from each weekly remittance, which covers services and guaranties. Patrimonio Hoy, for example, provides an architect to plan and organize in situ with participants and all family members. In addition, the cost of materials is held fixed over the course of work, protecting customers from price fluctuations and other macroeconomic instability. Patrimonio Hoy also offers customers the option to take a break from material delivery, if customers run into periods of inconsistent employment or wish to delay construction.
> 
> By adding value to the customer relations, Patrimonio Hoy sells complete enabling solutions, which include financing, technical assistance, guarantees through fixed prices, and all kind of building and finishing materials. By using this model, the Patrimonio Hoy venture has provided affordable home improvement solutions to more than 425,000 families (equaling more than 2 million people) in Latin America and supported the construction of more than 3 million square meters of space. More than US$280 million has been granted in credits, with a repayment rate of 99 percent.
> 
> Source: GIZ 2014.

## B) Mortgage Guarantee Programs

Guarantee schemes aimed at incentivizing lenders to serve the poor and low-income groups are rarely used successfully in sub-Saharan Africa, given the small size of housing loan portfolios and the lack of the reliable data required to adequately price risks. Ghana, Kenya, and South Africa have developed a product called Collateral Replacement Indemnity

(CRI), which has had a moderate impact in increasing access to housing finance. The Home Loan Guarantee Company (HLGC), a nonprofit company in South Africa, launched the CRI product 25 years ago to replace the need for down payments. CRI enables potential loan borrowers to have an LTV of up to 100 percent. This product is often targeted to low- and moderate-income households. Through this product, the HLGC has enabled over 300,000 low-income South Africans to become homeowners. The HLGC has facilitated over R 40 billion (US$3.2 billion) in home loans to lower-income South Africans to date. An attempt in Mali to launch an LTV-based mortgage insurance has not been successful, at least for now. In Burkina Faso, a guarantee fund had also been developed for medium-term housing loans extended by Caisses Populaires du Burkina. However, this pilot project was never scaled up. In Nigeria, a state-backed guarantee scheme aimed at fostering more lending to lower-income groups is in the process of being created.

One of the major reasons why traditional lenders do not venture into the moderate to lower end of the housing finance market is the predominance of informal employment, a risk category they have failed to accurately assess. Creditworthy customers in this segment are ignored by mainstream financial institutions but may not find adequate products in the microfinance channel, which largely explains the "no man's land" between the two types of financial institutions. The capacity to serve informal income earners with loans larger than microcredits should be a powerful driver of significantly broadening the coverage of housing finance systems. Safely lending to the low- and informal-income segment is possible, as demonstrated in Morocco. Doing so requires conventional financial institutions to go the extra mile and learn how to better assess the creditworthiness of this population and not simply use the standard underwriting processes that clearly do not fit the purpose of pushing housing finance down market.

In Morocco, the government has developed an innovative and successful guarantee scheme, Fonds de Garantie pour les Populations à Revenus Irréguliers ou Modestes (FOGARIM), which encourages banks to finance informal- and low-income households by securing their loans against credit risk. This guarantee covers 70 percent of the mortgage loan, and up to 80 percent for loans under the Villes Sans Bidonvilles (VSB) program (see Chap. 5). Loans can be made available for up to 100 percent of the LTV or 80 percent in the case of VSB. The premium charges are fixed at between 0.25 percent and 0.5 percent annually, depending on the LTV (for LTVs less than 50 percent) and up to 0.65 percent (for LTVs above 90 percent). In addition to being a first-time homebuyer, borrowers must have life insurance and the house needs to be secured with a mortgage. Over 115,000 loans, or about 20 percent of all mortgages in Morocco, have been serviced under this scheme since its creation in 2004. The success of this program has been largely due to the strong political will and effort of the government in favor of implementing a housing policy.

India provides valuable examples of how two housing finance companies (HFCs)—Dewan Housing Finance Corporation and GRUH Finance Limited—are catering to the housing finance needs of the underserved low- and lower-middle-income households. GRUH, for instance, extends loans of between US$1,500 and US$15,000 for up to 20 years. These loans are secured both by mortgages and by personal guarantees, with LTVs not exceeding 65 percent. Borrowers are existing customers with a multiyear savings history. GRUH has a good knowledge of typical incomes generated by various trades in specific areas. It has developed an internal scoring model on which interest rate scales are based. The credit performance of GRUH portfolio is outstanding: the NPL rate fell to 0.32 percent in fiscal year 2013. In the wake of the market-deepening efforts initiated in 2008, new lenders have entered the informal population segment as they see the demonstrated lucrativeness of this housing market segment.

It is clear from these examples that know-your-customer principles are of particular importance in the low-income housing finance segment. It is recommended that borrowers must have built a credit record with their lenders, who need to have the ability to assess the cash flows of their customers over time, especially for undocumented income streams.

### 3.2.5.6 Financing Rental Housing

Affordable rental housing has significant potential in expanding access to housing to low-income families. However, this housing tenure option has been overlooked and neglected in many national housing policies across the continent. In Tunisia, for instance, the government has targeted a homeownership rate of 80 percent as a key part of its housing policy. In many African cities, a vast number of African households are currently tenants. Therefore, it is imperative for governments to adopt policies that could help develop and regulate rental housing. In Johannesburg, 42 percent of households are tenants compared with 63 percent in Cairo, while in Nairobi, 80 percent of dwellers are tenants. In Lagos, 60–65 percent of business professionals are tenants due to the high home prices and the lack of affordable mortgage products, according to Residential Auctions Company, a real estate research company in Nigeria. This trend is also prevalent across informal settlements in many African countries. In some cities, a majority of slum dwellers live in rented accommodations. In Dakar, an estimated 25.5 percent of slum dwellers are tenants, compared with 91.5 percent in Nairobi (Peppercorn and Taffin 2013).

The masked reality is that there remains a large segment of African households that cannot afford to buy a house, even one that is heavily subsidized. For many households, renting is a cheaper alternative to homeownership. Unlike in developed countries, rental housing is not yet an important component of national housing policies in Africa. Some obstacles to the growth in Africa's rental housing market include a high cultural bias in favor of homeownership, weak or nonexistent legal frameworks, and the lack of equity options to support rental property projects. As discussed in Chap. 5, part of the solution to the housing crisis has to come from mentality and behavioral changes to reflect the fact that not everyone can be a homeowner. Some people will have to settle for flats, implying some densification of construction. The economics of rental markets have already been well chronicled in other studies. Peppercorn and Taffin (2013) and UN-Habitat's "A Policy Guide to Rental Housing in Developing Countries" contain relevant proposals on how to increase the supply of affordable rental stocks in emerging markets.

The development of an affordable rental market in Africa largely depends on the commitment of governments to create an enabling environment in terms of regulation, taxation, and the necessary legal framework. Laws are needed that clearly outline tenant rights and obligations, as well as provide effective legal protection to landlords. Improved legal frameworks are currently in place or are being drafted in countries such as Egypt, Tunisia, Morocco, and South Africa. Prior rental legislation in Egypt froze rental values and enforced the renewal of contracts between tenants and landlords, with apartments sometimes passing down through generations (Egypt Independent 2012). In 2012, over 4 million rental units in Egypt were vacant, an unintended consequence of rent controls, which further strangled growth in rental housing stocks. The Egyptian government is currently revising its rental framework to address these obstacles. In 2014, Morocco took measures that significantly improved its legal framework. The revised rental law outlined the obligations of tenants and landlords, and clearly defined conditions for lease renewals and termination. An 8 percent rent increase every three years was also enshrined in the new legislation. This improved legal environment has attracted new investments to the rental market.

On the financial front, regulators need to create an enabling environment that ensures financial institutions can raise long-term funds from financiers at an affordable cost. Balanced landlord-tenant relationships are critical to attract capital in this important segment, while ensuring tenure security to families. Rental frameworks are however not widespread, and sometimes are very constraining. South Africa's 1999 Rental Housing Act provides a rare example of a relatively investor-friendly framework. In developed countries, the government provides tax incentives and grants to improve the quality and quantity of private rental stocks. The Low Income Housing Tax Credit (LIHTC) program in the United States is one example of methods used by governments to attract private capital for rental housing targeted to low-income households. The Caisse des Dépôts model (see Chap. 1) can also be a source of long-term funding for rental housing.

Most important, a real estate investment trust (REIT) can be a novel investment vehicle for channeling resources from the capital market to rental investments in Africa. Given the fact that capital markets on the continent are in their infancy, this instrument can be realistically envisioned only in the medium to long term, to allow time for African capital markets to mature. A REIT is a special purpose vehicle (SPV), company that invests in both residential and commercial real estate. REITs can also invest in mortgages and mortgage-backed securities. As an investment vehicle, REITs enable investors to own equity stakes in the assets it owns in a way similar to owning shares in any other company open to the general trading public. Shareholders receive rental income in the form of dividends from property assets and also benefit from the growth of these assets overtime. Being traded on the local stock exchange also makes this asset very liquid. Fideicomiso Hipotecario, or FHipo, the first mortgage REIT in Latin America, established in November 2014, is a case in point. FHipo's initial public offering on the Mexican Stock Exchange raised more than US$633 million, with U.S. investors accounting for about 60 percent of this amount.

Residential REITs have proven successful in many countries. However, so far there are none in Africa, owing certainly to the shallowness of the capital markets, low risk-adjusted investment returns, the lack of large-scale residential assets, and the lack of adequate legal and regulatory frameworks. Nevertheless, Kenya, Nigeria, Rwanda, and South Africa have all adopted REIT frameworks, the usual first step in institutionalizing this investment vehicle. However, only South Africa has taken the next step to actually create one. Morocco is reportedly crafting a REIT framework; however, this legislation is intended to support commercial real estate for the time being.

Facilitating the expansion of this new asset class in line with global best practices would attract international investors to Africa's affordable rental and housing market. Moreover, doing so will provide an avenue for both individual and institutional investors to invest in Africa's housing market. A good starting point will be for governments to adopt legislative changes that will facilitate the development of capital markets and authorize the creation and successful rollout of REITs for affordable housing. These changes would include income tax deductions; a generous depreciation allowance, especially for newly constructed buildings; permitting a portion of rental income losses to be transferred to other assets for tax purposes; or reductions in capital gain taxes, all methods that could be used to increase the rate of return on investment (Oxley et al. 2010). Moreover, conditional subsidies and grants can also be provided to private developers for the construction of affordable rental housing. On the demand side, governments should also support a favorable regulatory environment, not just for landlords, but also for tenants, and provide rebates or voucher programs to increase demand from low-income households.

DFIs, in partnership with the private sector, should consider pioneering the development of an affordable housing REIT in order to provide long-term equity and debt financing for housing. However, DFIs should take the lead role in structuring, coordinating, and financing this groundbreaking venture. An example of a possible REIT is displayed in Fig. 3.4, whereby DFIs such as the African Development Bank (AfDB), IFC, Shelter Afrique, and other institutional investors—such as pension funds, regional banks, and insurance companies—could be anchor sponsors on this project. DFIs' early involvement in structuring such a project is expected to instill confidence among potential financiers, especially international investors.

On the basis of its investment criteria, a REIT vehicle can make investments in numerous affordable housing projects. Initially, the REIT could focus on financing new and existing properties, and gradually expand to purchasing affordable mortgages backed by real estate assets. Initiatives such as the US$300 million IFC-CITIC investment platform to develop affordable housing projects ranging in size from 2,000 to 8,000 units should make it possible to build a REIT portfolio across the continent that can yield a risk-adjusted return of at least 6 percent or slightly higher. The portfolio of this company could consist primarily of affordable housing projects; say, 70 percent for instance, with upper-income housing, investment in land acquisition, and commercial real estate accounting for the remaining 30 percent. Rental yields in Africa are quite high compared with those in other emerging markets. Table 3.7 provides a comparative overview of rental yields in selected emerging markets. Such a mixed portfolio holding would provide comfort to investors on the quality, viability, and sustainability of an affordable housing REIT in the long term.

The tax-neutral structure of this SPV will be an added benefit, as all net rental income will be passed along to shareholders, thereby avoiding the problem of double taxation. Moreover, each investment project should be financed through its own unique SPV. Doing so will help mitigate risks by ring-fencing each project from other REIT-backed investments.

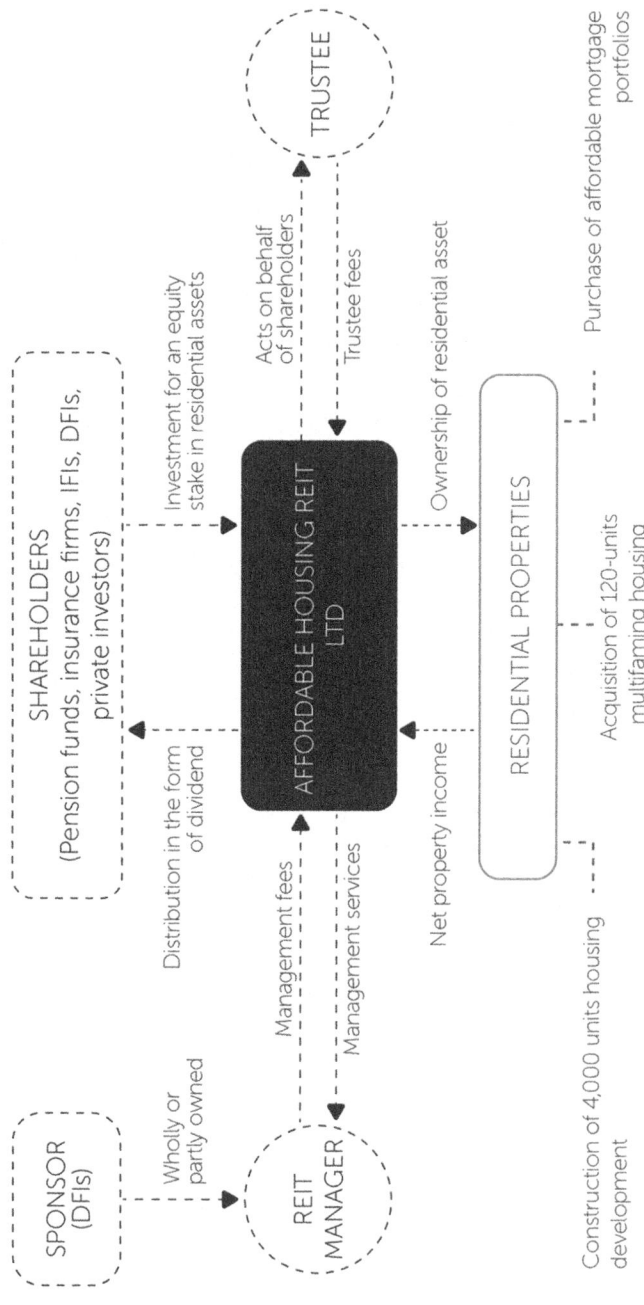

**Fig. 3.4** An illustrative REIT structure for affordable housing projects (Source: Author.)

Table 3.7 Rental yields in selected emerging markets

| Country | Price/m² (US$)ᵃ | Rent/month (US$) | Yield p.a. (%) |
|---|---|---|---|
| Africa | | | |
| Egypt | 831 | 977 | 9.40 |
| Gambia | 667 | 330 | 5.94 |
| Kenya | 1188 | 820 | 6.90 |
| Madagascar | 520 | 320 | 7.38 |
| Morocco | 2015 | 1217 | 6.04 |
| South Africa | 4214 | 1636 | 3.88 |
| Tanzania | 700 | 500 | 8.57 |
| Other Emerging Markets | | | |
| Argentina | 2632 | 2032 | 7.72 |
| Brazil | 3751 | 1765 | 4.71 |
| Cambodia | 2913 | 1553 | 5.33 |
| Ecuador | 1278 | 1027 | 8.04 |
| El Salvador | 1193 | 1013 | 8.49 |
| India | 11,455 | 2540 | 2.22 |
| Malaysia | 2873 | 1004 | 3.50 |
| Mexico | 2635 | 2045 | 7.76 |

Source: Global Property Guide
ᵃAverage buying price per square meter

Eventually, the shares of such a REIT should be listed on local exchanges in countries where REIT legislation has been adopted, in line with global best practices. Cross-border listings will increase liquidity in the trading of shares, reduce the cost of capital, and expand sources of capital for Africa's affordable housing market.

## 3.3 Conclusion

In this chapter, we attempted to provide a succinct description of the housing finance market in Africa. In order to draw a more complete, continent-wide picture, we used regional and country examples to illustrate the depth of the housing finance market. We also looked at critical components in the housing value chain, including the often-neglected rental housing finance market.

Given the continent's shallow mortgage market, it is obvious that a viable alternative for a majority of African families, particularly poor and low-middle-income households, is to use products such as HMF and contractual housing saving schemes. These alternative products can play an important complementary role to the mortgage market. Other promising initiatives in increasing access to finance for consumers and developers were also showcased. However, our analysis has demonstrated that some sort of creativity and ingenuity is needed to circumvent the risk problem, if one is determined to push the housing finance frontier and extend access to those in need. This then requires actions and measures within the housing finance system geared toward devising and promoting innovative business models that deal with the associated risks. Initiatives geared toward derisking housing finance should be facilitated and supported by governments, which could cover some of the risk and help reduce the risk of transactions. Better still, governments can work together with private investors to develop some credit-enhancement facilities. We provided policy considerations for developing the continent's housing finance market and expanding private lending for housing.

Designing and implementing institutional, legal, and regulatory frameworks to promote affordable housing finance is critical for making potential housing demand effective. In this regard, the design and implementation of subsidy programs, mechanisms for increasing access to long-term funding, and the strengthening of prudential frameworks present opportunities for expanding access to affordable housing finance for low- and middle-income families, including informal-income households. Following are some specific policy measures and initiatives. It is important to note that, given that specific housing finance policies should be local, each country is call for to develop an actionable affordable housing policy that suits the need of its population.

*Strengthening safeguards including prudential frameworks without stifling innovations for affordable housing finance* is critical to the health and stability of the financial system and economy. Governments and regulators, with the support of development partners, should develop and implement prudent lending standards, particularly for low-income households. This effort should include financial awareness programs, consumer protection and advisory services to borrowers, frameworks for asset-liability mismatches, and mandatory stress tests, particularly for adjustable-rate mortgages and housing loans. Model frameworks include the National Foundation for Financial Literacy, housed at the Central Bank of

Morocco, and South Africa's National Credit Act, which includes provisions to limit over-indebtedness, provide debt counseling, and establish both a national credit regulator and a consumer tribunal. Promoting housing finance inclusion through financial literacy campaigns and consumer protection is a key prerequisite for the stability and sustainability of a well-functioning housing finance market.

In the long term, standardizing mortgage underwriting practices and procedures is key for developing secondary mortgage markets. However, in the short term, particularly in the low-income housing market, customizing underwriting requirements to the specificities of this market segment is crucial. Key prudential lending criteria for low-income households should include developing the capacity of lenders to assess undocumented income such as requiring prior savings history. Once the income level is ascertained, lenders should assess the disposable income of low- and low-middle-income borrowers rather than simply applying standard debt-to-income ratios. Moreover, loan-to-value ratios (because of prior savings requirements) and debt-to-income ratios (to cushion against income stream fluctuations) should be lower than average.

Noncollateralized lending, which should only be done to accommodate households that lack full title to property, should only be considered in the case where a long-term relationship exists with customers, as well as an established cash flow and credit history. Nonetheless, alternative guarantees such as personal guarantees or savings placed in an escrow account should be sought during the life of the loan, as well as some form of tenure security. This is the method adopted in the community-based lending approach in the popular savings and loan sector in Mexico, where unsecured lending for housing with maturities of up to 10 years is supported by the second-tier government refinancing entity, Sociedad Hipotecaria Federal.

In addition, loan profiles could be adjusted to reflect the irregular income streams of low-income households. The HFC of Kenya provides an illustrative example. Under its "cyclical mortgage," repayments are set on pre-agreed cycles—quarterly, biannually, or yearly. However, this product primarily targets self-employed borrowers whose employment is at least partially formal, as it requires audited accounts and three-year cash flow projections. Another approach developing in some sub-Saharan

African countries is the opening of social security schemes to nonsalaried households, such as Kenya's Mbao pension plan, and in Côte d'Ivoire, where both private-and public-sector pension organizations are in the process of offering protection on a voluntary basis. Such approaches can have an indirect but important impact on the opportunities for informal households to access housing finance. One can expect this development to foster the progressive integration of informal-sector households into the formal financial system. It can also contribute in improving the access of informal households to housing finance in the various functions that pension funds can fulfill such as building a savings and credit record, and providing collateral or direct lending.

*Supporting the development of necessary housing market infrastructure* is another important initiative. One condition for a successful housing finance market is the existence of a credit bureau with a comprehensive credit profile on potential borrowers. Credit bureaus provide lenders with the information needed to ascertain borrowers' repayment capacity. It is imperative for governments and development partners to build and strengthen credit information registries so as to overcome one of the major barriers in the low-income housing market. The IFC, through its Africa Credit Bureau Program, is already working with numerous governments and the private sector to develop their credit information sharing and reporting systems. This program provides advisory services to market stakeholders such as central banks, creditors, lenders, consumers, and banking associations on effective and efficient ways of building credit registries. Supporting such initiatives should also promote responsible lending and reduce credit losses.

Furthermore, there is a need for a formal appraisal of residential mortgages in many countries so as to help address transactional inefficiencies. Information gathered from a consolidated housing database, as described below, is a crucial part of any valuation system. This will require well-trained and qualified valuators to ensure properties are accurately valued on the price that could be obtained in the market. There is a need for accepted standards of property valuation in many countries, which should be based on sound principles and best practices.

Strengthening institutions, including the legal and regulatory framework, is critical for a more efficient housing market, as well as for the development of a secondary mortgage market. This could include strengthening the legal infrastructure by building the capacity of the judiciary system to fairly and efficiently handle mortgage foreclosure cases or adopting legislative reforms that permit nonjudicial foreclosures, as in Ethiopia, where the central bank is tasked with administering the foreclosure process and reviewing mortgage contracts.

*Promoting credit-linked subsidy programs that leverage private savings with strong monitoring and evaluation systems* is another important initiative. Developing segment-specific products is important for expanding access to housing finance to various income groups. One such product could include a housing-linked contract savings scheme, as in Ethiopia and some European countries. This product should primarily target economically active poor households that may be able to afford a mortgage or a housing loan to purchase or construct a house but do not have access to finance. Once customers attain a minimum savings threshold, they become eligible for a mortgage or housing loan to be provided by the financial institution. This savings would provide a basis for assessing the borrowers' repayment capacity and could also serve as collateral for the housing loan. Similar to the Ethiopian model, eligibility criteria for the subsidy amount should be designed on a progressive scale. Doing so would enable the government to maximize the effectiveness of its subsidy programs, while attracting private capital into the underserved housing market. Subsidies could also be done through real estate tax deductions, land grants, and infrastructure provision.

*Expanding the range of innovative low-cost HMF products and services* would improve access to finance for low-income and informal-earning households. HMF is critical for expanding access and providing viable services to low- and moderate-income families. As evident in many African and Latin American countries, this form of microlending has enabled many poor households to incrementally build, improve, and expand their houses. Meeting this unmet demand for HMF should be accompanied by prudential lending policies and procedures. Similar to a savings-for-housing scheme, clients with no preexisting savings or lending history should be required to show a minimum period of savings—12 months, for instance. In the absence of documented evidence of income, this mandatory period of savings can be used as an income proxy and to ascertain the creditworthiness of clients. This eligibility criterion can also serve as an income proxy for informal-sector workers, as well as a risk management tool.

*Supporting the provision of construction technical assistance and housing support services* is important, given its crucial role in successful HMF lending aimed at low-income families. Construction technical assistance is compatible with the practice of self-construction, which accounts for over 70 percent of new housing supply in most African countries. This technical assistance could include training self-help builders on construction techniques, building capacity in MFIs, preparing layout drawings, optimizing bills of quantities, supervising construction sites, and providing access to lower-cost building materials. The provision of construction technical assistance will ensure a minimum level of quality and safety for houses financed by MFIs, while also promoting customer loyalty. Successful models include LafargeHolcim's partnership, CEMEX discussed above, and the WAT Human Settlement Trust in Tanzania. The construction technical assistance pilot programs of Habitat for Humanity provide other practical approaches also.

Deepening, broadening, and scaling up this innovative product to sustainability will require expanding access to long-term credit and diversifying the investor base for HMF lenders. In South Africa, for instance, through the National Housing Finance Corporation and Rural Housing Loan Fund, the government provides wholesale finance to specialist housing microlenders for on-lending to low-income households. It is recommended that commercial banks partner with MFIs to enable the continuous and dependable flow of finance for lenders. Doing so can open new markets to mainstream banks, while providing MFIs with the resources and expertise required for housing finance. These linkages could include servicing arrangements, information exchange, or ownership relationships. The Mutuelle Communautaire de Croissance (MC2), a microfinance network established by Afriland First Bank in Cameroon, provides an illustrative model of the MFI-Bank linkage. MC2 relies on Afriland for funding and also mobilizes savings at the base of the pyramid for Afriland. Afriland manages or supports the internal control and regulatory reporting, and accounting and provides capacity building for MC2's staff. In India, notable examples are the self-help group and bank linkage models and the nonbanking financial company–MFI partnership. The tripartite partnership arranged by the BHS is another successful strand of this model. This successful and sustainable MFI-bank partnership can be useful in overcoming the challenges traditionally faced by the financial sector in serving low-income families.

*Partnerships between commercial banks and MFIs* can be another important initiative. It is proposed that MFIs that pass a rigorous due diligence enter into a servicing arrangement with commercial banks. Under this arrangement, the MFI, for a servicing fee, will originate housing loans and undertake monitoring and collection functions for the bank. The bank, in turn, provides funding to the MFI to originate some or all of their housing loans to existing customers, with the bank holding the housing loans originated on its balance sheet. In order to mitigate the credit risk borne by the bank, the MFI needs to share the risk of default by providing a first-loss guarantee up to a specified level. For instance, 20 percent of the housing portfolio originated by MFIs could be provided in the form of cash collateral to the funding bank as a first-loss guarantee to cover each loan default. This will ensure a high quality of origination, as the MFI will have some skin in the game. In order to incentivize banks to lend to MFI clients, some form of guarantee is imperative. An intermediary, such as a government housing agency, a guarantee fund, or a DFI, should provide second-loss guarantees to the bank. The second-loss guarantee should cover the principal and interest payment defaults up to an agreed-upon threshold, after the first-loss guarantee is depleted. After the second-loss guarantee is exhausted, it is proposed that the funding bank begin the process of taking possession of the acquired property through sales or other outlets. Under this proposed structure, the role of DFIs and other market facilitators should include supporting market studies, conducting product design and pilots, providing capacity building to the MFI and bank staff, promoting partnerships between MFIs and banks, and incentivizing financial institutions to serve low-income families, as well as generating and disseminating knowledge products and industry best practices.

*Supporting the development of risk mitigation instruments such as guarantee or insurance mechanisms is vital to increase the effective demand and supply of housing for the poor.* In order to increase the appetite of lenders to extend access to housing finance to irregular- and low-income families, it is imperative for governments and development partners to promote innovations that primarily target low-income groups. Feasibility studies are a necessary prerequisite for the development and implementation of such risk mitigation instruments.

*Designing and implementing an effective household targeting system is vital for the efficient channeling of resources to the poor.* Developing data collection strategies should be the starting point in designing these systems. A consumer survey, such as data collected in a census, is one approach that could be used in collecting data and developing a concrete understanding of households. An adequate information management system, such as a national database, is crucial for avoiding duplication, tracking beneficiaries, and controlling fraud. Equally important is the institutional arrangement (centralized vs. decentralized system) selected for implementing the household targeting systems. However, institutional roles should be tailored to country needs and the available institutional capacity. Last, strong instruments for monitoring and evaluating targeting systems, such as random checks and verification of information provided, are crucial for ensuring transparency and preventing leakages. Best practices from Latin America, such as Chile's Ficha CAS system, Colombia's SISBEN system, and Costa Rica's SIPO system, can be used to design strategies and outline procedures for household targeting systems in Africa.

*Developing a consolidated housing market database* is vital for supporting the sector's development and overcoming informational inefficiencies. Governments, with the support of development partners, should facilitate the construction of national information systems to collect the housing data necessary for a well-designed and targeted housing policy. This real estate information portal should contain information on housing demand and supply, and the housing finance market. Data collected should include information on housing and rental stocks, land value estimates, the housing price index, the construction cost index, property information, and other relevant data. Data collated from public agencies, relevant government ministries, financial institutions, and real estate developers would be valuable for time series analyses of country data, trends analysis, and policy setting. DFIs have a critical role to play in supporting this market development activity. Institutions such as the AfDB and the World Bank Group could engage in capacity-building activities, advocacy campaigns, and provide incentives to market actors to collect data. DFIs can also partner with NGOs such as the Centre for Affordable Housing Finance in Africa (CAHF) and the Housing Finance Information Network to develop a continent-wide web portal with standardized indicators, which will facilitate cross-country comparisons of housing programs, policies, laws, and regulations in a central location.

## Notes

1. For a detailed assessment of the achievements of the South African Financial Sector Charter, see Center for Affordable Housing Finance in Africa, *Housing Finance in Africa*, 2013, 2014, and 2015 Yearbooks.

## Bibliography

Adams, Z., and R. Füss. 2010. Macroeconomic Determinants of International Housing Markets. *Journal of Housing Economics* 19 (1): 38.

Al Aissami, Nouaman, and Hicham Talby. 2013. Morocco Covered Bonds Project. In *Law in Transition 2013: Financial Law Reform: From Moscow to Casablanca*. London: European Bank for Reconstruction and Development.

BCEAO (Banque Centrale des Etats de l'Afrique de l'Ouest). 2014. *Note d'Analyse sur les Conditions de Financement Bancaire de l'Habitat dans les Pays de l'UEMOA*. Dakar: BCEAO.

Beck, T., M. Munzele, I. Faye, and T. Triki. 2011. *Financing Africa: Through the Crisis and Beyond*. Washington, DC: World Bank Publications.

Buckley, Robert. 1996. *Housing Finance in Developing Countries*. London: Macmillan.

Chen, J., and A. Zhu. 2008. *The Relationship Between Housing Investment and Economic Growth in China: A Panel Analysis Using Quarterly Provincial Data*, Working Paper. China National Social Science Foundation.

Economic Commission for Europe. 2005. *Housing Finance Systems for Countries in Transition: Principles and Examples*. New York: United Nations.

*Egypt Independent.* 2012. *Antiquated Rental Law Distorts Housing Market,* October 12. http://www.egyptindependent.com/news/antiquated-rental-law-distorts-housing-market.

GIZ (Deutsche Gesellschaft für Internationale Zusammenarbeit). 2014. *My Home, Your Business. A Guide to Affordable Housing Solutions for Low-Income Communities.* Bonn: Eschborn GIZ.

Goldberg, Michael, and Marialisa Motta. 2003. Microfinance for Housing: The Mexican Case. *Journal of Microfinance* 5 (1): 51–76.

Goodhart, C., and B. Hofmann. 2008. House Prices, Money, Credit, and the Macroeconomy. *Oxford Review of Economic Policy* 24 (1): 180–205.

Habitat for Humanity (HfH). (2011). *Annual Review 2011 INTERNET.* http://www.downloads.habitatforhumanity.org.uk/AnnualReview2010-2011.pdf

Hassler, Olivier, and Simon Walley. 2012. *Mortgage Liquidity Facilities,* Policy Note. World Bank, Washington, DC. http://documents.worldbank.org/curated/en/2012/01/16388290/mortgage-liquidity-facilities.

Hongyu, Liu, Y. Park, and Z. Siqi. 2002. The Interaction Between Housing Investment and Economic Growth in China. *International Real Estate Review* 5 (1): 40–60.

Houston, Anthea. 2010. *Housing Support Services for Housing Microfinance Lending in East and Southern Africa: A Case Study of the National Cooperative Housing Union (NACHU).* FinMark Trust, Midrand, South Africa, and Rooftops Canada, Toronto.

Kihato, Michael. 2013. *State of Housing Microfinance in Africa* (January 24, 2013). Available at SSRN: https://ssrn.com/abstract=2384688

Lea, Michael J., and Bertrand Renaud. 1995. *Contractual Savings for Housing: How Suitable Are They for Transitional Economies?* Policy Research Working Paper WPS 1516. Washington, DC: World Bank. http://documents.worldbank.org/curated/en/1995/09/697085/contractual-savings-housing-suitable-transitional-economies.

Mali, Aurelien, and Cyril Audrin. 2013. *International Sovereign Issuance in Africa 2013–14: A Rating Agency Perspective.* Moody's Investor Service.

Manson, Katrina. 2014. Private Equity Remains a Rarity in African Pension Portfolios. *Financial Times,* October 5. http://www.ft.com/intl/cms/s/0/ec152992-1e52-11e4-ab52-00144feabdc0.html?siteedition=intl#axzz3cfxVjhXX.

Masetti, Oliver, and Aila Mihr. 2013. *Capital Markets in Sub-Saharan Africa,* Research Briefing. Deutsche Bank, Frankfurt.

Oxley, M., R. Lishman, T. Brown, M. Haffner, and J. Hoekstra. 2010. *Promoting Investment in Private Rented Housing Supply. International Policy Comparisons*. London: Department for Communities and Local Government. https://www.dora.dmu.ac.uk/bitstream/handle/2086/7535/CLG%20PRS.pdf?sequence=1. Viewed 20 Feb 2014.

Panagiotidis, Theodore, and Panagiotis Printzis. 2015. *On the Macroeconomic Determinants of the Housing Market in Greece: A VECM Approach*, GreeSE Papers No. 88. Hellenic Observatory, European Institute, London.

Peppercorn, Ira Gary, and Claude Taffin. 2013. *Rental Housing: Lessons from International Experience and Policies for Emerging Markets*. Washington, DC: World Bank.

Ratha, Dilip, and Sonia Plaza. 2011. *Harnessing Diasporas, Finance & Development*. Washington, DC: International Monetary Fund.

Serrano, Loretta. 2008. *Construmex: Facilitating Remote Housing Investments for US-Based Mexican Migrants*, GIM Case Study No. A013. United Nations Development Programme, New York.

Taffin, Claude. 1998. 'Epargne logement' in France. *Housing Finance International* 4: 27–33.

UNECA (UN Economic Commission for Africa). 2014. *Private Equity and the Growth of Pension Funds Provide a Massive Opportunity to Finance Investment*. Press Release. http://amediaagency.com/private-equity-growth-pension-funds-provide-massive-opportunity-finance-investment/.

Uy, Willie. 2006. *Medium-Rise Housing: The Philippine Experience*, Presentation Paper for the 5th Asian Forum, Tokyo.

Vittas, Dimitri. 2003. *The Role of Occupational Pension Funds in Mauritius*, Policy Research Working Paper 3033. Development Research Group, Finance, World Bank, Washington, DC.

Williams-Stanton, Sonya. 2012. *Housing, Economic Growth, and Poverty: A Review of the Literature*. IFC working paper

World Bank. 2014. *Migration and Remittances: Recent Developments and Outlook*. Washington, DC: The World Bank.

**Open Access** This chapter is licensed under the terms of the Creative Commons Attribution 4.0 International License (http://creativecommons.org/licenses/by/4.0/), which permits use, sharing, adaptation, distribution and reproduction in any medium or format, as long as you give appropriate credit to the original author(s) and the source, provide a link to the Creative Commons license and indicate if changes were made.

The images or other third party material in this chapter are included in the chapter's Creative Commons license, unless indicated otherwise in a credit line to the material. If material is not included in the chapter's Creative Commons license and your intended use is not permitted by statutory regulation or exceeds the permitted use, you will need to obtain permission directly from the copyright holder.

# 4

# Unlocking Land Markets and Infrastructure Provision

## 4.1 Introduction

Land, along with the provision of bulk infrastructure, is central to any discussion on housing development in Africa. As the continent rapidly urbanizes and its population continues to grow, demand for urban and peri-urban land is increasing. This strong demand, fueled in part by the rising income of urban households, has translated to high land sales and rental values. In most African cities, the high cost of urban housing is often due to several issues including inadequate land governance policies that encourage speculative acquisitions, poor urban planning that generates urban sprawl, and the lack of critical infrastructure that has significantly increased the cost of serviced land. Land servicing costs adds to the housing development costs. As a consequence, the available serviced land is limited and out of reach for the majority.

Moreover, high land prices are, in most cases, the consequence of inadequate land policies that result in inefficiencies in the process of making land available for housing development. It is noted that high land prices, weak land markets, and inadequate land administration processes have been the main drivers of informal land market developments in many countries across the continent. As a result, the proliferation of informal settlements is a common feature in most large African cities. Today, over 60 percent of urban households in sub-Saharan Africa, consisting mainly of low- and middle-income families, live in informal settlements, compared with about 13 percent in North Africa (UN-Habitat 2010).

In sum, multiple tenure regimes, costly and rigid land administrative procedures, and inefficiencies induced by the political economy of land policies—the usual problems that bedevil formal land markets in Africa—are to blame for the continent's dysfunctional land market. Overall, it is important to note that it is the weak governance in many countries that continues to breed corruption, inefficiency, and speculation in land markets. As a result, most African urban households cannot afford to access formally titled land and intrinsically formal housing.

Moreover, much of Africa's urban expansion is occurring through the unplanned and low-density consumption of rural land. Long-standing cultural preferences for freestanding homes and the lack of formal high-density housing developments have accelerated urban sprawl patterns and the growth of informal settlements across many countries. Africa's growing urban sprawl not only affects rural livelihoods and the future growth patterns of urban settlements, it also entails financial, social, and environmental costs. Most important is the cost of upgrading or putting in place infrastructure and services after the development of peripheral urban settlements, which is excessively prohibitive, especially in informal settlements.

The lack of critical infrastructure further inhibits housing developments in many parts of the continent. Most local and even central governments in Africa today are unable to provide the requisite bulk infrastructure such as roads, electricity, water, sewerage, and road connections to residential properties. As a result, plenty of potentially promising land is not readily available for the housing market.

The result of the above-mentioned constraints is a housing market sharply divided between the haves and the have-nots. At one extreme, a small elite benefit from easy access to land, quality housing, and mortgage products. At the other, the majority of households are stuck in the vast informal sector, reliant on alternative forms of credit, the informal land market, and self-provided housing as well as infrastructure and service connections.

This chapter attempts to describe Africa's dysfunctional land markets for housing. It is organized around four important land market phenomena that have major implications on formal sector provision of land and infrastructure for affordable housing in Africa: (1) poor land governance and administration systems; (2) implications of unclear land tenure rights and regime; (3) urban sprawl; and (4) how to increase land supply and the provision of basic infrastructure services.

## 4.2 Land Governance and Administration in Africa

Current land policies and administrative frameworks in Africa have been significantly influenced by various social, economic, and political factors inherited during the colonial era. Under colonialism, titled land was reserved for Europeans and the colonial administration; many Africans could access land only under customary user rights. This is particularly true in former British colonies, wherein Crown land was governed under English law, whereas land occupied by indigenous people was administered under customary law, as in Kenya (Doebele 1983; Wanjala 1990; Musyoka and Musoga 2015).

### 4.2.1 Multiple Tenure Regimes and Unclear Land Rights

The coexistence with the formal system of a customary system of land holding and statutory land rights is prevalent across Africa. Often, government institutions responsible for demarcation of plot boundaries, land registration, record-keeping, and adjudication of land rights are poorly coordinated, with a poor governance system, largely ineffective and lack capacity. This failure has partially contributed to the existence of multiple, parallel, and sometimes even overlapping land tenure regimes across Africa. Although some countries have adopted improvements in the security of land rights, for a majority of African governments, land reforms and the enforcement of property rights remain a challenge.

Today, an estimated 10 percent of land in Africa is formally registered to individuals as private (freehold) property, although wide variations exist across regions. In West Africa, for example, only 2–3 percent of land is titled—most of it situated around major cities. In Cameroon, 31 years after the legislation requiring land titling was enacted in 1974, less than 2 percent of land or an estimated 125,000 titles have been registered (USAID 2011). Likewise, in Burundi, as in most African countries, less than 1 percent of land is registered. In Uganda and Kenya, less than 15 percent of the country is covered under the land titling and cadastral system (Augustinus and Deininger 2005).

Besides creating optimum conditions for entrenching inequalities and failing to protect vulnerable groups, this dual-tenure system has been primarily used to serve the interests of elites in postcolonial Africa. Although legal frameworks for land titling and property rights have been established in many African countries today, these policies have often failed to achieve an efficient and equitable land market because most reforms have been ad hoc and top-down. Moreover, in most African countries there is a lack of a well-defined and coordinated institutional framework to implement the policies effectively. This is exemplified in the constant wrangling between the Ministry of Lands in Kenya and the National Lands Commission over their mandates and responsibilities.

Nowadays, despite the development of comprehensive land reforms promoting statutory land rights in many countries (Table 4.1), customary tenures remain predominant. Today, a vast majority of land sales and rental transactions take place outside statutory legal systems. In sub-Saharan Africa, customary or informal land markets account for 30–90 percent of all land transactions (Durand-Lasserve 2003). A study conducted in six African countries—Botswana, Kenya, Lesotho, Nigeria, Uganda, and Zambia—showed that 50–70 percent of land transactions for housing take place in the informal markets (Rakodi and Leduka 2004). In Zambia, for example, about 94 percent of urban land is governed under customary laws, with statutory land accounting for only 6 percent of available urban land (UN-Habitat 2012a). In Uganda and in Ghana, customary tenure covers about 60 percent and 78 percent of the

Table 4.1 Land reforms in selected African countries

| | |
|---|---|
| Land policy with legal recognition of customary land | Ghana (1999), Guinea (2001) |
| Land laws enacted with formal recognition of customary or user rights to land and security of customary land tenure | Niger (1993), Benin (2007), Burkina Faso (2009), Côte d'Ivoire (1998), Ethiopia (2005), South Sudan (2009), Kenya (2012), Tanzania (1999), Angola (2004), Namibia (2002), Zambia (1995), Botswana (1968/1993), South Africa (1998), Madagascar (2005), Mozambique (1998), Uganda (1998), Rwanda (2005), Malawi (2002) |
| Consultative process to establish new land laws with recognition of customary rights | Gambia (1990), Mali (2009), Senegal (2005), Nigeria (2009), Lesotho (2008/2009), Sierra Leone (2010), Guinea-Bissau (1998) |
| Land is nationalized | Ethiopia (1975), Mozambique (1975) |

Source: Amanor (2012); national sources

countries' total areas, respectively (AUC-ECA-AfDB 2012). In South Africa, an estimated 40 percent of available land parcels is still under customary land tenure.

In many parts of the continent, land governance frameworks are weak and are often restricted by the complexity of land systems. Attempts to achieve greater efficiency and equity in land markets have resulted in the nationalization of land for public good in some countries, such as Ethiopia and Mozambique. However, very few governments that have chosen the path of nationalization have achieved equitable and transparent land distribution, particularly for the benefit of poor households and marginalized groups. Our fact-finding field visits revealed that even for those countries where land belongs to the state *de jure* as stipulated in the country's Constitution (e.g., Côte d'Ivoire), in practice, the existence of a customary land regime in parallel makes the law null and void. There is a *de facto* dual land regime which complicates the land governance system. Processes for obtaining formal land rights and individual titles remain onerous, expensive, and inefficient for the majority of households. Merging the systems of customary and formal land rights is a major challenge faced by most African governments today. In subsequent sections, we discuss efforts made to strengthen and enforce land rights in Africa while highlighting the impediments induced by the existence of a dual–land tenure regime.

## 4.2.2 Poor Land Administration and Management Systems

Efficient and effective land management and administration is imperative to sustain affordable housing development. In many countries, urban land management and administration remain heavily centralized, particularly in francophone sub-Saharan Africa relative to anglophone sub-Saharan African countries. The reluctance to decentralize land management and administration to city governments has hindered the development of effective land markets able to satisfy the large demand of urban land. Moreover, the complex administrative procedures and high centralization of land management breed more corruption in land markets.

Even though some countries have adopted policies to decentralize land management to local governments and streamline the registration procedure, in many countries the process of land titling remains long and arduous, with many steps and documents still required. In Kenya, even government officials acknowledge that for many households the steps to register land are not easy to understand. As a consequence, many Kenyans abandon the land registration process or seek tenure security through informal means such as giving "gifts" to speed up the land titling process. In other countries, the registration process can also be exclusive, as in the urban areas of Cameroon, for example, where land in some parts can be allocated only to indigenous people or "autochtones." As a result, land information systems cover only a small portion of available land in most countries, resulting in unclear ownership rights. This reflects the lack of an adequate land registration system including up-to-date maps and registries that can identify and prove who owns land.

Furthermore, in many countries, land data and registries are still maintained manually due to a lack of capacity to acquire and use modern technologies. As a result, information on registered land and land rights is often inconsistent and difficult to gather. Efforts to put together efficient land information systems have often been hampered by the lack of adequate resources (AUC-ECA-AfDB 2010). Consequently, it is not uncommon for land registries to issue multiple titles to different people for the same plot of land. Moreover, inaccuracies in boundary limits are commonplace, resulting in land disputes and conflicts. To ensure precision in land record management, governments will need to adopt modern, computerized land registry and cadaster systems. According to the World Bank's Doing Business 2016 report, economies that have digitized their land registry and property systems have seen a 38 percent reduction in the time required to transfer property since 2011, compared with a drop of just 7 percent in countries that have not. Rwanda provides a good example of how computerization can increase transparency, security, and efficiency in land administration and management. In that country, the time required for transferring property dropped significantly from over a year to just one month following the implementation of a computerized land information system (Box 4.1). However, before digitizing land records, governments need to develop a legal and institutional framework, as well as put in place an appropriate technology system, among other preparations.

> **Box 4.1 Improving Land Governance in Rwanda**
>
> Before the development of the National Land Policy in 2004 and the enactment of the Organic Land Law in 2005, which determined the use and management of land in Rwanda, there was a juxtaposition of customary tenure and statutory tenure. Most rural land in Rwanda was accessed through inheritance and through leasing under customary tenure arrangements, and most urban land was accessed through purchase and leasing under statutory tenure arrangements. Other methods of acquiring land included government land allocation, borrowing, gift, first clearance, and informal occupation. Within nine years of the law's enactment, the government adopted policies and enacted comprehensive reforms that produced an efficient land administration and management system that guaranteed land tenure security through land registration and titling, among other mechanisms.
>
> The government undertook the following key actions:
> - Development of a legal and institutional framework: refinement of land policy, development of secondary legislation, and development of land management organizations at the central and district levels (the Land Centre and Office of the Registrar of Land Titles, Land Commissions at the central and district levels, District Land Offices, and Land Committees at decentralized levels)

> - Development of a national system and program for land tenure regularization: to systematically bring land to first registration and to allow all citizens equal access to the new systems
> - Development of low-cost, effective, and simplified land administration system at the national and decentralized levels and operational guidelines: to secure land rights and promote investment through regulated land transactions
> - Development of a national land use master plan: for land planning and development control, to ensure rational use of land and effective development as well as environment protection
> - Development of a land administration information system: with a digital register as a tool that facilitates land data maintenance and flexibility to accommodate new changes (parcel updates, personal and land rights information) and land transactions, contributing to ease of doing business
>
> By the end of December 2012, all of the estimated 10.3 million parcels had been demarcated, adjudicated, and digitized (100 percent); 10.3 million parcels had been entered in the Land Tenure Regularization Database (LTRSS) with full information on 8.3 million parcels; 7 million leasehold titles had been approved; 7 million leasehold titles had been printed for distribution; and 4 million leasehold titles had been collected by owners. Only 11,840 disputes were registered countrywide.
>
> Future developments in the pipeline are linking the digital land information system to mortgage registration, as well as connecting banks to landowners and linking geographical data to land rights.
>
> Source: Rurawanga (2013).

### 4.2.3 Inefficient Regulations and Poor Land Use Policies

Many countries on the continent have official standards and regulations that are unnecessarily costly and outdated, including unrealistic minimum plot sizes and expensive forms of infrastructure that raise the cost of housing and land development. Although planning standards vary significantly across Africa and within countries, overall there is a trend toward standards that are too high. On average, the minimum plot size for residential property in Africa is 262 $m^2$, ranging from a high of 500 $m^2$ in countries such as Angola, Eritrea, and Guinea-Bissau to a low of 60 $m^2$ in Djibouti and Morocco (Fig. 4.1). High standards, for minimum plot sizes in particular, have a significant effect on housing costs and affordability as plot size can significantly inflate construction costs.

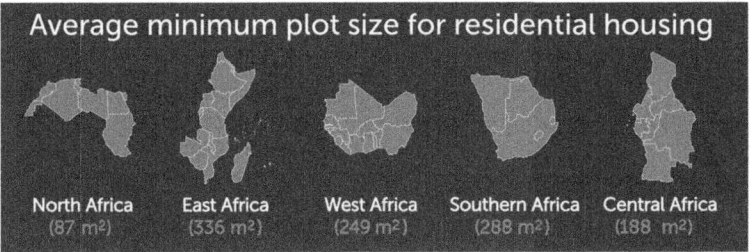

**Fig. 4.1** Average residential plot size by region (Source: *Author based on* CAHF (2015) Annual Survey data)

Many of these standards in Africa are still based on regulations created under colonial rule and were originally instituted for use only within areas of the colonial city that were inhabited by "non-natives" (Satterthwaite 2009). In many cases, urban planning and density restrictions from the colonial era have not been updated to reflect current needs.

In Kenya, for example, land policies and official codes, used as of 2014 were inherited from the colonial government and replicate British building regulations, most of which are not appropriate in today's Kenya. There have been calls on the government to revise these regulations, taking into account the unique characteristics of Kenyan society and housing market dynamics. In neighboring Tanzania, by contrast, minimum plot sizes are unaffordable for most households, particularly the poor, and are too expensive for the government to service owing to prohibitive infrastructure costs (Silva 2015). Using examples from Ghana, South Africa, and Tanzania, Silva concludes that the urban planning concept and the amended regulations adopted in many former British colonies are ill suited for the needs and realities of these countries today. This is largely due to the weak capacity of governments to adopt and implement changes on building standards, their limited financial resources, and the rapid growth rate in urban Africa. There are also emotional and cultural factors that need to be taken into account and which require a mentality change. In the majority of African countries, people have a sentimental relationship with land. In some African communities, the size of land owned reflects someone's wealth and may confer him a certain status in the society. This cultural factor is nonnegligible constraint to the revision of certain standards.

### 4.2.4 Onerous and Complex Land Titling Processes

It is within the purview of government to establish proper legal frameworks to guide land tenure and transfers. However, in many African countries, the procedure for acquiring and transferring land is fraught with uncertainties. Moreover, the high costs of accessing land and providing secure property rights are major obstacles to the development of land and housing markets. During our fact-finding consultations, housing stakeholders across the continent decried the long, onerous, bureaucratic, and expensive land titling process as a major constraint. While it is reported that formal registration of a property in Africa takes on average slightly less than two months and the associated costs are estimated at 8.1 percent of the property value (Table 4.2), this masks a certain disparity between countries. In 22 African countries today, it takes between 6 and 12 months to register property; in 9 countries, it takes 3–6 months; and in 16 countries, it takes up to 3 months (Table 4.2).

Although onerous titling procedures represent a challenge for all population segments, it is the poor who are disproportionately affected, given that they cannot afford the high administrative costs and typically are less politically connected. In Luanda, Angola's capital city, the waiting period

Table 4.2 Registering property: Inefficient land administration systems in Africa

|  | Procedures (number) | Time (days) | Cost (% of property value) | Quality of the land administration index (0–30) |
|---|---|---|---|---|
| Africa | 6.3 | 57.1 | 8.1 | 8.3 |
| North Africa | 6.2 | 47.2 | 4.9 | 9.7 |
| Central Africa | 5.9 | 61.4 | 12.5 | 6.4 |
| East Africa | 7.1 | 44.2 | 6.2 | 9.5 |
| West Africa | 6.2 | 68.8 | 8.7 | 6.9 |
| Southern Africa | 6.1 | 54.7 | 7.6 | 10.4 |
| Latin America and Caribbean | 7.0 | 63.0 | 6.1 | 11.5 |
| South Asia | 6.4 | 97.6 | 7.2 | 7.6 |
| OECD high-income countries | 4.7 | 21.8 | 4.2 | 22.7 |

Source: Based on data from World Bank Doing Business 2016

to obtain full legal occupation rights can last between 15 and 20 years, according to conversations with land experts on the ground. Because of such constraints, over 75 percent of peri-urban residents around Luanda do not have land titles and land rights that are recognized under the law. In Cameroon, an estimated 80 percent of urban land transactions occur in the informal market even though the government streamlined its land registration procedure in 2005. The current process still entails 12 steps, involves 17 organizations, costs 18 percent of the property value, and takes about 93 days. This trend is common across the continent. It highlights the costly and cumbersome land titling process faced by many Africans across the continent.

### 4.2.5 Land Administration and Management: A Laissez-Faire Approach of the State

In the 1960s and 1970s, public land development agencies in several countries had a mission to acquire and develop large land parcels, which were then sold to various social groups, including low- and middle-income families, at below-market prices. This government-controlled land delivery accounted for an estimated 10–40 percent of all land transactions in Africa at the time (Durand-Lasserve 2003). In Cameroon, for instance, agencies such as the Mission d'Aménagement et d'Equipement des Terrains Urbains et Ruraux (the Urban and Rural Lands Development Authority, better known by its French acronym, MAETUR) built tens of thousands of housing units through large-scale programs. MAETUR supplied over 30,000 land plots at its peak in the 1970s.

At the end of the 1970s, several African countries experienced severe macroeconomic difficulties including balance of payments and fiscal deficits, high inflation, and low GDP growth rates. For many analysts, including the IMF and the World Bank, the excessive interventionist role of governments was seen as the main culprit. This triggered the design of massive macroeconomic and structural reform programs, called structural adjustment programs (SAPs). SAPs consisted of the elimination of subsidies, a reduction of government expenditures, the privatization of state-owned enterprises, and the introduction of cost-recovery principle with the goal to move service delivery from the public to the private sector. It is against this backdrop that the SAPs were rolled out in a number of African countries during the 1980s–90s. Although its implementation took different forms, the SAPs substantially curtailed budget expenditure in the public sector, which caused the state to gradually lose its capacity to deliver a wide range of services, including the supply of land for housing.

In fact, policy adjustments in the SAPs era led to the gradual withdrawal of the state from the delivery of land for housing. Many state and parastatal land development agencies had to withdraw from land markets as government budgetary support for housing developments dried up; in most cases, the housing developments were canceled. Consequently, many governments adopted a laissez-faire approach to land management, administration, and the regulation of urban housing. This has contributed in the growth of informal settlements and unplanned neighborhoods.

In Côte d'Ivoire, the parastatal called Compte des Terrains Urbains (Urban Land Agency, or CTU), which was established to finance the acquisition and development of land for housing, has not conducted any activity since 1992 owing to the withdrawal of government budgetary support. Since its creation, the CTU has completed just two operations, in 1988 and 1989, resulting in the delivery of a meager 4480 land parcels. During the structural adjustment era, concessionary funding and technical assistance from multilateral agencies and governments dried up, precipitating the collapse of many public land development and servicing agencies, even as the demand for serviced land plots continued to soar. As far as the land market is concerned, the SAPs have not been helpful; they were trying to promote free-market principles in a context where markets were dysfunctional or simply failing. Even though policymakers have learned from their policy mistakes and have been implementing corrective measures such as gradually reviving sites-and-services programs in many countries (Box 4.2), the laissez-faire approach adopted during the structural adjustment era has been detrimental to affordable housing development across the continent.

## Box 4.2 Increasing the Supply of Low-Cost Serviced Land in Côte d'Ivoire

Côte d'Ivoire was one of the many countries that launched sites-and-services programs in the 1970s. As in many other African countries, the program was abandoned following the implementation of the SAPs.

In 2014, however, the Ivorian government launched a new sites-and-service scheme called Lotissement à Equipement Modéré, popularly known by its acronym LEM. LEM is one component of the presidential housing program for low-income households. It is in a pilot phase; four planned sites totaling 58 hectares are reserved around the city of Abidjan for this program.

LEM targets social groups with irregular income streams, particularly households living in slums and first-time homebuyers. The program was created to help slum dwellers to build better self-help housing, in a planned environment. LEM makes use of existing land reserves through a form of developer contribution—donation (natural contribution) from private developers worth 2.5–5 percent of the serviced land that the state has approved for private formal development. Stakeholders have lauded LEM as the most affordable and realistic means to rehouse low-income households in better conditions.

LEM beneficiaries in the district of Abidjan receive serviced and titled plots of either 80 square meters ($m^2$) or 108 $m^2$, while recipients outside Abidjan get plots with a minimum size of 120 $m^2$. The 80 $m^2$ plots can accommodate a three-room house, while the 108 $m^2$ plots can accommodate three to four rooms. All LEM plots will come equipped with services such as water, electricity, sewerage, and access to paved primary and secondary road infrastructure. The government has identified future land reserves of 850 hectares across the country for LEM. To improve affordability, land for LEM is based on an emphyteutic lease, a flexible system. After 20 years, the lease can be transferred into purchase when the lease has been paid off.

LEM plots will be located in zoned and well-planned areas, and will make provision for commercial real estate and more expensive housing, thus ensuring a mixed-use community. Moreover, a large proportion of each planning zone will be dedicated to community spaces, access roads, green spaces, and social facilities, such as schools, clinics, and commercial centers. The zones will also be equipped with collective parking lots and garbage disposal sites. Land titles will be provided to beneficiaries who meet all requirements.

Source: Based on information obtained during fact-finding mission in Côte d'Ivoire, November 2014.

## 4.3 Implications of Unclear Land Tenure Regimes and Rights

Notwithstanding that African governments have been adopting some policies to increase the supply of land for affordable housing, very few have succeeded in opening up access to land for a vast swath of their populations. Governments are finding it increasingly difficult to locate large land parcels in urban areas for mass housing projects. Even in countries where land belongs to the state and citizens have land use rights, accessing vast swaths of land for housing remains a major challenge. For example, to meet the demand for affordable housing in Addis Ababa in Ethiopia, where the state owns all land and no customary land regime is in play, the government needs to build 50,000 units per year, for which it needs 650 hectares of land. However, finding such vast land in the city limit of 54,000 hectares has been a challenge. As a result, most new housing developments are located far from the city center and have limited basic infrastructure services such as water, electricity, roads, and sewerage systems. This challenge is even more prominent in countries operating under a pluralistic land tenure system.

The effects of these multiple tenure regimes on formal housing markets are manifold. Not only do they diminish the security of land rights of housing consumers, they also create an artificial land shortage, which further inhibits the delivery of land for housing developments. Moreover, unclear land tenure regimes, which often are fraught with loopholes and inconsistencies, dissuade private investment in the housing market. The result has been greater land speculation and rising housing prices. In order to address the continent's growing housing crisis, African governments need to take a stand on the debate over the formalization of land rights in order to increase the efficiency of land delivery systems.

### 4.3.1 The Land Formalization Debate

The establishment of a regime of individual property rights in land and housing is considered the cornerstone of an enabling housing policy regime (Angel 2000). In Africa, however, there is an ongoing debate on the relative merits and wisdom of recognizing statutory individual property rights as a universal solution to tenure security, particularly for the poor. The policy debate on land formalization was given a new impulse by the arguments of the Peruvian economist Hernando De Soto in 2000.

De Soto (2000) argues that the registration of informal land assets and their transformation into formal individual property rights would be the main way for rural and urban poor households in developing countries to join the formal market. By so doing, he argues, households would achieve the benefits of development, investment, and economic growth. Indeed, some research in the African context supports these claims. One school of thought argues that a clear demand for accessible and affordable processes of land formalization is emerging anyway. For example, Benjaminsen et al. (2008) point out that in the peri-urban areas of the cotton zone in Mali, private and alienable land holdings are fast replacing the customary tenure system. This growing demand for titled land is significantly driven by rapid population growth and the commercialization of agriculture.

However, critiques of land formalization programs highlight the weak capacities of governments and the fallacy of assumptions such as those from de Soto mentioned above. It is reported that although the incidence of titling is higher in East and Southern Africa, titling does not necessarily provide sufficient tenure security in these regions (Toulmin 2008). In addition, the critiques point to the dangers of such programs in aggravating socioeconomic inequalities. The larger critique of land formalization programs in Africa is that they represent the "imposition of alien [i.e., Western] legal and cultural practices" in an institutional setting that "differs so profoundly from the legal and cultural setting from which they are taken" (Bromley 2008: 21–23). Furthermore, the "object of transplantation" (i.e., land titles) does not function like it is supposed to in the Western environment, as it lacks the same cultural, legal, and economic institutions (Bromley 2008: 21–23). As Deininger and Feder (2009) argue, it is important to note that the "formalization of land rights should not be viewed as a panacea and that interventions should be decided only after a careful diagnosis of the policy, social, and governance environment."

Although it is important to acknowledge the limitations of land formalization programs, it is also clear that much of the urban expansion

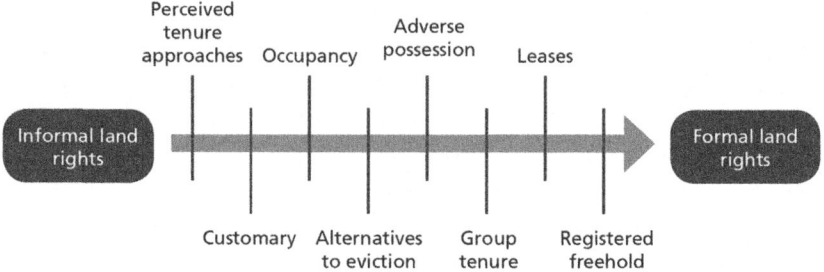

**Fig. 4.2** Continuum of land rights (Source: UN-Habitat (2012b))

now taking place in Africa is following market principles that are primarily driven by households and businesses. For this reason—whether formally or informally—land market pressure will continue to be exerted onto urban, peri-urban, and even rural areas.

There is a growing consensus in land policy circles that, in the long run, individual property rights are needed to provide the degree of land tenure security that will be the basis for a functioning formal land market, mortgage financing, and private investment in housing (World Bank 2003). The Global Land Tool Network (GLTN) advocates that land rights should be seen as a continuum—from perceived and *de facto* tenure at the informal end of the continuum to registered freehold at the more formal end (Fig. 4.2). This continuum underscores that land tenure involves a complex set of informal and formal rights that range from various rights of occupancy and use to full rights of ownership and disposal of the land.

Better efforts to formalize land rights are required to guide this new development. Formal and informal rules governing property acquisition, sale, development, and use will be critical in creating predictable, vibrant, and efficient housing markets in Africa. In the long run, individual property rights are needed to provide the degree of land tenure security that will be the basis of a functioning formal land market, mortgage financing, and private investment in housing. The question for the housing sector is thus not whether formalization of land rights needs to occur, but how best it can be done to avoid some of the known pitfalls of land registration. Deininger et al. (2009) "suggest not only that implementing a decentralized, transparent, and cost-effective process of land registration is possible but also that failure to do so may squander significant economic and possibly social benefits." Nonetheless, it is worth noting that, not all social groups need or benefit from formal land rights, at least in the short to medium terms.

## 4.3.2 Land Delivery Systems

Land for housing in most African countries is provided through three main delivery systems.

*Formal Private Delivery System* The formal private land delivery system most closely resembles the system of private property prevalent in developed countries. In this system, land parcels are developed and sold by private actors such as property development companies. These transactions usually come with full legal rights, a property title, or equivalent documentation. Second are public, formal, or government-controlled land delivery systems, which allocate residential plots to various social groups at below-market prices. Through this delivery channel, the state can also provide large parcels of land to developers and cooperatives for affordable housing construction. The third and predominant land delivery system is the customary and informal system, in which unserviced land is sold or transferred with no legal guarantees or property title.

As discussed above, most African countries today are characterized by an uneasy coexistence of customary and statutory land delivery systems, giving rise to a variety of tenure situations. Moreover, as African cities rapidly expand into the urban-rural periphery, there is frequently a direct clash between state power and legal claims to land management and those of customary authorities. As a result, the general spatial pattern of land tenure modes is that the more secure, formal tenure modes are usually to be found nearer to city centers (Mattaei and Mandimika 2014).

Durand-Lasserve et al. (2013), for instance, found that plots obtained under private and public land access modes in Bamako generally occupied relatively central locations of the city. The authors also found that plots with secure forms of tenure are on average more expensive than plots with less-secure forms of tenure. In Bamako, plots with property titles were estimated to be worth 1.4–5.7 times the price of similar plots with no legal rights. This demonstrates the high value of tenure security and legal transferability. These findings may probably be applied to most African cities. They indicate the steady growth of land markets, even in locations that were previously not urban. However, African governments will need to create flexible tenure systems that are simple and provide secure tenure in order to accelerate land delivery.

*The Customary Delivery System* Customary authorities, including traditional chiefs, continue to play an important role in land management and land allocation in many African countries. Particularly in rural areas, these authorities often have more power to allocate land than formal land administration systems do. Their legitimacy is based on their claim to represent local populations and customs. In Ghana, for instance, the system of customary land rights enshrined in the 1992 constitution is seen as progressive and egalitarian, with checks and balances (UN-Habitat 2011).

However, elsewhere on the continent customary land allocation is not held in as high regard as in Ghana. In neighboring Côte d'Ivoire, for example, officials and notaries claim that many chiefs have long gone beyond their traditional roles and have become land brokers, merely out to make a profit rather than primarily serving as custodians of ancestral land. Rather than enshrine customary land allocation in the constitution, as Ghana has done, the government of Côte d'Ivoire has adopted compensation framework for the acquisition of customary land (Box 4.3).

**Box 4.3 Purging Customary Land as a Land Delivery Mechanism in Côte d'Ivoire**

Since 2013, the buying of customary land has been the law in Côte d'Ivoire. The policy was instituted to help the state achieve three main objectives: (1) reduce the cost of land and housing, (2) reduce the risk of litigation from customary owners, and (3) reduce the incidence of land speculation. According to decree n° 2013-224 of March 22, 2013, all purchases of customary land must be done at scheduled rates: a maximum of 2000 FCFA (~US$3.22) per square meter in the main city of Abidjan; a maximum of 1500 FCFA (~US$2.42) per square meter in Yamoussoukro, the capital; and a maximum of 600 FCFA (~US$1) per square meter in all other districts and cities around the country.

New land acquisition negotiations for projects considered to be in the public interest take place between the government and multiple landowners with chiefs in the background. Government officials draw up a land map to be able to demarcate and register the land (cadaster) with the property owners to assess how much the state has to pay and to whom. Then it implements the decree and establishes a protocol of payment. In the case of housing projects, the state then buys the parcels and distributes them to developers. Beforehand, to preempt litigation, the state prepares a general urban plan (like a master plan). The process is successful as a way of removing the risks of dealing with customary land. It is only property owners themselves who often do not know how to deal with the cash payments. To reduce the risk of conflict among property owners, the state allows them to opt for a new house in the development instead of an instant cash payment.

Source: Based on information obtained during fact-finding mission in Côte d'Ivoire, November 2014.

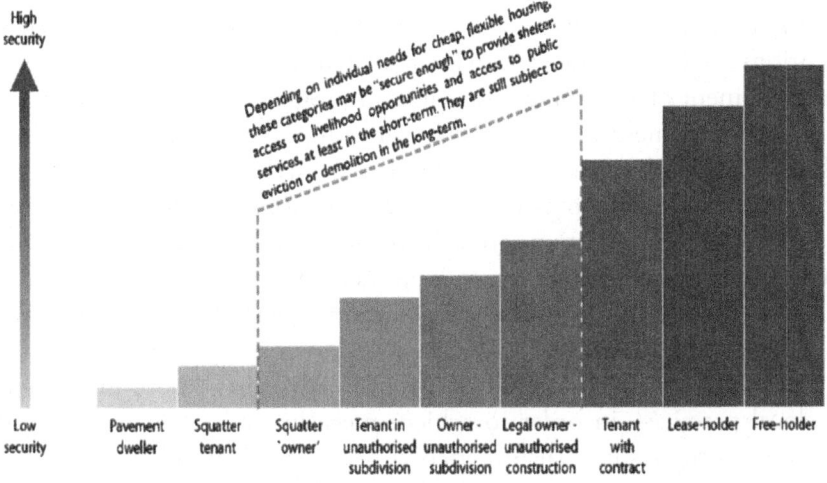

Fig. 4.3 The urban tenure continuum (Source: Payne et al. (2014))

*The Informal Delivery System* A fundamental problem for poor urban households across the continent is their inability to access secure, well-located, and affordable land for even the most basic housing needs. Figure 4.3 illustrates the continuum of tenure arrangements that typically exist in urban centers in many developing countries, including African cities. The least secure tenure arrangements are those on the left, with tenure security increasing progressively as one moves to the right. However, the progressively higher steps between tenure statuses also represent the increasing difficulty of moving into a more secure tenure status.

As highlighted in Fig. 4.3, urban land markets operate on multiple levels, ranging from the most informal to the highly formalized. If the market is understood as a series of transactions and exchanges, supported by sets of rules and institutions, it is clear that the market is at work even in the alternative, informal mechanisms through which most people meet their needs for land and housing. Indeed, the market influences the value of land and housing built on it and, hence, affects affordability (Napier 2013). In other words, land markets do exist in Africa, although a majority of these transactions occur informally. The inefficiencies related to that informality and related issues discussed above have deleterious effects on affordability.

*The Pragmatic and Flexible Delivery System* A number of practical interventions can be implemented to incrementally improve tenure security in the continent's land market, as well as in programs to upgrade slums or informal settlements. However, there are a number of contextual factors that will have a bearing on the potential for incremental tenure security. They include good governance and democratization through a more advanced decentralization process, policy and legal frameworks; the state's capacity and willingness to innovate, especially at municipal levels; and the strength of civil society organizations that actively support vulnerable communities.

It is more efficient to build on what already exists—both in law and in local practice—in order to achieve more immediate upgrading and tenure security results. The experiences of the cities of Johannesburg and Huambo, respectively, in South Africa and Angola show that one way to do this effectively is to identify the laws that can be adapted innovatively (see Royston 2013 for more on the legal discussions). In Johannesburg, for instance, the city municipality legally recognized several informal settlements, which paved the way for the provision of basic infrastructure services, tenure security, as well as land use planning and integration into the municipal administrative system. Another is to consider confirming the status of local practices and adding municipal or administrative weight to them, as in Huambo, Angola. In Huambo, the council adopted temporary and flexible resolutions that enabled households to obtain upgradeable land occupation licenses, known as *Licença de arrematação*. This administrative recognition helped in closing gaps in the Angolan land law.

A Community Land Trust (CLT) is another model that can be used to provide access to land and housing to people who are otherwise denied access. A CLT can be a useful tool in keeping housing affordable, as it prohibits speculation and manages land for the common good of the community. The CLT model has been experimented to provide tenure security in an informal settlement upgrading project in Voi, Kenya (Bassett 2005). In Nigeria, Gusah (2012) has proposed the adoption of a CLT model based on the shared equity housing approach that evolved in the United States in the late 1960s. A CLT is seen as a possible compromise between the country's primary land policy instrument, the Land Use Act of 1978, which vests ownership of all land in Nigeria's federal and state governments, and the traditional, historic claims of local communities, such as those in Nigeria's capital, Abuja, which provide the city with its most affordable housing. The title documentation under the CLT would not be issued in the names of individuals, but rather in the name of the community as a whole, as a trust on behalf of all the land-owning individuals—in keeping with the traditional concept of the communal ownership of land (Gusah 2012).

Similarly, the Namibian government has developed the Flexible Land Tenure System (FLTS) as an innovative way to provide affordable tenure security for residents living in informal urban settlements. The FLTS concept derives from the government's need to create upgradeable alternative land tenure options for informal settlements to complement the current formal system of freehold tenure, which is cumbersome, costly, and out of reach of the urban poor. The FLTS is a community-driven process that offers the possibility of registration of individual rights under group ownership, an approach that is currently unique to this process.

## 4.4 Low-Density Urban Expansion and a Massive Infrastructure Deficit

Over the last two decades, the concept of urban sprawl has gained considerable attention in Africa, partly owing to the continent's rapid pace of urbanization. Today, much of Africa's urban expansion is occurring through unplanned and low-density consumption of rural land. On the one hand, this urban sprawl is being driven by cultural preferences. Some housing experts argue that African households, even in urban areas, prefer to own a detached house, surrounded by a plot of land. This long-standing cultural preference fuels the growth of both formal and informal housing areas. On the other hand, poor urban planning, which is a function of a lack of political will and vision, as well as limited government capacities, appears to be the key factor contributing to urban sprawl in many countries. Land prices also play an important role in sprawling, low-density developments: it is significantly less expensive to buy a strip of land in peri-urban or rural areas than in the city center in many countries. As explained above, this is related to the fact that higher land tenure security is associated with city centers.

As African cities rapidly expand into rural areas, this presents both opportunities and challenges. Africa's low-density urban sprawl entails long-term financial, social, and environmental costs for rural livelihoods and future urban settlements. On the one hand, significant swaths of new land may become available for housing and other urban uses. Exploiting the full potential of this new land for housing depends on the availability of transport, infrastructure, and service connections being built by the state and private-sector actors. There exists a real opportunity for African governments to move away from congested large cities to build new satellite cities that are well connected with all required services to host the growing population. However, the limited capacity of both national and local governments presents a major obstacle to providing basic bulk services and infrastructure. On the other hand, rural livelihoods and agriculture will also come under threat as African cities rapidly grow and put pressure on agricultural land. As approximately 60 percent of the continent's population still derives its livelihood and income primarily from

**Table 4.3** Africa's infrastructure deficit

| % of population with access | | | | |
|---|---|---|---|---|
| Infrastructure | Africa | South Asia | Latin America and Caribbean | OECD Countries |
| Electricity | 43[a] | 78 | 96 | 100 |
| Improved water source | 66 | 92 | 95 | 93 |
| Improved sanitation facilities | 40 | 45 | 83 | 98 |

Source: World Bank (data for latest year available)
[a]Data from IEA, World Energy Outlook 2013

farming, livestock production, and related activities, it is imperative to identify and promote promising rural-urban linkages as well as positive externalities through an efficient allocation and use of the land to avoid jeopardizing the livelihood of rural dwellers.

Furthermore, the expansion of cities across Africa is accentuating the clash between customary and statutory land tenure systems and cultures as noted in the preceding section. In most countries today, towns and cities are gradually swallowing up villages whose land development modes are still largely dominated by customary systems. As observed by some land experts, these village inhabitants presently do not see the need to apply for a formal land title since they believe the land belongs to them. The absorption into newly urbanizing areas of previously rural land thus engenders a clash in terms of perceptions of property rights that will cause future conflicts and complicate efforts to clarify land rights.

The urban sprawling problem goes hand in hand with the lack of adequate infrastructure. African countries lag behind other developing countries in terms of infrastructure provision (Table 4.3). For instance, this infrastructure deficit is largest in access to electricity as well as water and sanitation services.

For instance, only 43 percent of African households have access to electricity compared with 41 percent of households in low-income countries outside Africa. Even though the continent's stock of paved roads and the population's access to pipe-borne water and sanitation have increased over the years, the continent still lags behind other developing economies when it comes to the provision of infrastructure and basic services. Moreover, in many countries, the overstretched infrastructural network compounds the problem. For instance, Luanda in Angola, which was built for approximately 1 million residents, currently houses over 6.5 million. The influx of new populations coupled with the natural growth in urban expansion is putting increasing pressure on the poorly maintained infrastructure networks, not only in Luanda but also in many African cities including Lagos, Nairobi, Dakar, Cairo, and so on.

This extensive infrastructure deficit has severe implications for the continent's housing sector, given that decent and adequate housing requires basic infrastructure services such as roads, good transportation access, electricity, water, and sewerage. In South Africa, for instance, the provision of infrastructure and bulk services accounts for 23 percent of the total cost for an affordable house. Likewise, in Kenya, the lack of infrastructure and serviced plots emerges as a major constraint to affordable housing, accounting for over 20 percent of the cost of new housing. The high cost of land in Kenya is a major impediment to the provision of roads and other bulk infrastructure, according to government officials. In neighboring Ethiopia, the provision of trunk infrastructure accounts for 15 percent of the total cost of housing under the government's social housing program.

Infrastructure, in particular access to efficient transport infrastructure, shapes cities. As a result, affordable housing cannot be looked at in isolation from reliable transport links and transport costs. In most countries, available land parcels and new housing developments are far from the city center and are often not connected to it by public transit. Besides putting considerable strain on household budgets, poor transport networks reinforce physical barriers, resulting in urban residential segregation. The housing developments in Kilamba and Zango offer a glimpse of the divided housing market in Angola. Residents in these cities must commute for 25–40 km a day to and from their places of employment in the city center in Luanda. With commuting times of up to two hours, many households wake up as early as 5:00 AM to go to work and return only at about 9:00 PM when traffic has lessened. In our discussions with housing stakeholders in South Africa, it was noted that many households living in the periphery of Johannesburg spend about 40 percent of their monthly income on the costs of commuting to and from work. As a result, these households are left with very little income to spend on goods and services such as housing, health care, and education, among others. A lesson that could be learned from this situation is that effective urban planning and management systems should always make provision for integrated transport networks, particularly so for peri-urban housing development projects.

High costs and extensive delays in providing bulk infrastructure intrinsically affect housing affordability in Africa. Governments, in partnership with the private sector, need to find cost-effective solutions to meeting the capital costs of providing basic bulk infrastructure. In most countries, the responsibility for the provision of basic physical infrastructure, land use planning, and development rests with the government. However, limited resources, weak institutional capacities, and lack of coordination between multiple government agencies entrusted with the tasks of service delivery further complicate the infrastructure challenge.

Furthermore, the level of investment required for infrastructure provision in peri-urban settlements (whether formal or informal) can be prohibitive, owing to the cost of retrofitting bulk infrastructure, especially in unplanned areas. Without careful urban planning and the timely delivery of basic infrastructure to support new housing developments—particularly in urban peripheries—the costs of providing physical infrastructure are likely to increase significantly. This is simply due to the economics of densification: it is cheaper to provide physical infrastructure and basic services in denser areas than in low-density settlements because the fixed costs can be spread over many households.

The infrastructure challenge highlights the important link between planning, land, and finance. Collier and Venables (2014) suggest that inadequate urban planning and the failure of many African governments to build local tax systems have widened the infrastructure gap in cities. In addressing this challenge, the starting point is to plan properly and be able to map out the available land.

## 4.4.1 Financing Land and Infrastructure

Africa suffers from an acute shortage of infrastructure. The continent's ageing infrastructure continues to prevent it from realizing its full economic potential. Overall, Africa needs an estimated US$93 billion per year to fill its infrastructure deficit. Mckinsey (2016) suggests that Africa will need to double its annual investment in infrastructure to US$150 billion, which is equivalent to about 4.5 percent of Africa's GDP, in order to accelerate infrastructure development and contribute to the realization of the potential of Africa's economy. Urban and housing infrastructure could account for about US$23.25 billion to US$31 billion of this financing deficit. In South Africa, for instance, frequent power outages weigh heavily on the manufacturing sector's growth. In Angola, the city of Luanda, the infrastructure stock is under heavy pressure to serve a population that is 6.5 times bigger than what it was built for. These situations are rather common across African cities and highlight the fact that Africa's population growth and urbanization are placing enormous pressure on the stock of limited infrastructure. Inadequate financing has been considered as one of the major obstacles constraining Africa's infrastructure development. Lessons learned in terms of infrastructure development and recent development regarding the financing of development suggest that African governments will need to attract more private capital and mobilize resources domestically to finance its infrastructure needs including, particularly, urban and housing development.

Pinpointing how the government should pay for infrastructure services, including resource mobilization through municipalities and local governments, should be a fundamental aspect of any urban planning discussion. Some revenue tools that could be used to pay for infrastructure services include developer levies, land value capture allowing for user fees, taxes and public-private partnership (PPPs).

### 4.4.1.1 Moving from the Dominance of Public Finance to Mobilization of Private Capital

Financing flows into Africa's infrastructure have been dominated by public budgets and equity finance, as well as investment from traditional and new development partners such as China, whose investment has grown appreciably over the years, from US$313 million in 2000 to US$4.4 billion in 2012 (Gutman et al. 2015). Funding from multilateral development banks such as the African Development Bank (AfDB) and World Bank has also supported infrastructure financing and technical assistance on the continent. These institutions continuously refine their instruments and create new facilities to help fill the financing gap. The AfDB's US$3 billion Africa50 fund and the World Bank's Global Infrastructure Facility are some investment vehicles established to close the infrastructure gap. The Africa50 Fund aims at pooling resources devoted specifically to the financing of Africa's infrastructure development.

In recent years, African governments have relied on international capital markets to raise funds for infrastructure projects, through the issuance of bonds. The overreliance on Eurobonds, especially in West Africa, as a means of raising capital to finance infrastructure projects poses risks as local currencies depreciate against the dollar, with commodity producers—such as Ghana and Nigeria—being the most exposed. Mozambique and Zambia have been similarly exposed. As the dollar strengthens, this places pressure on Eurobond yields and increases the cost of borrowing in capital markets. Moreover, compared with the energy and telecommunications sector—which have raised 78 percent of the financing mobilized through PPPs on the continent (Paulais 2012)—such mechanisms have not been widely used for urban and housing infrastructure development purposes in Africa. The difficulties of crowding in the private sector in the financing of Africa's residential real estate market and urban infrastructure are due to (1) the paucity of reliable data to guide investment decisions, (2) inadequate institutional and legal frameworks, and (3) a lack of awareness among investors. One way to attract private capital is to boost the equity investment in infrastructure. Equity investments account for 80 percent of infrastructure funding in sub-Saharan Africa. This has become an asset class that is attractive to several equity investors including pension funds, sovereign wealth funds (SWFs), and bank-sponsored investment funds. Capital raised by infrastructure funds has also been increasing (Faye and Geh 2016). As of September 2016, the total amount raised by private equity infrastructure funds with a primary geographic focus of Africa since 2013 stands at over US$2.3 billion, according to Preqin. The challenge is to attract part of those equity investments in the urban and housing development sector. In so doing, political leaders and decision-makers around the continent need to put urban and housing infrastructure development high on their agendas and among their top priorities along with energy and telecommunications. They should also be eager to put in place an enabling environment conducive to attracting such private capital.

### 4.4.1.2 Tapping into the Contractual Savings Industry: Expansion of the Caisse des Dépôts Model

Financing urban and housing infrastructure development is a big-ticket item and as such requires long-term financing. The contractual savings industry is one of the natural channels through which long-term resources could be mobilized domestically. This includes insurance companies, pension funds, and SWFs. Between 2009 and 2014, it is reported that assets under management (AUM) by African SWFs grew by about 34 percent, from US$121 billion in 2009 to US$162 billion in 2014. The AUM by pension funds in 10 sub-Saharan Africa countries was estimated at US$379 billion in 2013. As per the African insurance companies, the AUM in 2012 was estimated at US$273 billion, and projected to grow to reach US$378 billion by 2018, equivalent to a 37 percent increase. Despite, the sizeable amount of long-term resources it manages, the contractual savings industry has until recently been untapped, but new developments show an increased interest in leveraging savings from institutional investors.

Inspired by Morocco's state-owned Caisse de Dépôt et de Gestion (Deposit and Management Fund, or CDG), many French-speaking countries in sub-Saharan Africa have sought to replicate the success of this nonbank financial institution, which manages the savings of many institutional investors such as the National Savings Bank and the National Social Security Fund. With about US$25 billion in assets under management, CDG is the biggest financial institution in Morocco, with a market share of about 10 percent. Such government-backed institutions typically have a dual mandate to (1) mobilize regulated funds and deposits for long-term investments and (2) invest these resources in urban development, infrastructure, and housing projects, particularly low-income housing. When well established, the volume and the stability of their resources channel quasi-monetary resources into illiquid long-term investments. In addition, their fiduciary functions can be extended to a wide range of activities, from the sponsoring of PPP arrangements to the management of pension funds.

The Caisses des Dépôts model exists in Gabon, Mauritania, and Sénégal, while Benin, Cameroon, Madagascar, and Togo have recently created or are in the process of creating similar institutions. The potential of the Caisse des Dépôts model is promising, provided that they succeed in mobilizing a significant part of national savings that often stay idle outside the formal banking sector. However, a few risks must be carefully managed in order for this model to be successful. The first is linked to possible governance issues that result from the politicization of these institutions by governments using it as a financial tool for noncommercially viable projects. A rigorous project evaluation system and strong corporate governance, with an independent management team operating under strict processes, must be in place to ensure that this model functions successfully. Second, the Caisse des Dépôts model should avoid adopting market-distorting actions. These institutions should be designed as complementary, and not competitors of commercial institutions. Third, the legal and regulatory framework should be conducive enough to avoid stifling the potential of these types of institutions to contribute to financing housing development.

### 4.4.1.3 Land Value Capture

As discussed in Chap. 2, the absence of a reliable land registry database in many African countries is due to capacity constraints faced by government entities and agencies entrusted with land registration and administration activities. Moreover, there is a lack of a comprehensive and up-to-date mapping of the available land, including information on ownership, size, and value, which takes into account its agro-ecological features, the quality of infrastructure to service the land and other characteristics. Government entities in charge of land such as cadaster offices are still using obsolete and manual techniques and do not have the capacity to use modern technology including computerized system using real-time data supplied by GPS, geospatial, or satellite imagery systems. This has significantly undermined the ability of countries to properly value land, effectively manage the available land, or negotiate fair land concessions. In many countries, the lack of adequate land valuation system and weak land markets prevents several African governments to effectively mobilize domestic resources through land value capture to finance urban infrastructure.

In the current challenging and difficult global economic environment that has been exacerbated by a decline in donor funding and the scarcity of long-term financing, land value capture is an innovative financing mechanism which should be harnessed to raise domestic financing for urban infrastructure (such as transport infrastructure, education and health facilities, as well as recreational infrastructures, social facilities, and parks), which contributes to the well-being of urban dwellers. As discussed in the literature (Palmer and Berrisford (2015) and others), land value capture (LVC) is a possible solution that governments (both central and local) could apply to capture a share or all of the increase in private land value that results from public infrastructure investments or from some public decision, such as approved land use changes. For instance, public investments in transportation or sewerage often positively affect adjacent land value as it becomes more productive and valuable. Moreover, such public capital investments also increase property values, with residents willing to pay a premium in order to benefit from the positive externalities—such as increased accessibility, better schools, and employment opportunities—that often come along with the provision of most public infrastructure. The LVC is a benefit sharing mechanism that could take several forms depending on the instrument used as shown in Table 4.4. In fact, sharing the benefits created by the provision of public infrastructure can often be done through property taxes, sale of government-owned land or via preemption rights, and so on. International experiences have shown that the LVC solution has worked very well in Latin America (e.g., Colombia and Brazil), China, and Mexico.

**Table 4.4** Land value capture mechanisms

| Instruments | Description |
|---|---|
| Betterment levies/taxes | Any tax or charge on an increase in value resulting from some public action, such as the issuing of development rights or the provision of infrastructure. |
| Sale of development rights | The sale of the right to convert rural land (agricultural or unzoned) to urban use; and the right to build at greater densities than normally would be allowed by zoning rules or height restrictions. |
| Public land leasing | If the relevant local authority owns the land, it would lease the land out for a period of time, thus generating revenue. |
| Land acquisition and resale | The purchase of land around a development, and subsequent resale of that land by the public sector or relevant authority is a method to capture the full value of the gains that an infrastructure investment may create. |
| Land sales | This instrument relates to the sale of publicly—preferably city—owned land. |
| Developer exactions | Exactions are requirements a local government places on a developer to dedicate land, construct, or pay for all or a portion of the costs of capital improvements needed for public facilities as a condition of development approval. |
| Impact fees | Impact fees are designed to cover the costs of the bulk and connector infrastructure required for a new property development or property development improvements. |
| Negotiations and voluntary contributions | A bilateral negotiation, before the investment occurs, is used to determine a rate that property owners in the area of influence should pay for the improvement. |

Source: DfID and African Centre for Cities (University of Cape Town (2015))

According to Palmer and Berrisford (2015), as far as sub-Saharan Africa is concerned, all the instruments in Table 4.4 except betterment taxes could be applied. Findings in the literature regarding the applicability of the betterment taxes method in Africa have not been unequivocally conclusive. However, the DfID-ACC report highlights the fact that public land sales, land leasing, and direct contributions from owners or developers (exactions and impact fees) are the main land-based value capture methods which are likely to be implementable in Africa.

The reality is that the use of LVCs to finance infrastructure in Africa is fairly limited. However, African cities and municipalities are gradually adopting property taxes to guide and finance the development of urban infrastructure. This approach has been commonly used in rapidly growing cities in other parts of the world, particularly in developed economies. An important feature of such taxes is that they must be closely linked to the provision of basic services. As citizens see an improvement in service delivery, their willingness to pay taxes will generally increase. However, building local tax systems is a necessary step toward developing sustainable infrastructure financing for cities. The approach used by Lagos illustrates how municipalities can build their tax systems to finance basic infrastructure and satisfy the huge demand for public services. Since 2001, successive Lagos state governments have streamlined the property tax rates, developed an electronic property database, which has digitized and enlarged the property tax registry. The Lagos state government has also increased its public outreach and community engagement practices, educating its residents about the benefits of compliance. The results have been an increase in tax receipts, while at the same time engaging residents to ensure that their tax contributions are well spent. In Ethiopia, the government has begun implementing policies that would enable it to introduce the LVC tool to raise financing for municipal infrastructure. With funding from the Bill and Melinda Gates Foundation, the government has introduced a modernized property tax system in Ethiopian cities. The new property tax system was piloted in the cities of Mek'ele, Bahir Dar.

Developer contributions and development levies are also two possible options that some municipalities on the continent have been using to finance infrastructure. Although this source of funding can be adequate for financing infrastructure within the boundaries of a development area, it is not a sufficient or sustainable source of funding for new infrastructure needs. In order to increase housing affordability for low- and middle-income families, developer levies should closely reflect the capital cost of putting the infrastructure in place. However, in situations where the government can fund infrastructure construction through tax receipts, development levies should not be used.

## 4.4.1.4 Financing Urban and Housing Infrastructure: Specialization Matters

Urban and housing infrastructure development is a complex and very demanding field and requires dedicated teams of professionals, technical resources, and instruments relevant to the sector. Some countries are cognizant of those requirements. Burkina Faso, Cameroon, Ghana, Kenya, Mali, Nigeria, Sénégal, and South Africa, for instance, have created dedicated facilities to support public investments in the housing market. However, most of these facilities depend heavily on government budgets. Apart from the Development Bank of South Africa (DBSA), most of these institutions do not have a sustainable mechanism for mobilizing domestic resources as they rely heavily on government budgetary allocations and merely serve as conduits for donor support. The DBSA, by contrast, has diversified funding sources including bonds, money market paper, and committed foreign lines of credit with commercial banks. As of November 2013, the DBSA had raised R 20.25 billion (US$1.7 billion) in the domestic bond market, with the proceeds used to finance infrastructure development even at municipality level. However, only a small portion of this funding has been allocated to housing. Another notable example of a specialized institution supporting domestic infrastructure financing is The Infrastructure Bank (TIB) of Nigeria. TIB, which is majority owned by the private sector, is mandated to finance large-scale, long-term infrastructure projects in Nigeria such as mass housing, water provision, and transport, among other municipal services. More efforts are needed to put in place specialized institutions able to successfully deliver the requirements needed. There is therefore a need to think about appropriate institutions or facilities dedicated to urban and housing infrastructure development with adequate governance structure, mechanisms, and procedures that could enable them to raise adequate financing for housing development.

New and more adequate instruments are needed to mobilize market resources for urban infrastructure and housing developments in Africa. In mature markets, structured finance instruments are used to ring-fence cash flows generated by newly developed infrastructure, which are then allocated to capital market investors. Revenue bonds provide a good example of such a structure. These are municipal bonds that finance income-generating projects and are secured by a specified revenue source, such as lease payments, tolls, or tax income. Typically, a special purpose vehicle (SPV) or an ad hoc project company is created to ring-fence the revenue streams and ensure their transfer to bondholders. Generally, the creditworthiness of the sponsoring entity needs to be enhanced by an external guarantor, or, as it is often done in the United States, through a reserve fund capitalized by public resources. The economics of revenue bonds is simpler than securitization, and can be used in place of sukuks where Islamic finance is needed. Several Nigerian states have already issued revenue bonds, and the DBSA plans to launch this instrument in the near future.

Revenue bonds can help municipalities reduce their dependence on conditional cash transfers, such as in Uganda and Ethiopia, or on ad hoc revenue, such as land transfer taxes in Kenya, to fund infrastructure and service delivery. Some countries have also created specialized financing tools to support municipalities such as the Municipal Infrastructure Fund (Fonds d'Équipement Communal, or FEC) in Morocco, the Fund for Mutual Assistance (Fonds Spécial d'Equipement et d'Intervention Intercommunale, FEICOM) in Cameroon, or the Municipal Development Agency (Agence de Développement Municipal, ADM) in Sénégal. In Cameroon, for instance, FEICOM funds infrastructure projects and housing developments of local governments. In March 2014, FEICOM signed a partnership agreement with Crédit Foncier du Cameroon (CFC), Cameroon's leading mortgage lender, wherein the latter committed to provide a CFAF 10 billion (US$19.9 million) line of credit to finance low-income housing projects through local municipalities. If properly managed and structured, such an initiative has the potential to empower local governments, which are closer to the population, to address the housing and infrastructure needs in their municipalities.

Hybrid instruments can also be envisaged for the provision of urban infrastructure, depending on the degree of capital market development as well as institutional investors' expertise. New financing modalities can widen the funding bases, particularly of investors with a high risk-return appetite. Developing new financing mechanisms to support urban infrastructure development is crucial for building sustainable cities as the continent rapidly urbanizes. The availability of reliable data to guide investors' decision will be vital in mobilizing the required private capital for infrastructure and housing developments. In recent years, two regional initiatives have made significant strides in this respect, the Africa Infrastructure Diagnostic, although this has been a one-time initiative, and the Sokoni internet platform. However, more still needs to be done in unifying data collection efforts for infrastructure projects and housing finance among stakeholders, including DFIs, development partners, governments, and the private sector.

## 4.5 Increasing Land Supply and Infrastructure

The preceding discussions have clearly identified the key challenges related to the provision of land and infrastructure, which hamper affordable housing development delivery. Experience indicates that increasing the supply of land and infrastructure is a crucial part of solving issues of housing availability and affordability. Measures successfully implemented in some countries have included reforms to increase efficiency in land markets and expand access to land for residential development. The provision of basic infrastructure and services is another critical component of housing supply that is often overlooked but has a huge impact on affordability. Strengthening certainty, reducing costs, and ensuring timeliness are key ingredients in expanding the provision of services and infrastructure for affordable housing. To this end, it is necessary to put emphasis on three key areas, which are crucial prerequisites for the provision of land and infrastructure for affordable housing: build efficient and equitable land administrations, adopt flexible mechanisms to increase the supply of land for housing, and integrated urban infrastructure and services planning into related urban development strategies. Although a range of measures have been used in countries to increase both land supply and infrastructure, the policy proposals in the following sections focus on measures that are more appropriate for the continent's land supply and planning systems.

## 4.5.1 Build Efficient and Equitable Land Administrations

Simplifying procedures and increasing flexibility in land use is critical in expanding access to land for housing. To adequately address the continent's housing crisis, governments must make land markets work for the poor by streamlining bureaucratic procedures and reducing the associated costs for acquiring and registering land. The complex regulatory system in many countries is often based on contradictory land laws, which, as mentioned above, hinders transparency, propagates inefficiencies, and breeds corruption in land administration and management. Regulatory frameworks on land use, land development, as well as on housing and building standards have immense implications for the ability of low- and middle-income households to buy, build, or rent good-quality housing. Consolidating the myriad legislation, including administrative frameworks, laws, and regulations governing land markets, is not just a priority but also a crucial first step in building efficient land markets. Kenya's passage of a new and consolidated suite of land laws in 2012 demonstrates how this can be done.

## 4.5.2 Introduce Flexible Land Tenure Regimes to Accelerate Land Delivery

Governments should adopt flexible and innovative approaches in order to incrementally formalize land markets and secure tenure rights. At best, land formalization programs in Africa have had mixed results. This failure has as much to do with the pace as it does with the scale of reforms. Rather than implementing a one-size-fits-all land formalization program, any land titling initiative should recognize the existence of a continuum of land rights that recognizes different sources of land access and land use patterns.

The important implication of the continuum of land rights is that populations in different land tenure situations have distinct land formalization needs and priorities: there is no one-size-fits-all recipe that applies to all categories. This observation is illustrated in Fig. 4.4, which shows the case of three common groups of housing stakeholders.

First, buyers of homes in formally planned housing developments will require formal land rights in the form of individual, freehold titles, in large part because these are required as collateral for mortgage loans. Individual titles are thus a standard element of housing projects planned and developed by the formal private sector. However, the needs of slum dwellers will vary depending on their circumstance and legal position. Those residents of urban slums whose land occupations are legally disputed or otherwise unresolved will not be eligible for formal freehold titles. Instead, the short-term priority for this group of housing stakeholders will be to obtain a moratorium on eviction, and secure tenure through land occupancy permits, or other such legal certificate. Once legal occupancy has been secured, the medium- to long-term priority for these populations may be to obtain formal, freehold title, if needed. Even

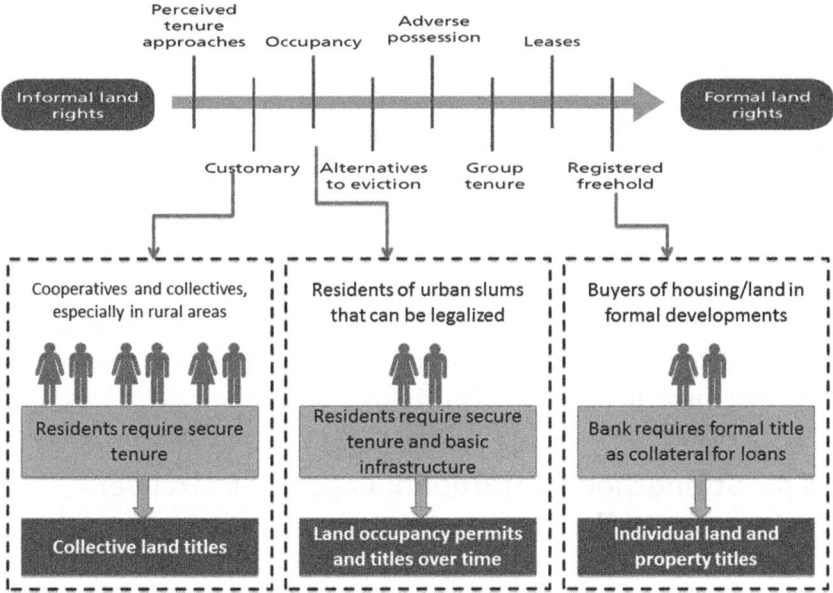

**Fig. 4.4** Land titling priorities for selected housing stakeholders (Source: Adapted from UN-Habitat's continuum of land rights)

in the latter case, however, freehold title may not necessarily be desirable for these residents, if it is accompanied by massive displacement as a result of rising land values following titling.

Last, rural and peri-urban villagers, cooperatives or collectives, may not need to title their land at all, provided that their land occupation is uncontested. In many countries, the land of these communities will have been allocated and secured through customary channels. Even if their land occupation is informal, these communities may enjoy sufficient tenure security, provided there is no active land market that will threaten to displace them. Therefore, formal and individual land titles will not be necessary. In fact, in the case of some rural communities, individual title will even be considered harmful—and culturally alien—to the collective, and may therefore be rejected as inappropriate to the needs and practices of these communities.

### 4.5.3 Promote Community Participation in Land Formalization Processes

In rural areas and informal settlements in particular, governments should be open to alternative approaches to land formalization, involving local partners and using informal approaches. In some areas, such as informal settlements, state agencies may not be the best-placed institutions to carry out enumerations of local residents and rights holders, because of their lack of knowledge of the area or because of potential hostility toward the state in these communities. In such cases, community-based approaches may be more suitable. Community-based organizations are able to implement a local enumeration process in the settlements that they cover much more effectively than the state can.

### 4.5.4 Strengthen Institutional Capacity to Deliver on Land Reforms

Governments need to strengthen the capacities of land institutions and actors in order to promote good land governance and management. In most African countries today, governments, including local administrations, are increasingly playing an important role in land management and planning. However, most of these efforts have been piecemeal. Half-hearted decentralization efforts, as in Cameroon, have failed to improve efficiency in land administration and registry records management. Complete fiscal decentralization, implying the transfer of resources from the central government and the empowerment of municipalities to mobilize financial resources must accompany the delegation of decision-making powers from central to local governments. Most importantly, the provision of technical skills enhancement programs through appropriate and continuous professional training as well as the adoption of modern technology, including remote sensing toll for land demarcation and mapping, will improve the management capacity of governments to increase the quality of services provided and increase efficiency in land administration.

### 4.5.5 Revive Sites-and-Services Programs

Increasing the availability of low-cost serviced land for housing is critical for increasing the supply of housing at prices affordable to low- and middle-income households. Between the 1960s and 1980s, sites-and-services programs played an important role in increasing the supply of affordable housing in many African countries. These programs involve the development of land and the provision of bulk infrastructure, which is then sold to various social groups and developers at below-market rates. They have the potential to better reach many more households at the bottom of the income ladder than conventional social housing programs. Well-planned sites-and-services projects have the potential to increase the supply of titled and serviced land strips to poor families that would otherwise be impossible for them to access due to their limited household budgets. As mentioned above, Côte d'Ivoire's rebirth of its sites-and-services program, LEM, demonstrates how these programs can be the product of collaboration with private developers, with land as a key contribution from the public sector. Another component of LEM worth noting is the mixed-use and mixed-income nature of planned LEM sites. These are positive features that can help LEM neighborhoods avoid some of the pitfalls noticed in single-use social housing areas.

## 4.5.6 Leverage Land Readjustment Programs for Urban Redevelopment

Land readjustment is another method governments can use to assemble and increase the availability of land for housing and infrastructure. This mechanism basically involves the exchange of plots or property rights between private and public entities in a way that is mutually beneficial to the parties involved. Land readjustment has the potential to be useful in Africa as it addresses the major impediment of assembling fragmented land sites for housing redevelopment programs and projects. In cities with a high degree of private landownership, local governments might apply a land readjustment policy to access land for the development of infrastructure, particularly in the urban periphery. Typically, a municipality, local government, or a professional organization works on behalf of the state with local landowners to obtain a right of way for the proposed infrastructure networks in order to get them to agree to a land readjustment or assembly process. The landowners are compensated for the loss of part of their properties through land value gains. In return, the government builds roads, public amenities, utilities, and social spaces within the area and may reserve some land for sales to recover its infrastructure costs. Some land can also be set aside for development of affordable housing. Many forms of land readjustment or pooling are possible, depending on the capacity of the local administration and the willingness of the landowners to participate in the process.

## 4.5.7 Control Illegal Land Invasions and Speculation

Land speculation and hoarding pushes up prices and artificially restricts the supply of land for housing developments. In this instance, the state's intervention in checking such practices is warranted. Instituting an idle or vacant land tax is one method some governments around the world are using to curb hoarding and speculation. In Ethiopia, for example, where land prices have been sharply increasing, leaseholders are expected to add value to land before transferring their leasehold rights, in order to curb speculation. In instances where land has been acquired for residential purposes, leaseholders are also required to begin construction within five years; otherwise, they lose their tenure rights. Leaseholders that transfer freehold rights without completing construction are barred from participating in future bids. Moreover, individuals who transfer leasehold rights without completing at least half of the construction are entitled to just 5 percent of the transfer lease value, assuming they satisfy all other leasehold transfer modalities.

## 4.5.8 Create Land by Upgrading Slums

Slum upgrading is another potential source of land for housing as informal settlements often represent an important and often well-located reservoir of available land. A key challenge for using this land creation mechanism is to expand the formal rights of informal residents to occupy the new land so that these residents may upgrade their housing situations over time. Governments can play an active role in such a situation. In situations of stalemate within slums between structure owners and community residents who are tenants, as noticed in Nairobi, governments are in a unique position to break the impasse that stops upgrading from taking place. A solution could be found through some kind of arrangement giving tenure rights to long-standing, registered community members while compensating structure owners—either through additional housing units in a new housing development elsewhere, as in Morocco's third-party slum-upgrading program, or through other incentives. Governments should also partner with NGOs in slum-upgrading initiatives so as to leverage the collective knowledge of these stakeholders, who often have an inside knowledge of slum dynamics. Moreover, it is critical to involve local residents in major land transactions, especially during the planning phases. Continuously engaging the relevant stakeholders and residents through awareness campaigns at all stages of the slum-upgrading projects is key to ensuring successful outcomes.

Finally, if all other measures fail, governments can use their eminent domain powers to release land for development in the public interest—for building public infrastructure or low-income housing purposes. However, compensation should reflect market rates if the tool is to be acceptable to civil society. This land acquisition mechanism should be used only as a last resort, given its controversial nature as well as the associated costs—financial, political, and legal. In many African countries, civil society is becoming better organized and more powerful politically, as recent events in Tunisia and Burkina Faso have demonstrated. People are also becoming more aware of their rights. This will have important implications for land and housing markets in a subtle but crucial way: it will make it more difficult for the state and private parties to grab land, as resistance will grow. Moreover, citizens will increasingly demand better access to secure tenure and affordable, decent housing and services.

### 4.5.9 Better Coordinate Transportation and Housing Programs

Priority must be given to public transport infrastructure as the costs of traveling to and from work and accessing social facilities are intertwined with housing affordability. Transport is not often considered as a land instrument, but in fact, land strategies and transport should be considered together when planning housing developments. The availability and quality of transport options is an important infrastructure and service issue for housing—particularly, but not solely, for the urban poor. Decent public transport connections act to increase the area of land that is within reach of housing areas, business districts, or industries. Around the world, attempts to develop affordable housing on the urban periphery have frequently failed, due to the lack of infrastructure in newly urbanized areas. The ghost cities in Angola, Mexico, and Egypt provide illustrative examples. When housing is built in remote areas, cut off from social and economic activities, the risk is that these projects will either become ghost towns or fail to attract their target populations. Many policymakers frequently suggest that because the overall housing deficit is so large, even new housing in remote areas will attract buyers or tenants. However, this line of thinking underestimates the problem of "downward raiding"—when higher-income households occupy housing meant for lower-income groups—for public policy objectives of housing affordability, especially when public subsidy is involved. It also underestimates the costs and difficulty involved in "retrofitting" infrastructure once settlements have already developed. Hence, governments should play a lead role in improving connectivity across cities, particularly so for new housing developments in urban fringes.

### 4.5.10 Integrate Infrastructure Planning in Urban Development Policies

It is important to develop a comprehensive and integrated infrastructure plan as part of the urban planning process. The starting point in the infrastructure planning process should include a forecast of population growth so as to estimate the demand for housing, the land space required to accommodate the urban growth, and issues surrounding settlement density. This information will serve as a baseline for assessing infrastructure needs, as well as estimating future replacement needs. This will also enable local governments to strategically plan for future displacement costs when establishing user fees and tax levies for various type of infrastructure. It is crucial and cost-effective for infrastructure planning to precede settlement development in order to avoid the scenario of retrofitting infrastructure, and the associated prohibitive costs. What is more, the development of physical infrastructure is vital to reaping the full benefits of urbanization, improving the quality of life of African households, and increasing the industrial capacity of cities. Hence, African governments need to accelerate the construction of infrastructure such as water and sanitation, electricity, and roads, as well as other physical infrastructure, in order to transform cities into industrial economies and regional hubs.

## 4.6 Conclusion

In this chapter, we discussed the challenges and opportunities related to the provision of land and infrastructure for affordable housing in Africa. The chapter suggests that three principal challenges currently confront the formal housing sector in Africa: poor land governance, weak property rights and tenure security owing to the multiplicity of land tenure regimes, and the growing low-density urban expansion, which raise the cost of service provision.

Our analysis suggests that there is a need for African governments to play a decisive role in land markets. Examples of land governance reforms across Africa and in other regions highlight effective ways of dealing with issues of land access and management. Rwanda provides a good example of how to improve land rights and security. However, it is important to note that a copy-and-paste solution is not recommended. The uncertainties in land tenure regime and enforcement of property rights have significant implications related to the land formalization debate and land delivery. Even though it is clear that individual property rights are needed for the land tenure security required for a well-functioning formal land market, mortgage financing, and private investment in housing, it remains that land formalization should not be seen as a panacea and should be customized depending on the country context and market dynamics. The importance of community engagement and participation in land reforms cannot be overemphasized. In some areas, such as informal settlements, civil society can play a vital role in ensuring equity and efficiency in land market access and distribution. In many countries, civil society is becoming better organized and more powerful politically. As such, governments need to involve local residents in major land transactions and to sensitize residents to the law and the importance of collective interests.

Delivering large-scale housing developments and urban infrastructure is very demanding in terms of long-term finance. The discussion in this chapter has shown that the resources needed goes beyond what African governments' budgets can afford. It is therefore imperative, for those concerned with delivering large affordable housing developments, to put in place innovative financing mechanisms to help raise sufficient resources for land and infrastructure. These include financing schemes geared toward crowding in private capital through PPPs, putting in place necessary conditions to attract investments from the contractual savings industry and ensuring that the prerequisites are in place for increased domestic resource mobilization, through land value capture in particular. The success of such financing mechanisms would heavily depend on the existence of a conducive enabling environment including enforcement of property rights, appropriate legal and regulatory frameworks, security of land tenure and ownership, well-functioning financial systems and adequate information and transparency systems. More specifically, for land value capture schemes to work, there is a need for an active central government putting in place the required policies, and a well-functioning decentralized system with capable and functional local governments, as well as a dynamic class of private developers.

Unlocking land supply and infrastructure for housing would require governments around the continent to adopt and enforce simple regulatory frameworks and land governance systems. Doing so will help clarify land rights and strengthen tenure security. In addition, making regulations and official standards flexible, such as by allowing smaller minimum plot sizes, can directly reduce housing costs. However, these efforts may not be helpful, if efficient and well-equipped land administrations are not in place and their capacity strengthened to deliver on land reforms.

It is also clear from the analysis in this chapter that unlocking land supply and housing infrastructure development requires efforts to ensure that infrastructure planning are integrated in urban development policies to avoid the onerous costs of retrofitting the required infrastructure entailed by poor urban planning. This includes making sure there is a better coordination of transportation and housing programs. Similarly, more efforts would be needed to take courageous and corrective measures geared toward making the land available to those in need, particularly low- and lower middle-income households and individuals. In so doing, several actions could be taken depending on the country context: (1) rekindle sites-and-services programs, given that well-planned sites-and-services projects have the potential to make land acquisition more inclusive; (2) take advantage of land readjustment programs to assemble fragmented land sites for housing redevelopment programs and projects; (3) establish appropriate legal and regulatory frameworks to avoid illegal land evasions and speculations; and (4) make more land available through slum upgrading, as informal settlements often represent an important and often well-located reservoir of available land.

# Bibliography

AfDB (African Development Bank). 2009. *Cameroon—Diagnostic Study for Modernization of the Lands and Survey Sectors*. Abidjan: Country Regional Department Center.

African Centre for Cities. 2015. *Urban Infrastructure in Sub-Saharan Africa – Harnessing Land Values, Housing and Transport. Literature Review on Land Value Capture and Infrastructure Finance*. Rondebosch: African Centre for Cities, University of Cape Town, v + 51 pp.

Amanor, K.S. 2012. *Land Governance in Africa: How Historical Context Has Shaped Key Contemporary Issues Relating to Policy on Land*, Framing the Debate Series No. 1. Rome: International Land Coalition.

Angel, S. 2000. *Housing Policy Matters: A Global Analysis*. New York: Oxford University Press.

AUC-ECA-AfDB Consortium. 2010. *Land Policy in Africa: A Framework to Strengthen Land Rights, Enhance Productivity and Secure Livelihoods*. Addis Ababa: Land Policy Initiative of the African Union Commission–United Nations Economic Commission for Africa–African Development Bank Consortium.

———. 2012. *Tracking Progress in Land Policy Formulation and Implementation in Africa*. Addis Ababa: Land Policy Initiative of the African Union Commission–United Nations Economic Commission for Africa–African Development Bank Consortium.

———. 2014. *Guiding Principles on Large-Scale Land-Based Investments in Africa*. Addis Ababa: United Nations Economic Commission for Africa.

Augustinus, C., and K. Deininger. 2005. *Innovations in Land Tenure, Reform, and Administration in Africa*, Paper presented at the CGAIR System-wide Programme on Collective Action and Property Rights, United Nations Development Programme, and International Land Coalition workshop, "Land Rights for African Development: From Knowledge to Action," Nairobi, October 31–November 3.

Bassett, Ellen M. 2005. Tinkering with Tenure: The Community Land Trust Experiment in Voi, Kenya. *Habitat International* 29 (3): 375–398.

Benjaminsen, T.A., S. Holden, C. Lund, and E. Sjaastad. 2008. Formalisation of Land Rights: Some Empirical Evidence from Mali, Niger, and South Africa. *Land Use Policy* 26: 28–35.

Bromley, D.W. 2008. Formalising Property Relations in the Developing World: The Wrong Prescription for the Wrong Malady. *Land Use Policy* 26: 20–27.

Byamugisha, F.F. 2013. *Securing Africa's Land for Shared Prosperity: A Program to Scale Up Reforms and Investments*. Washington, DC: World Bank and Agence Française de Développement.

CAHF (Centre for Affordable Housing Finance in Africa). 2015. *2015 Yearbook—Housing Finance in Africa: A Review of Some of Africa's Housing Finance Markets*. Parkview: CAHF.

CFS (Committee on World Food Security). 2012. *Voluntary Guidelines on the Responsible Governance of Tenure of Land, Fisheries, and Forests in the Context of National Food Security*. Rome: Food and Agriculture Organization.

Colin, J.-P., and P. Woodhouse. 2010. Introduction: Interpreting Land Markets in Africa. *Africa* 80 (1): 1–13.

Collier, P., and A.J. Venables. 2014. *Housing and Urbanization in Africa Unleashing a Formal Market Process*. Washington, DC: World Bank.

Crisp, B.F., and M.J. Kelly. 1999. The Socioeconomic Impacts of Structural Adjustment. *International Studies Quarterly* 43 (3): 533–552.

De Soto, H. 2000. *The Mystery of Capital: Why Capitalism Triumphs in the West and Fails Everywhere Else*. New York: Basic Books.

Deininger, K., and G. Feder. 2009. Land Registration, Governance, and Development: Evidence and Implications for Policy. *World Bank Research Observer* 24 (2): 233–266.

Deininger, K., D. Ayalew Ali, and T. Alemu. 2009. *Impacts of Land Certification on Tenure Security, Investment, and Land Markets: Evidence from Ethiopia*, Environment for Development Discussion Paper Series, EfD DP 09-11.

Doebele, W.A. 1983. Concepts of Urban Land Tenure. In *Urban Land Policy: Issues and Opportunities*, ed. H.B. Dunkerley, 63–107 (A World Bank Publication). London: Oxford University Press.

Durand-Lasserve, A. 2003. *Land Tenure, Property System Reforms, and Emerging Urban Land Markets in Sub-Saharan Africa*. Cambridge, MA: Lincoln Institute of Land Policy.

Durand-Lasserve, A., M. Durand-Lasserve, and H. Selod. 2013. *A Systemic Analysis of Land Markets and Land Institutions in West African Cities*. Washington, DC: World Bank.

ECA (Economic Commission for Africa). 2009. *African Women's Report: Measuring Gender Inequalities in Africa—Experiences and Lessons from the African Gender and Development Index*. Addis Ababa: Economic Commission for Africa, UN.

Faye, Issa, and Zekebweliwai Geh. 2016. *Meeting Africa's Long-term Housing Finance Needs: A Journey of a Thousand Miles?* European Investment Bank Report.

Gusah, S. 2012. Community Land Trusts: A Model for Integrating Abuja's Urban Villages within the City Master Plan. In *Changing Cities: Climate, Youth and Land Markets in Urban Areas*, ed. Lauren E. Herzer, 141–159. Washington, DC: Wilson Center.

Gutman, Jeffrey, Amadou Sy, and Soumya Chattopadhyay. 2015. *Financing African Infrastructure: Can the World Deliver?* Brookings Institute, Washington, DC.

http://www.brookings.edu/~/media/Research/Files/Reports/2015/03/financing-african-infrastructure-gutman-sy-chattopadhyay/AGIFinancing AfricanInfrastructure_FinalWebv2.pdf?la=en.

Matthaei, E., and P. Mandimika. 2014. *The Flexible Land Tenure System in Namibia: Integrating Urban Land Rights into the National Land Reform Programme*, Paper presented at the Annual World Bank Conference on Land and Poverty 2014, "Integrating Land Governance into the Post-2015 Agenda," Washington, DC, March 24–27.

Mayo, S.K., and D.J. Gross. 1987. Sites and Services-and Subsidies: The Economics of Low-Cost Housing in Developing Countries. *World Bank Economic Review* 1 (2): 301–335.

MGI (McKinsey Global Institute). 2014. *A Blueprint for Addressing the Global Affordable Housing Challenge*. San Francisco/Seoul/Shanghai: McKinsey Global Institute.

———. 2016. *Lions on the Move II: Realizing the Potential of Africa's Economies*. New York: McKinsey Global Institute.

Musyoka, R.M., and H. Musoga. 2015. *Typologies of Land Tenure and Their Impact on Urban Form in Africa: The Case of Eldoret City in Kenya*, Paper presented at the Annual World Bank Conference on Land and Poverty 2015, "Linking Land Tenure and Use for Shared Prosperity," Washington, DC, March 23–27.

Napier, M. 2013. Land and Markets in African Cities: Time for a New Lens? In *Trading Places: Accessing Land in African Cities*, ed. Mark Napier et al., 1–21. Cape Town: African Minds.

Olvera, L., D. Plat, and P. Pochet. 2003. Transportation Conditions and Access to Services in a Context of Urban Sprawl and Deregulation. The Case of Dar es Salaam. *Transport Policy* 10 (4): 287–298.

Palmer, Ian, and Stephen Berrisford. 2015. *Final Report on Land-Based Financing for Urban Infrastructure in Sub-Saharan African Cities*. Cape Town: African Centre for Cities.

Paulais, Thierry Tristan. 2012. *Financing Africa's Cities: The Imperative of Local Investment*, Africa Development Forum. Washington, DC: World Bank.

Payne, G., A. Piaskowy, and L. Kuritz. 2014. *Land Tenure in Urban Environments*, Issue Brief. Washington, DC: United States Agency for International Development (USAID).

Pejovich, S. 1990. *The Economics of Property Rights: Towards a Theory of Comparative Systems*. Dordrecht: Kluwer.

———. 1995. *Economic Analysis of Institutions and Systems*. Dordrecht: Kluwer.

Rakodi, C., and C.R. Leduka. 2004. *Informal Land Delivery Processes and Access to Land for the Poor: A Comparative Study of Six African Cities*, Policy Brief 6. University of Birmingham, International Development Department.

Royston, L. 2013. *Incrementally Securing Tenure: Promising Practices in Informal Settlement Upgrading in Southern Africa*, Paper presented at the Annual World Bank Conference on Land and Poverty 2014, "Integrating Land Governance into the Post-2015 Agenda," Washington, DC, March 24–27.

Rurawanga, E. 2013. *Land Tenure Reform. The Case Study of Rwanda*, Paper presented at the Land Divided Conference 2013, "Land and South African Society in 2013, in Comparative Perspective," University of Cape Town, March 24–27.

Satterthwaite, D. 2009. Expanding the Supply and Reducing the Cost of Land for Housing in Urban Areas in Low- and Middle-Income Nations. Background Note. *World Development Report: Reshaping Economic Geography*. Washington, DC: World Bank.

Silva, C.M., ed. 2015. *Urban Planning in Sub-Saharan Africa: Colonial and Postcolonial Planning Cultures*. New York: Routledge.

Toulmin, C. 2008. Securing Land and Property Rights in Sub-Saharan Africa: The Role of Local Institutions. *Land Use Policy* 26: 10–19.

UN-Habitat. 2010. *State of the World's Cities 2010/2011: Bridging the Urban Divide*. Nairobi: United Nations Human Settlements Program.

———. 2011. *Ghana Housing Profile*. Nairobi: United Nations Human Settlements Program.

———. 2012a. *Zambia Urban Housing Sector Profile*. Nairobi: United Nations Human Settlements Program.

———. 2012b. *Handling Land: Innovative Tools for Land Governance and Secure Tenure*. Nairobi: United Nations Human Settlements Program.

USAID (U.S. Agency for International Development). 2011. *Cameroon Country Profile: Property Rights and Resource Governance*. Washington, DC: USAID.

———. 2013. *Côte d'Ivoire Country Profile: Property Rights and Resource Governance*. Washington, DC: USAID.

Wanjala, S.C. 1990. *Land Law and Disputes in Kenya*. Nairobi: Oxford University Press.

Weru, J. 2004. Community Federations and City Upgrading: The Work of Pamoja Trust and Muungano in Kenya. *Environment and Urbanization* 16 (1): 47–62.

World Bank. 2003. *Land Policies for Growth and Poverty Reduction*. New York: Oxford University Press and World Bank.

———. 2012. *Doing Business 2012: Doing Business in a More Transparent World*. Washington, DC: World Bank Group.

———. 2013. *Doing Business 2013: Smarter Regulations for Small and Medium-Size Enterprises*. Washington, DC: World Bank Group.

**Open Access**  This chapter is licensed under the terms of the Creative Commons Attribution 4.0 International License (http://creativecommons.org/licenses/by/4.0/), which permits use, sharing, adaptation, distribution and reproduction in any medium or format, as long as you give appropriate credit to the original author(s) and the source, provide a link to the Creative Commons license and indicate if changes were made.

The images or other third party material in this chapter are included in the chapter's Creative Commons license, unless indicated otherwise in a credit line to the material. If material is not included in the chapter's Creative Commons license and your intended use is not permitted by statutory regulation or exceeds the permitted use, you will need to obtain permission directly from the copyright holder.

# 5

# The Construction Cost Conundrum in Africa

## 5.1 Introduction

Demand for affordable housing among low- and middle-income households across Africa is high and unmet. Fueled by the continent's rapid urbanization rate and large housing deficits, this demand is projected to grow tremendously in the coming decades. This presents both a huge opportunity and a challenge for the construction industry. The opportunity is to transform the sector in order to respond to this demand, eventually resulting in job creation, industrialization, and ultimately poverty reduction. The challenge stems from the inability of most small and medium-size construction companies to deliver large-scale housing developments, in light of their limited financial and managerial capacity. Moreover, it is noted that there is a mismatch between the supply and the demand for housing.

The high cost of building materials and inefficiencies in the construction process make housing unaffordable for the vast majority of Africans. As formal housing built by real estate developers remains out of reach for the majority of households, self-built housing is the preferred and prevalent option for home acquisition. In Cameroon, for instance, 93 percent of the houses are built through owner-driven construction, while in Dakar, Senegal, over 80 percent are self-built. Chaotic urbanization, lack of affordable serviced land, and difficulties in acquiring both an official land title and a construction permit result in the majority of homes being informal. Today, formal housing represents only 10 percent of housing built in African cities. This chapter analyzes the drivers of high construction costs in Africa and provides recommendations for lowering these costs and possible pathways for transforming the sector.

## 5.2 The Importance of the Construction Sector

Although the need for housing construction is important, both residential and nonresidential housing represent a small share in construction spending. The construction sector is undergoing major shifts, with strong demand for construction services fueled by large investments in infrastructure, especially transport and energy. With a huge infrastructure gap to fill—about US$93 billion per year—and renewed efforts by national governments and development partners to invest in infrastructure development, the demand for construction is expected to increase further in the coming years.

The value of projects under construction that are worth over US$50 million had increased from US$222 billion in 2013 to US$326 billion by June 2014 (Deloitte 2014). This sharp increase was driven by the rise in the number of megaprojects valued at more than US$1 billion, although the number of projects actually fell from 322 to 257. The 2014 distribution by sector shows that transport (40 percent) and energy (39 percent) are by far the largest beneficiaries of these construction projects, with real estate representing only 3 percent of the value of construction in the continent.

Construction investment as a share of GDP varies widely across countries, from a low of 1.5 percent in Liberia to a high of 28.5 percent in the Republic of Congo, with an average of 10.6 percent and a median of 11.5 percent. Construction spending can also be analyzed as a proportion of total investment. Figure 5.1 shows that in most African countries, the largest share of total investment is directed toward construction spending. Although the median share is 52 percent, 14 countries had shares above 60 percent. This suggests that most countries are largely making efforts to fill their infrastructure gap rather than accumulating machinery and equipment, a move that is important for industrialization.

Although real estate construction is a small share of overall construction spending (3 percent), spending on housing represents a larger share of households' individual consumption expenditures (Fig. 5.2). The average share is 16 percent and varies from a low of 5 percent in Algeria to a high of 33 percent in Comoros. However, these data should be treated with a degree of caution as housing expenditure varies widely between urban and rural areas and will be certainly influenced by levels of urbanization between countries. Spending on housing also depends on housing prices and government transfers to households.

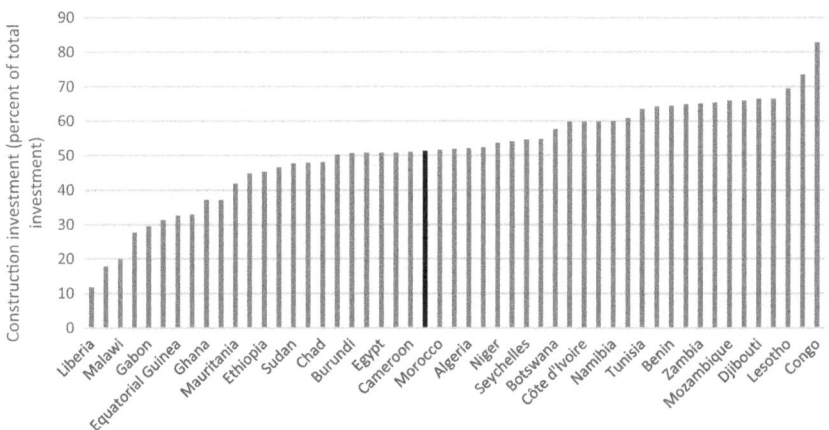

**Fig. 5.1** Construction investment as a share of total investment, by country (Source: World Bank, International Comparison Program 2011)

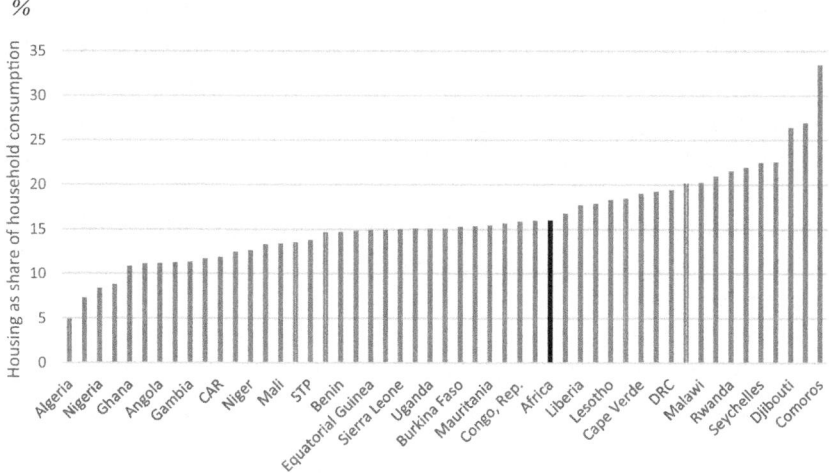

**Fig. 5.2** Housing spending as a share of total household spending, by country (%) (Source: World Bank, International Comparison Program 2011; Note: *STP* São Tomé and Principe)

## 5.3 Housing Construction Costs

The high construction costs and the lack of affordable land are the two biggest factors affecting housing affordability. As discussed in Chap. 4, Africa's rapid urbanization has generated a scarcity of land across major cities and the unaffordability of well-located plots, resulting in high land prices and urban sprawl. Construction costs are the largest component of home prices in Africa. Data from the South African market apparently suggests that growth in construction costs has been going on for quite some time and the recent trend does not seem to be significantly reversed. This shows the acuity of the affordability issue driven by construction costs in that country.

In Kenya, for instance, construction costs represent 60 percent of overall costs (Fig. 5.3). Land acquisition and infrastructure costs represent another 20 percent. This cost structure contrasts with that of South Africa, where profits and overhead costs are high (31 percent), the bulk and link infrastructure alone represent 23 percent, and construction costs account for 38 percent of the housing costs. This difference suggests that

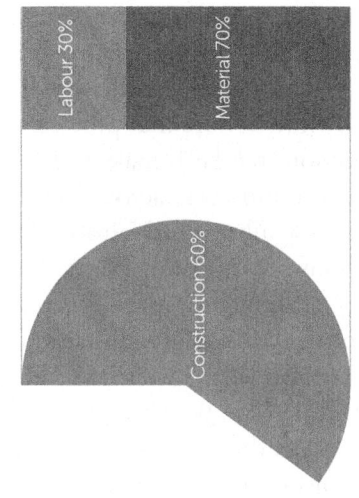

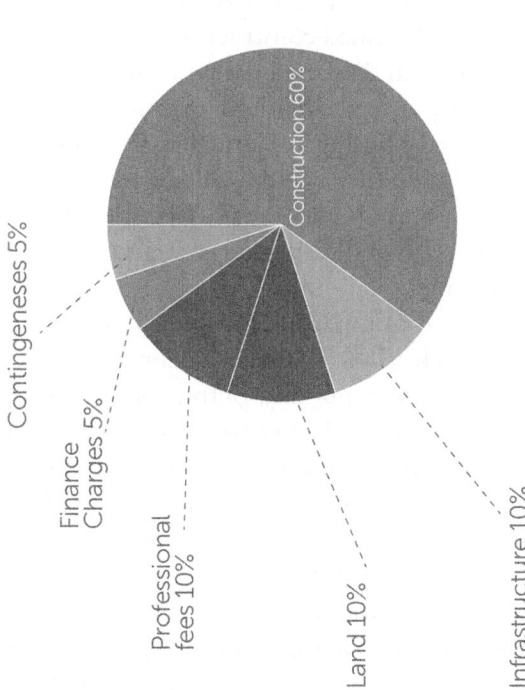

**Fig. 5.3** Formal housing cost structure, Kenya (Source: AFDB 2012)

there may be a room to lower construction costs in Kenya taking South Africa as a benchmark. One possible way to bring construction costs down in Kenya could be through the reduction in the costs of materials.

However, it is worthwhile to note that product differentiation and the lack of unified construction standards make it difficult to gather data and compare housing construction costs across countries. For instance, the cost of a 40 m$^2$ house in a suburb in Nairobi, Kenya, is quite different from a similar-sized house in Niamey, Niger. Moreover, differences in climate, the availability of different types of materials, and varying levels of efficiency among construction companies lead to different costs.

A standard form of cost measurement that seeks to address these differences is the bill of quantities (BoQ) technique. A BoQ provides a detailed view of the necessary inputs, their quantities, and the unit prices for each type of construction project. The project cost is obtained by adding overhead costs to the sum of the product of quantity and unit price for all components, including the hiring of local construction professionals. The implementation of this approach in a large number of countries is thus difficult due to the lack of unified construction standards and the multiplicity of construction materials used across countries. Nonetheless, it remains a feasible and practical approach to consider by governments undertaking standardized housing construction. For instance, the BoQ method is being used by the city of Addis Ababa for the construction of standardized condominiums on a large scale. It enables the city to control costs by supplying materials and managing contracts with a large number of construction companies.

The 2005 International Comparison Program (ICP) introduced a variation of the BoQ approach called the Basket of Construction Components (BOCC), a combination of input and output pricing. Calculating the BOCC involves collecting the prices of basic inputs such as cement and reinforcing steel, as well as the prices of composite components, which are intermediate outputs that are similar across countries. Weights are then used to aggregate the composite components to arrive at the final project costs. To circumvent possible implementation challenges, a simplified input method was used in the 2011 round of the ICP. Data from the ICP 2011 round are summarized in Table 5.1.

Table 5.1 Construction costs in Africa

| Price per square meter in US$ (2011 exchange rates) | | | | |
|---|---|---|---|---|
| | Single-story, detached house, average quality, masonry (brick or block) or timber frame | Two-story attached house, mass market, center unit in terrace/ row of four units | Low-rise apartment, mass market, concrete frame, brick or block infill, walk-up | High-rise apartment, average quality, concrete frame, brick or block infill |
| Morocco | 173 | 161 | 161 | 185 |
| Central African Republic | 181 | 174 | 252 | – |
| Mali | 196 | 223 | 403 | 456 |
| Tunisia | 251 | 299 | 334 | 348 |
| Tanzania | 254 | 382 | 286 | 445 |
| Benin | 278 | 479 | 589 | 747 |
| Kenya | 281 | 360 | 315 | 394 |
| Niger | 306 | 494 | 943 | 627 |
| Burkina Faso | 313 | 493 | 886 | 1250 |
| Ethiopia | 314 | 385 | 402 | 444 |
| Burundi | 317 | 396 | 476 | 515 |
| Egypt | 319 | – | 335 | 302 |
| Malawi | 321 | 449 | 642 | 770 |
| Chad | 350 | 424 | 583 | 848 |
| Gambia | 373 | 543 | 238 | 509 |
| Cameroon | 424 | 371 | 530 | 901 |
| Djibouti | 456 | 439 | 619 | 563 |
| Senegal | 477 | 668 | 689 | 785 |
| Comoros | 537 | 494 | – | – |
| Algeria | 548 | 548 | 466 | 535 |
| Guinea | 549 | 631 | 652 | 694 |
| Ghana | 595 | 554 | 537 | 496 |
| Mozambique | 601 | 1201 | 801 | 1752 |
| Zambia | 613 | 720 | 350 | 613 |
| Nigeria | 617 | 705 | 975 | 1429 |
| Côte d'Ivoire | 626 | 678 | 1007 | 1272 |
| Congo, Republic | 865 | 989 | 1024 | 1219 |
| Average | 412 | 510 | 557 | 724 |
| Median | 350 | 486 | 533 | 613 |

*Source:* World Bank, International Comparison Program 2011

There are large variations in construction costs across countries, as seen in Table 5.1. The price per square meter for a single-story house varies from a low of US$173 in Morocco to a high of US$865 in the Republic of Congo. The variations are large not only across countries but also within regions. The average price per square meter of a single-story detached house is lowest in North Africa (US$323), followed by East Africa (US$360), West Africa (US$428), Central Africa (US$455), and Southern Africa (US$512). It is only in North and East Africa that the prices are below the African average of US$412. Within regions, the lowest variation is within Southern Africa, where the price per square meter for a single-story detached house in Zambia is about 1.9 times than that in Malawi. The largest variation is within Central Africa, where prices range from US$180 per square meter in the Central African Republic to US$865 in the Republic of Congo. The ratio of the highest to the lowest prices is 2.11 in East Africa, 3.16 in North Africa, and 3.19 in West Africa.

## 5.4 The Construction Value Chain and Construction Costs

A detailed analysis of the housing delivery chain is necessary to identify the determinants of high house prices. The first step in the value chain, as shown in Fig. 5.4, is the acquisition of land and provision of bulk infrastructure. As discussed in Chap. 4, rapid urbanization and the lack of urban planning have contributed to soaring land prices in major urban centers across the continent, making well-located land unaffordable to the majority of households. Finance, another critical input of the construction value chain, was discussed at length in Chap. 3 highlighting its contribution to housing prices. Like finance, the government is also present in all stages of the value chain, as a regulator, controller, or producer/customer. Other important inputs in the construction value chain are design, materials, and labor. The following subsections discuss and analyze each of the main housing delivery value chain input and their contribution to high construction costs.

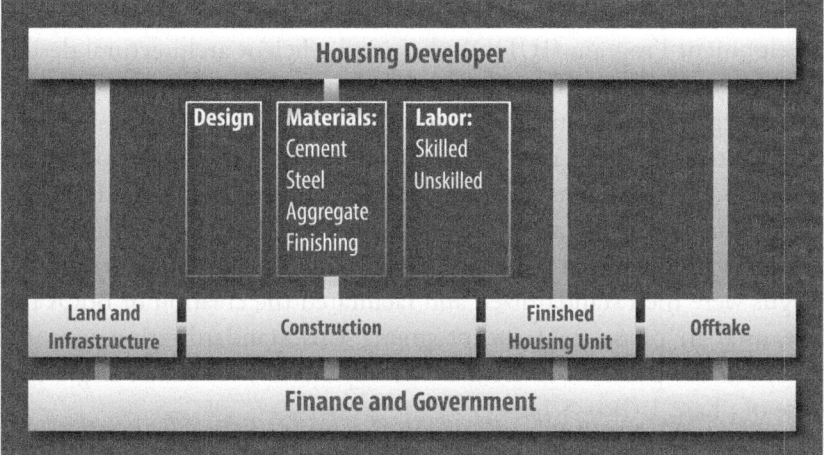

**Fig. 5.4** Housing delivery value chain (*Source*: Author)

## 5.4.1 Design

The value of architectural design is often neglected in the conception of affordable housing development projects. Although the services of an architect may be expensive for a small project of a few housing units, the benefits generally outweigh the costs for large projects. An optimized architectural design can lower construction costs significantly, not only by reducing the quantity of material used but also by minimizing material waste. Simply limiting the number of corners or reducing the number of convex or concave corners reduces construction costs. In addition, using dimensions that are proportional to the standard measures of building materials in the country reduces cutting time and wastage. For instance, flooring work can involve a lot of tile cutting and wastage if the areas are not proportional to the tile sizes available in the market. The 2016 winner of the Pritzker prize in architecture, the Chilean Alejandro Aravena, has demonstrated how good design can be used to build low-cost, functional houses. He has constructed 100 flexible and functional houses in Iquique in Chile costing only US$7500 per house. For this price, he managed to build houses which are twice the size of the ones the construction industry in Chile could have built (30 m$^2$).

Phase 1 (2006–2010) of the Ethiopian Integrated Urban Housing Development Program (IUHDP) has used efficient architectural designs extensively to reduce costs. First, the design preparation embraced compact, integrated, and mixed-use settlements (business and residential), consideration of social mix (low- and middle-income households), and density. Building designs included different housing typologies for different income levels to allow for cross-subsidy and cost optimization. Designs were improved continuously through design competitions. The designs were then standardized and facilitated the creation of BoQs that were used in phase 2 of the program. This standardization was very important for phase 2, given that the objectives were much larger than those of phase 1 (Box 5.1).

> **Box 5.1 Large-Scale Affordable Housing: Ethiopia's Integrated Urban Housing Development Program**
>
> The IUHDP is part of the government's effort to address the housing challenge in Ethiopia, where the housing deficit is estimated at 1 million units. The IUHDP was launched in 2005 as a pilot program, supported by GIZ, to build 5000 housing units annually in Addis Ababa. In 2006, the program was scaled up, with a target to build 396,000 housing units in the first phase of the project (2006/2007–2009/2010) and 231,288 housing units in the second phase (2010/2011–2014/2015).
>
> Given the shortage of land in urban areas and the high costs of infrastructure, the IUHDP decided early on to choose condominium-style housing, despite local habits favoring groundfloor living. New services to facilitate condominium living emerged and preferences changed over time. The program was executed under the form of public-private partnership (PPP). The government, in collaboration with municipality officials, managed procurement of materials and project control, while large private contractors undertook construction. Each large contractor was expected to subcontract 40 percent of the work to micro and small enterprises (MSEs). The centralized bulk purchase of building materials, combined with tax exemptions, contributed to lowering construction costs. The success of the centralized procurement system rested upon the use of standardized designs and the adoption of standardized BoQs. The government also provided land and bulk infrastructure before the start of construction projects.
>
> In response to the shortage of required skills that were identified as a bottleneck early in the planning, the program included a component to build capacity with assistance from GIZ. New graduates from engineering and design schools received skills training, and contractors received both

skills training and microfinance loans for equipment. This assistance helped create and equip over 4300 MSEs, which were involved in different stages of the program from the local production of building materials to finishing works in condominium projects. A national overall skill-upgrading program was implemented at the same time through reforms of tertiary education and technical and vocational education and training (TVET).

Facing rising housing construction prices, the Ethiopian government undertook import substitution strategies that led to a dramatic increase in cement production (see Box 5.3). As a result, cement prices declined by more than 50 percent. Similar efforts to increase the production of steel materials are ongoing.

Although the program continues to experience skill shortages and high costs for some building materials, overall it is a commendable success. As of January 2015, it had built and delivered 329,301 housing units and over 60,000 were under construction. This performance is better than any other large-scale affordable housing program in any sub-Saharan African country, with the exception of South Africa. Moreover, as a result of the labor-intensive delivery method of the program, which does not use cranes and heavy machinery, the IUHDP has created 737,256 job opportunities, of which 175,400 arose in the first phase and 561,856 in the second phase.

The most important success factor, cited by the majority of stakeholders, is the government's vision and leadership. Pragmatism, the ability to solve problems as they appear, and a supply chain–driven approach were also important factors that led to the large-scale delivery of affordable housing in Ethiopia.

Source: Based on data gathered in November 2014 fact-finding mission and February 2015 regional workshops; Ermed (2015) and Mekuria (2015).

## 5.4.2 Building Materials

The timely supply of building materials of required specification and quality is a major concern for stakeholders in the construction and housing sector because of its direct impact on construction costs. In other words, affordable housing programs cannot succeed without timely availability of building and construction materials at an appropriate specification, quality, and price. As shown in Fig. 5.3, the cost of materials represents 40 percent of total housing costs in Kenya. This share can be even higher in countries that import the majority of their construction materials.

Given the huge infrastructure and housing deficits, the abundance of raw materials as well as large construction-related import bills faced by African countries below, it is clear that the construction and building materials sector can be a gateway for Africa's industrialization. In fact, the needs for large-scale affordable housing and infrastructure development programs are so glaring and pressing that the current model based on importation of construction and building materials is not sustainable. The sector is very large: it includes aggregates, cement, iron and steel bars, timber and wood, marble, tiles and stone, electrical and sanitary works, glass, paints and varnishes, electrical lighting, and so on. Some of the subsectors related to the production of these products provide great opportunities for import substitution and job creation. In some countries, it is noticed that the construction and building material sector has already been attractive to large companies.

Aggregates such as sand, gravel, crushed stone, and slag are typically mined in each country by quarrying companies and are not traded across borders. Their prices vary across countries and across cities, depending on the availability of mineral deposits, the cost of transportation, and the efficiency of quarrying companies. Most of other building materials are manufactured products with different degrees of sophistication. Given the limited size and capacity of the manufacturing sector in Africa, most countries import the majority of such products, especially finished products. For instance, in Ethiopia, only one plant makes sanitary products and it has a low production capacity. The exception is South Africa, which has a mature manufacturing sector able to produce most construction products. In the next subsection, we analyze the supply of cement and steel products and discuss how imports of building materials affect house prices.

### 5.4.2.1 Cement Sector

Africa's cement sector is undergoing unprecedented growth. Heavy investments in infrastructure and housing across the continent are fueling this high demand. Cement consumption Sub-Saharan Africa grew by 6.6 percent in 2014, the highest in the world (Business Day 2015). The Ethiopian Grand Renaissance Dam Project alone is expected to use 10 million tons of concrete. Despite the recent slowdown in economic growth, investment in infrastructure is expected to increase. This is in part due to the acknowledgment by African governments and their international development partners that the continent needs to address its infrastructure gap for its long-term development.

As a response to this strong demand, cement producers are increasing production capacity at a very rapid pace. Determined to dominate the cement industry in Africa, the Dangote group has invested an estimated US$5 billion since 2012, expanding operations to 16 countries (Ecobank 2015). It is estimated that by 2016, the group will have a capacity of 62 million tons per annum (mtpa) with the objective of reaching 81 million tons by 2020 (Adekoya 2015). Dangote's rapid expansion across the continent is pressuring its competitors to increase their capacity. LafargeHolcim, which has a very strong presence in North Africa, is planning to increase its investments in sub-Saharan Africa, where it is currently the second largest producer. Heidelberg Cement, a German company, has also increased its installed capacity in four African countries within the last two years. Ciments d'Afrique, a Moroccan producer, as well as some Chinese companies and local producers, are also increasing their investments throughout sub-Saharan Africa.

Production capacity in sub-Saharan Africa varies significantly across countries. Ecobank (2015) shows that Nigeria is by far the largest producer, with twice the capacity of the second largest producer, South Africa (Table 5.2). The Nigerian market is dominated by Dangote Cement, which has 68 percent of the market, followed by LafargeHolcim (20 percent) and BUA Cement (12 percent). Spurred by a large-scale housing program (see Box 5.1) and heavy infrastructure investment, Ethiopia's cement production increased from less than 2 million tons a year in the early 2000s to 15.1 million tons a year in 2015.[1] The next group of large producers is Kenya, Senegal, and Ghana, with installed production capacity between 6.7 mtpa and 8.9 mtpa. Capacity is also increasing in other countries, as Dangote recently opened factories in Cameroon, Tanzania, and Zambia; each country is now producing over 3 mtpa.

Table 5.2 Installed production capacity in various Sub-Saharan African countries, 2015

| Million tons per annum | |
|---|---|
| Country | Installed capacity |
| Nigeria | 42.7 |
| South Africa | 21.4 |
| Ethiopia | 15.1 |
| Kenya | 8.9 |
| Senegal | 8 |
| Ghana | 6.7 |
| Tanzania | 3.7 |
| Zambia | 3.2 |
| Cameroon | 3.1 |
| Uganda | 2.6 |
| Côte d'Ivoire | 2.5 |
| Angola | 2.5 |
| Benin | 2.1 |
| Mozambique | 1.9 |
| Togo | 1.8 |
| Zimbabwe | 1.7 |
| Guinea | 1.1 |
| **Total sub-Saharan Africa** | **133.3** |

*Source:* Ecobank 2015

Despite the growing production capacity, Africa remains a large importer of cement. Total imports of lime and cement, and fabricated construction materials (excluding glass and clay) by African countries increased from US$4 billion to US$5 billion between 2010 and 2014. At the regional level, North Africa, led by Algeria, experienced the largest increase, followed by Central and Eastern Africa (Fig. 5.5). Imports to West Africa have been stable at about US$1.3 billion, while Southern Africa experienced a 12 percent decline, from US$311 million to US$274 million.

Figure 5.6 shows import volumes per country in 2014, as well as the origin of the imports. Algeria is by far the largest importer, with total imports estimated at US$648 million. Libya and Egypt follow, with imports totaling US$422 million and US$307 million, respectively. In sub-Saharan Africa, Nigeria is the largest importer, although imports decreased from US$426 million in 2010 to US$280 million in 2014 as a

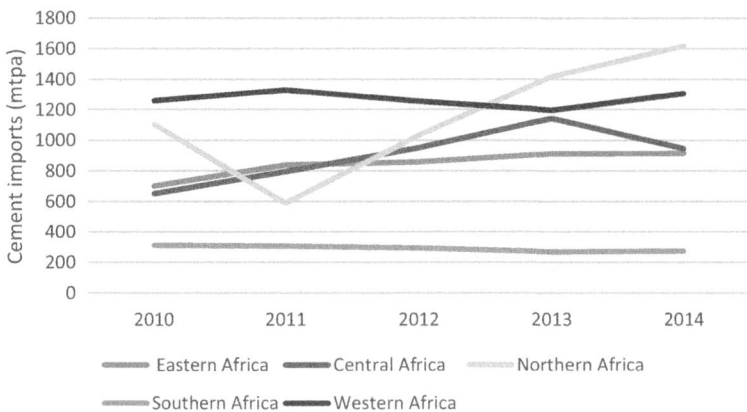

**Fig. 5.5** Imports of Lime, Cement, and Fabrication Construction Materials (Excluding Glass and Clay), 2000–2014 (*metric tons per year*) (*Source:* UNCTAD)

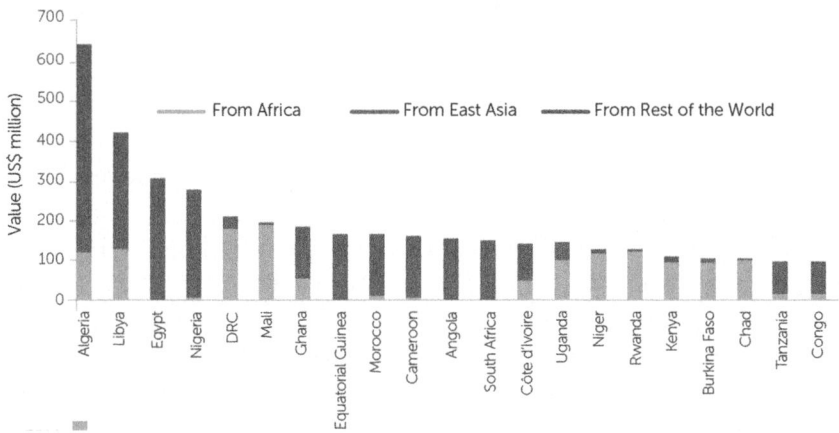

**Fig. 5.6** Cement imports by source for top 20 importers, 2014 (*US$ million*) (*Source:* UNCTAD)

result of the rapid increase in production and the adoption of protection policies. It is expected that continued expansion projects and greenfield investments by different actors will make the country self-sufficient in the near future. Following Nigeria, a number of countries in West and Central Africa imported between US$100 million and US$200 million per year. Overall, these imports contribute substantially to increasing construction costs. They are quite sizeable and alarming knowing that the majority of countries in these regions are low-income countries experiencing more or less substantial budget deficits.

The vast majority of cement imports in Africa originate from East Asia—specifically Indonesia and Pakistan—except in Algeria and Morocco, which, due to their proximity to Europe, have benefited from increasingly competitive European manufacturers. East Asian imports dominate the market in Central and Eastern Africa. However, intra-African trade has increased significantly during the last few years. For instance, Burkina Faso, Chad, the Democratic Republic of Congo, Mali, Niger, Rwanda, and Uganda import cement largely from other African countries. This represents a drastic change from 2010, as 17 of 51 African countries more than doubled their volume of imports from other African countries, while their overall imports recorded a smaller increase.

### 5.4.2.2 Steel Products

In addition to the extensive usage of steel in infrastructure projects, the large quantity of reinforcing steel bars used in Africa's housing construction contribute to the high demand for steel in the continent. However, the size of Africa's steel industry is still very limited. In 2013, for instance, total production of crude steel was estimated at 16.1 mtpa while imports amounted to 25 mtpa (World Steel Association Yearbook 2013). South Africa and Egypt were by far the largest producers in 2013, with production of 7.3 and 6.7 mtpa, respectively. Together, both countries produce 93 percent of Africa's crude steel output. Other countries, such as Angola, Kenya, and Nigeria, are trying to increase their production. The biggest importer in 2013 was Algeria with 5.1 mtpa, followed closely by Egypt with 4.2 mtpa. Other large steel importers were Nigeria, Morocco, and Kenya, with quantities estimated at 2.2, 1.6, and 1.3 mtpa, respectively.

The UNCTAD's trade database had been used to calculate the value of steel imports for all African countries.[2] Overall, Africa imported US$14.8 billion in 2014, which is 19 percent higher than the value of steel imported in 2010. The ranking across countries (Fig. 5.7) shows that in

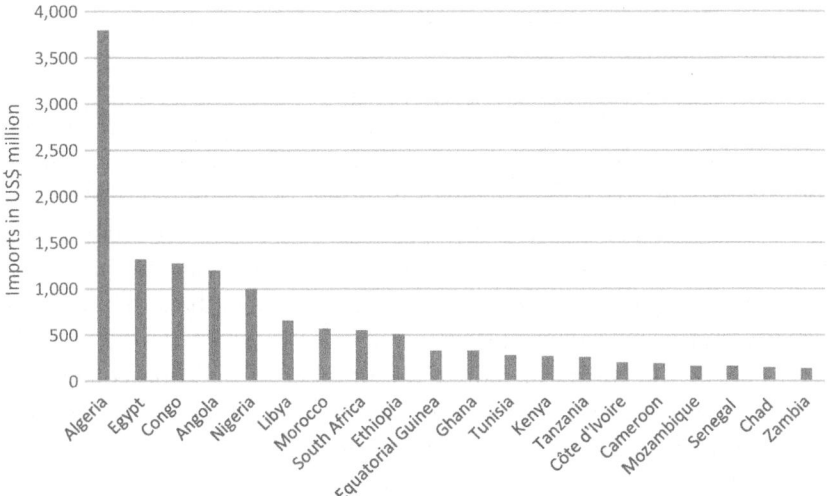

**Fig. 5.7** Top 20 steel products importers, 2014 (*US$ million*) (*Source:* UNCTAD)

2014 Algeria alone imported US$3.8 billion, a quarter of Africa's total imports. Imports of the next three highest ranked—Egypt, Congo, and Angola—came to about a third of Algeria's imports. The figure also shows that the top six importers are among the top oil producers in the continent, reflecting the heavy usage of steel in the oil industry. The fact that Algeria features as the first importer of cement and steel products is not fortuitous, this has a lot do with the ongoing large government infrastructure development and housing programs being implemented in the country. Similar to cement, the importation of steel contributes to increasing construction costs.

### 5.4.2.3 Building Materials Quality Standards

Improving building material standards is a necessity in most African countries. However, a blind adoption of standards from Europe or the United States would be counterproductive, as environmental and market conditions differ. This is a common challenge for most African countries, particularly in the context of importation of counterfeit goods and production of local building materials. Concerns have been raised in the industry about using materials and products that do not comply with national standards.

As response, several African countries have been working on creating and enforcing standards by creating regulatory institutions. Education and training are also vital components in the efforts to improve quality. For example, in 2010, the Ugandan National Bureau of Standards, with assistance from the Swedish International Development Cooperation Agency and TradeMark East Africa, began a five-year quality infrastructure and standards program to establish and strengthen the country's capacity to develop and implement standards.

As part of the efforts to reduce the number of building collapses in Nigeria, the Standards Organization of Nigeria and the Association of Block Molders of Nigeria have reached agreement that a 50 kg bag of cement should be used to produce only 24 blocks instead of the previous practice of 42 blocks. The Standards Organization then raised molders' awareness of the critical role that cement blocks play in stabilizing buildings and in construction work. The trade association agreed to use the prescribed standards, but this has resulted in a 70 percent increase in the unit price of blocks, from US$0.70 (₦120–130) to US$1.20 (₦200–250). While this provides a perfect illustration that getting the quality standards right in the construction sector comes with a cost which somehow end up affecting the house prices, it remains that such costs are economically and socially more acceptable than the ones that could be entailed by building collapses due to quality issues.

### 5.4.3 Labor

Labor is a critical input in the construction sector and generally represents 30 percent of overall construction costs. The industry requires both skilled and unskilled labor. Although unskilled labor is widely available, there is an acute shortage of skilled workers, especially well-trained technicians such as electricians, carpenters, plumbers, general construction workers, and, in some countries, engineers and architects. The Kenya Federation of Master Builders, representing 2500 contractors—of which 80 percent are small and medium enterprises (SMEs)—notes that there is a large skills gap in the construction sector both in terms of adequacy of human resources and in terms of the productivity and quality of workmanship. This is largely because training costs (about US$1200) are generally unaffordable for skilled workers, semiskilled workers, and SME contractors and because the curricula of most training institutions are out of touch with industry needs.

Local artisans who construct without respecting building codes dominate the incremental housing construction sector. The lack of the proper professional training and skills to comply with standards locks low-income households into a cycle of poor-quality, self-built housing. Habitat for Humanity in Kenya (2014) observes that the poor quality is a reflection of the low skills—in both budgeting and building design—of the artisans who influence the procurement process.[3] This increases the cost of construction and limits the ability to construct decent dwellings.

A challenge facing many African countries is the skills mismatch between the supply and labor demand in many productive sectors. Construction is not an exception. The education systems, which were modeled on European colonial systems, do not respond to local needs. A majority of pupils enrolled in primary and secondary schools end up dropping out before reaching the tertiary level. It is estimated that 90 percent of young people between ages 15 and 24 face a lack of training alternatives and eventually enter the informal sector without proper qualification (UNESCO n.d.). Furthermore, the majority of those who do finish secondary school enroll in general teaching universities whose programs or curricula are not adapted to produce the skills required in the labor market. The 2008 African Economic Outlook notes that, in contrast to sub-Saharan Africa, where enrollment in TVET as a share of total secondary school enrollment is about 5 percent, North African countries have enrollment rates averaging 23 percent. In addition to the limited availability of formal TVET programs in sub-Saharan Africa, progress is hindered by cultural biases in which people perceive such training as the mechanism of enrolling students who failed in the curriculum of general education. Concerted efforts to sensitize youth to their career choices at an earlier age would change such cultural biases. However, while promoting and implementing TVET programs is part of the solution, it is important to note that such TVET programs should be designed in such a way that it responds to potential employers' needs, to ensure that students not only get the necessary skills but also find employment upon completing their programs. The difficulty to get skilled labor in the markets and the costs associated to acquiring the adequate skills contribute definitely to increasing construction costs.

### 5.4.4 Construction Companies: Predominance of SMEs

In the housing delivery value chain, construction companies (or contractors) play a critical role, as they use inputs (land, design, construction materials, capital, and labor) to produce housing as output. The ability of these companies to deliver high-quality products at scale and in a cost-effective manner will determine whether Africa can reduce the huge housing backlog it faces. However, it is noted that in Africa these construction companies are for the vast majority SMEs with limited technical and financial capacity, unable to build more than a few hundred units per year, except in South Africa and in some North African countries where large local companies have emerged.

SMEs in the construction sector face several constraints. A large number of SMEs operate informally. Their poor governance structures and limited project management skills often lead to execution delays and cost overruns, which ultimately can lead to project failure. Shelter Afrique, a pan-African institution specializing in the provision of debt and equity financing to housing developers, cites the above-mentioned factors together with the lack of equity as the main drivers of the high risk in the sector.

In addition, low access to finance limits the ability of SME developers to deliver a high number of housing units and to grow. In Kenya, for instance, only 13.4 percent of all credits were allocated to building and construction in 2012 and the average interest rate was about 22 percent. The Kenyan Federation of Master Builders views the access to and costs of finance as a huge constraint for the SMEs in the construction sector. Poor access to finance is due in part to the underdevelopment of the financial sector and in part to the risks and constraints in the construction sector (see Chap. 3). This has contributed to making affordability a serious challenge for the SME developers.

Consequently, promoters of large-scale housing projects are often obliged to use foreign companies, particularly Chinese construction firms. Chinese companies can deliver large numbers of housing units at affordable prices. For instance, the CITIC (formerly, the China International Trust and Investment Corporation) Group has been involved in the delivery of several housing programs and infrastructure development in several countries on the continent including Angola, Kenya, and South Africa. This poses the sustainability question, given that Chinese contractors were criticized in the past because of their tendency to import cheap labor from China to do the construction work. In an interview with a Chinese construction company operating in Africa, representatives admitted that most of the skilled workers and managers whom they employ are Chinese (Chen et al. 2009). This situation is changing, as the wages of Chinese workers have been rising in recent years and the companies have started to employ low-skilled workers locally in Africa. Chinese construction companies also import most of their construction materials and equipment from China. Projects with a high share of imports for labor and construction materials have a low impact on the development of local economies. Therefore, it is recommended that African countries should have clear requirements for local content if they want to increase the developmental impact of their projects while delivering the needed housing units.

### 5.4.5 Government

The government intervenes at all stages in the housing value chain. It performs sovereign functions including establishing the legal and regulatory frameworks, carrying out inspections, putting in place a conducive business environment, protecting property rights, leveling the playing field to minimize exclusion, and ensuring laws are enforced. Depending on country context and needs, government can intervene from both the supply (producer) and demand (customer) sides of the housing market, to cater especially for low-income households. However, instead of being an enabler, government is often seen as an impediment despite the efforts made. As already discussed at length in Chap. 2, in the construction sector the government has failed to deliver on its mandate. This has in most cases translated into additional construction costs and delays. The first failure of governments in Africa is the lack of effective urban planning. Most countries have failed to update urban plans inherited from colonial times, leaving cities to experience informal growth. The second failure is the adoption of the building codes that do not take into account local realities, as they are mostly copied from colonial powers. Collier and Venables (2013) point out that the British Town and Country Planning Act applied in 1947 to British colonies was maintained after independence. The act set regulations that were inappropriate for African countries, given their levels of income then and even now. For instance, the minimum plot size for Nairobi was set at 253 $m^2$ while in Dar es Salaam it was 500 $m^2$. Given the stringent regulations, most households build outside the formal sector, avoiding the regulations altogether. Even those households who chose to work with the formal construction sector often resort to bribery in order to avoid complying with some aspects of the regulations.

Another area where government failed is in terms of the procedures to get construction permits. The procedures are complicated, long, and costly. The World Bank's 2015 Doing Business Report shows that obtaining a construction permit involves at least 10 steps in Namibia and 27 in Republic of Guinea. The time it takes to navigate all the steps varies from 77 days in Rwanda to 448 days in Zimbabwe, while the costs vary from 0.3 percent of the property value in Botswana to 30.8 percent of the value in Madagascar. This contributes to the high construction costs observed on the continent. Figure 5.7 shows the strong correlation between the time to get a construction permit and the cost of a 40 $m^2$ house. This association is due to the fact that beyond the official costs of the permitting process, delays are costly to construction companies.

Building inspection is the fourth area in which government's failure is adding costs and delays to the construction process. Although it is important to ensure that construction adheres to appropriate building codes, especially relating to safety standards, most governments do not have the capacity to perform those inspections due to a lack of sufficient well-trained building inspectors. That situation often leads to delays and an opportunity for corruption. A case in point is South Africa, where the shortage of qualified inspectors for the National Homebuilders Registration Council leads to inspection delays and, hence, increases in costs. The Doing Business Report has started computing building quality control index comprising of six subindices: the quality of building regulations, quality control before construction, quality control during construction, quality control after construction, liability and insurance regimes, and professional certifications indices The index ranges from 0 to 15 with higher values indicating better quality. Data for 2015 shows that 28 of 49 countries in Africa have scores lower than 8 and the average for Africa is 7.58. These are proof of the weaknesses in building quality control in Africa.

## 5.5 Reducing Construction Costs

The high costs of land, bulk infrastructure, and housing construction have made it very difficult and often impossible to provide affordable housing for the majority of middle-income and low-income households. Even though, the shortage of affordable housing is not specific to Africa, it has reached a critical level on the continent. It is clear therefore that finding ways to lower construction costs is imperative to meet the affordable housing demand.

This chapter explores several avenues for delivering affordable housing developments while reducing construction costs and house prices in Africa, including the following: (1) industrialized construction, (2) reducing waste of building materials, (3) process improvements to improve efficiency, (4) local production of building materials, (5) use of alternative building technologies, (6) densification, and (7) capacity building and skills training. This is consistent with the findings of the McKinsey Global Institute (Woetzel et al. 2014) report, which, in a global study addressing affordable housing issues, identified four levers that can narrow the affordability gap[4] by up to 48 percent. These include unlocking land supply, taking an industrial approach, achieving scale efficiency for operations and maintenance, and reducing the costs of and expanding access to finance.

## 5.5.1 Industrialized Construction

In order to fill the affordable housing deficit of more than 51 million units and deliver large-scale housing developments, Africa's construction sector needs to undergo an extensive transformation toward industrialization. Industrialization of the housing construction process is often mentioned as a way to cut costs, reduce the time of construction, and produce mass housing. It was used in Europe and the United States after World War II with various degrees of success. For instance, the US Housing Act of 1949 set a goal to construct 810,000 units in six years using industrialized methods; however, owing to political opposition to public housing and racial integration, the program was not very successful, as it reached its goal only in 1969 (Von Hoffman 2000).

### 5.5.1.1 Industrialized Construction: What Is It?

Industrialization of housing construction involves the use of prefabricated parts, manufactured in plants outside the project site, which are then assembled on-site. The objective of the approach is to save time and costs and to achieve gains in productivity (both capital and labor). Productivity in the construction industry is relatively low and has been falling in both developed and developing countries. The MGI report notes that between 1989 and 2009, while overall labor productivity in the United States increased by a third, in the construction sector it fell by a fifth. Bailey and Solow (2001) note that the economies of scale achieved through large housing developments in the United States and the Netherlands are important in explaining their superior productivity compared with other European countries, where small plots of land are allocated to housing projects. They also note that gaps in scale and managerial abilities explain the difference in labor productivity between the United States and Brazil.

Conventional construction methods that are labor intensive and in which most components are made on-site, often involving a lot of specialization, lead to long construction times and high costs. An estimated 33.4 percent of time is wasted in construction sites in Sweden, for example (Josephson and Saukkoripii 2007). A large share of this wasted time involves reworking, waiting, handling interruptions, and inaction. Preparation time also represents a large share—45.4 percent—of the total working time, whereas value adding time represents only 17.5 percent. Conventional methods also lead to material waste, as manufactured materials often need to be cut to fit the customized sizes. Another source of low productivity is the dominance of SMEs with low capital equipment and financial capacity. For instance, of the 163,000 companies registered in the United Kingdom in 1998, the majority employed fewer than eight workers (Construction Task Force 1998). Moreover, the firms retain very few skilled workers, as time between projects varies widely. It is argued in this book that adopting an industrial approach would go a long way to addressing the above-mentioned issues.

### 5.5.1.2 Is Industrialized Construction the Right Approach for Africa?

The public view of industrialized construction is limited to the use of precast components or systems. However, it is our conviction that it goes beyond that, although there is no consensus on its definition. There is not a unique way of defining or conceptualizing industrialization in the construction sector, and the use of prefabrication ranges from simple structures to complete houses. The definition depends on the objective and whether authors are considering either the process or the product (Zabihi et al. 2012). There is also a large variation in the extent of prefabrication. The objectives and experiences of such industrialization also differ by country. For instance, the definition of the US Department of Housing and Urban Development covers the range from prefabricated components or modules up to complete homes, such as mobile homes. In the United States, prefabrication has not taken off, due partly to geographic barriers and availability of low-cost migrant workers. In Malaysia, the use of industrialized building systems has failed to achieve the government's targets despite its implementation of encouraging policies (Chan 2011). In some developed countries, the goal of industrialization is to substitute high-cost labor with capital by increasing the usage of automation and equipment. Obviously, this may not be the type of industrialization one would like to experience in Africa, bearing in mind the need for the continent to take advantage of the demographic dividend while addressing the large youth unemployment. In fact, one of the key developmental challenges of African countries today is how to create jobs for the large shares of unemployed or underemployed youth populations and thus improve the livelihood of African people. This calls for housing construction policies that are biased toward more labor-intensive technologies. Prefabrication of complex structures using automation is thus not a viable option for Africa.

The goal of industrialized construction in Africa could consist in producing at massive scale, in shorter periods of time, at lower costs, while taking into account the countries stage of development and peculiarities, including features such as an abundance of unskilled labor and a shortage of capital. In so doing, it is important to ensure that housing and construction policies are integral parts of the country's development policy agenda.

Taking a value chain approach will improve the productivity of the sector and its ability to deliver affordable housing at scale. Moreover, given the role played by SMEs in African economies and their strong presence in the construction sector, industrialization of construction should be seen as a business opportunity for SMEs. In fact, the range of prefabricated materials is large, and simple structures can be made by SMEs with less capital intensity. Using simple and less bulky components makes installation less capital and skill intensive, and therefore could be delivered by SMEs. Indeed, complex components require high skills for installation. In Sweden, some prefabrication companies have failed because they created systems that require low tolerance in the installation process (Malmgren 2014).

A successful example of a labor-intensive construction method using prefabricated materials can be seen in Ethiopia. The first phase of the Ethiopian IUHDP trained and equipped MSEs to prefabricate a number of components and supply some materials such as aggregates. As a result, from 2000 to 2006, some 2600 MSEs employing 49,000 workers were created. The MSEs were involved in production activities for a variety of materials: aggregate, precast beams, hybrid composite beams, metal and wood, stone, etc. As the volume of construction increased under phase 2, the number of MSEs involved in prefabrication also increased. Phase 2 created 561,856 jobs and built 192,467 housing units between 2010 and January 2015 (see Box 5.1).

The following subsections describe the steps that are necessary in the industrialization process of the construction sector.

### 5.5.1.3 What Does It Take? Standardization is Key

Prefabrication or precasting of components such as doors, windows, and sanitary elements is already part of housing construction in Africa. However, the lack of standardized dimensions may prevent the production of these components at large scale. For instance, in self-built housing, each house has its own dimensions for the doors and windows, which are then built to order by carpenters. Moreover, housing superstructures are largely built using blocks that are made on-site or purchased from block molders. Therefore, laying brick for external and internal walls takes a large share of time in the building process. This time and the resulting costs can be cut by using prefabricated concrete or other types of panels. Examples in India, Mexico, and South Africa show time savings of 40–50 percent (MGI 2014). However, savings vary widely, from 10 percent to above 50 percent (Malmgren 2014). In South Africa, the use of precast concrete and optimized design has permitted overall cost savings of 25 percent for an affordable housing project (MGI 2014). The cost savings come from shorter project completion periods, which translate into lower labor and financing costs as well as to lower wastage of building materials. In addition to the time and cost savings, the quality of the superstructure can be increased as the concrete is not exposed to the natural environment and as adequate mixes of cement and aggregates are applied. This consideration is especially important during certain seasons, such as winter in temperate areas and the rainy season in tropical countries.

Prefabrication does not benefit only the superstructure and finishing elements; roofing can also benefit. In difficult working conditions, the roof is generally time consuming and costly. In Kenya's self-built housing, roofing costs constitute nearly 50 percent of the total building costs.

Roofing is ranked first in terms of the building stage that exerts the most financial pressure on self-built housing for low-income households. Often, roofing expenses dictate the size of rooms at the design stage.[5] Time and costs can be cut significantly using prefabricated roofing components. In the Republic of Guinea, as in most African countries, most of the affordable houses are roofed using corrugated iron sheets. In the past, the sheets were sold in small sizes, requiring a long time to install and the use of a large number of nails. However, it is noted that new producers of these materials in the market offer customized, longer sheets. This reduces the time and costs of roofing while offering higher quality.

For precast concrete to be a competitive alternative to on-site building, the most important requirements for efficient industrial production are standardization, large scale, and good logistics. Standardized sizes and higher-quality components facilitate large-scale production by component manufacturers and decrease the complexity of building processes. They provide the economies of scale necessary to justify large capital investments. Standardization also allows savings in the sense that it provides an opportunity to combine orders and make large-volume purchases. The Ethiopian Integrated Urban Housing Program, for example, uses bulk purchases to reduce the cost of materials.

Standardized component sizes, quality of building materials, and building codes are important not only within countries but also within regional blocs. For instance, an aluminum window manufacturer from Sénégal will not benefit from economies of scale in exporting its products to the Republic of Guinea if window sizes in the two countries are different. As some regions become increasingly more integrated, it is important to set common standards to enable the creation and growth of regional component manufacturers. In other words, industrializing the construction sector should be seen in a wider perspective of regional integration, if one is concerned with benefiting from economies of scale.

It is important to note that some precast components such as standard concrete panels, which are heavy and costly to transport, require high demand in a relatively small area. Clogged roads in poor condition across the continent constitute a significant constraint, which make the establishment of adequate logistics an important prerequisite for precast concrete. If components cannot be delivered on time and at competitive prices, the industrialized approach will not deliver on its goals to save time and costs.

Standardization should be introduced early in the process, at the design stage. Architects need to use available standard sizes in their designs in order to avoid multiple changes during construction (MGI 2014). A value chain approach, in which there is close coordination between designers, component suppliers, transporters, and construction companies, is therefore essential (Construction Task Force 1998). Box 5.2 shows how design, prefabrication, and good supply chain management have been used to reduce construction costs in Angola. It appears also from Box 5.2 that the model of Kora Housing is labor intensive at the assembly phase and required basic skills, which favored the employment of local labor, even in rural areas.

> **Box 5.2 Kora Housing: Lowering Costs Through Industrialized Construction**
>
> Kora Housing is building 40,000 housing units on 16 sites throughout nine provinces in Angola. It provides quality, affordable housing in community settings for the large and growing middle class emerging in Angola, thereby tackling the country's housing shortage, which is estimated at about 2 million units. From March 2012 to June 2014, the company built and sold 15,206 units to Angola's National Housing Fund. It is now well engaged in phase II of the project, which is to develop the next 7500 units.
>
> The concept behind Kora Housing is to adapt construction systems and materials used for the development of urban communities to local reality and needs. To this end, the company developed comprehensive know-how about industrialized construction systems using prefabricated panels of autoclaved, aerated concrete—lightweight concrete panels that incorporate air. These panels, imported from Europe, are green materials that meet European Union standards; they are available in numerous shapes and sizes, allowing for a wide range of construction applications for all types of buildings. Implementation of projects starts with urban planning, including social infrastructure and housing designs, adapted to the local environment. The construction is executed by subcontractors but managed by Kora. The success factors leading to large-scale delivery and lower costs are the following:
>
> - *Design:* Housing designs enable the standardization of elements and easy supply chain management, with close relationships between the design and supply chain management teams.

- *Supply chain management:* Kora manages the entire supply chain, from acquisition, transportation, and distribution to subcontractors. Purchasing is done in high volume through offtake agreements with material manufacturers and bulk agreements with transportation entities.
- *Technology:* The light weight of the concrete panels requires only small transport equipment; hence, the mobilization and initiation costs of contractors are very low. The technology also allows contractors to work with unskilled local workers who can be trained on-site.

The results of this construction system are 30 percent savings in construction costs and about 40 percent savings in time. Even though it works in remote provinces, Kora Housing is thus able to sell a house at 50–60 percent of market price. Moreover, despite the industrialized approach of the construction system, it is labor intensive; for instance, upon completion, the project is expected to have created 35,000 local jobs (9000 direct and 26,000 indirect).

*Source:* Based on Kora Housing Process document.

### 5.5.2 Process Improvement to Increase Efficiency

The low productivity in construction is related not only to the fact that production takes place on-site but also to how the production is organized. Poor project scheduling, with excessive sequencing of tasks, and poor management are important determinants of low productivity. Often, projects are executed the same way they have always been, with no effort to improve processes. The adoption of an industrial approach involves learning from process innovations in other industries and adapting them to the needs of the construction industry. Case in point is lean manufacturing and just-in-time production, which have been introduced in other industries with great success. For instance, rigorous project management and implementing techniques such as flowcharts showing all activities on a critical path to completion can reduce project completion times by making optimal use of the resources to perform some of the tasks simultaneously. The flowchart can also be used to make a better estimate of the demand for resources and to serve as a basis for a critical review of tasks. Such a review can lead to optimized processes that can be documented in an operational manual for employee training. Optimized and documented processes can also reduce rework, which is prevalent in construction projects. It is estimated that in developed countries, about 30 percent of the time spent on construction is used for rework (Construction Task Force 1998, Josephson and Saukkoriipi 2007).

Although consultants can be used to analyze and improve processes, construction managers are required to have good project management skills and to execute projects on time with the required quality level. However, during our fact-finding missions in Angola, Cameroon, Côte d'Ivoire, Ethiopia, Kenya, and South Africa, the shortage of managerial skills was often cited as a big constraint for scaling up affordable housing delivery. The Ethiopian government, with assistance from GIZ, undertook a capacity-building program to address this issue and other types of skills shortages. Although the situation has improved over the years, this skill shortage is still seen as a constraint in the sector.

## 5.5.3 Reducing Waste of Building Materials

Waste is a common feature in construction projects in both developed and developing countries. The two main types of waste are time and building materials, both contributing to cost overruns. We have already discussed the contribution of time wastage to the low productivity in the sector. Numerous studies have shown that in developed countries at least 10 percent of the costs of building materials are wasted in construction projects (Egan 1998). In Brazil, the wastage is estimated at about 20–25 percent (Bossink and Bouwers 1996). The extent of wastage of building materials in construction projects in Africa is not widely known but anecdotal evidence points to high shares of the total purchased. John and Itodo (2013) found that wastage contributes on average to 21–30 percent of project cost overruns in Nigeria, depending on the type of subcontracting arrangement. Using a case study in River State, Nigeria, Adewuli, and Otali (2013) show that the main factors contributing to the high levels of wastage are poor supervision, material handling, rework contrary to drawings and specifications, design changes, as well as revision and waste from uneconomical shapes. Similar studies conducted in other countries point to the same conclusion (Alwi et al. 2002, for instance, in Indonesia).

Given that material costs represent an estimated 50 percent of the overall costs of housing construction in most countries, it is clear that reducing waste will have a large impact on house prices. As discussed above, construction costs could be significantly curtailed by minimizing building material waste. In so doing, it is important that countries' rules and regulations related to the standard measures of building materials are enforced. Recognizing this as a major issue, the IUHDP in Ethiopia created an incentive scheme for contractors to minimize waste: the contractor gets 50 percent of the cost of saved materials exceeding the 10 percent agreed level. In addition to cost considerations, construction waste has environmental costs, as its bulky nature means that it occupies space in landfills. Cement is well known as a nonenvironmentally friendly product, its production, manipulation, and use in construction projects do not always comply with the required standards. The waste related to its production and use could entail nonnegligible public health and biodiversity degradation consequences, which can turn up to be fairly costly. The share of construction waste in total solid waste represents 20–30 percent in Australia, 13–15 percent in Finland, 19 percent in Germany, 26 percent in the Netherlands, and 20–29 percent in the United States (Bossink and Bouwers 1996). To the best of our knowledge, reliable estimates for Africa are not available. Moreover, there are indirect environmental costs as energy is used for the production and transport of materials that are later wasted.

### 5.5.4 Local Production of Building Materials

In recent years, the discussion of structural transformation in Africa has highlighted the pattern of labor moving from agriculture into low-productive services (Bah 2011, AfDB et al. 2015). What is more, sub-Saharan Africa has been deindustrializing as the contribution of manufacturing to output has declined in several countries, representing on average just 11 percent of output today (AfDB et al. 2015). It has been argued that this pattern of structural transformation leads to low overall productivity and undermines Africa's long-term development (McMillan and Rodrik 2011).

The need for Africa to undergo substantive structural transformation, which promotes industrialization has become an argument on which most development partners, such as the AfDB, have agreed upon. Moreover, policymakers and analysts are more or less convinced that industrialization should be high in country development policies and strategies. Recent reports from the United Nations Economic Commission on Africa (UNECA) have focused on how Africa can industrialize through trade, by leveraging its commodities (UNECA 2013, 2015). Manufacturing is seen as a catalyst for job creation and economic diversification (UNECA 2015).

In this book, it is argued that housing development in general, and the production of building materials, in particular, can be a channel through which countries could spearhead their industrialization. Producing building materials in Africa will not only create local jobs but also reduce construction costs. As discussed above, the demand for housing and infrastructure are fueling high demand for building materials, such as cement, steel, and finishing products, but this demand is essentially satisfied through imports, mostly from Asia. Interviews conducted during our fact-finding missions indicated that imports of building materials are an important driver of high construction costs, and this is likely to worsen in the near future due to large infrastructure investment programs on the continent. The effects of imports of building materials on construction costs are even more important in landlocked countries. For instance, it is estimated that transport costs represent 40 percent of building materials costs in Kigali, Rwanda.

This section analyzes the extent to which imports of building materials contribute to higher construction costs. Given the lack of data on the amount of building materials used, it is not possible to calculate the share of imports. Moreover, data on construction costs are available for only 27 countries, thereby making it more difficult to apply regression analysis. However, the available data do show that each of the six countries where we conducted fact-finding missions spent about US$400 million in 2014 for imports of building materials, supporting the view of stakeholders according to which imports are the main factor explaining the high costs of construction. Figure 5.8 shows that imports and construction costs are

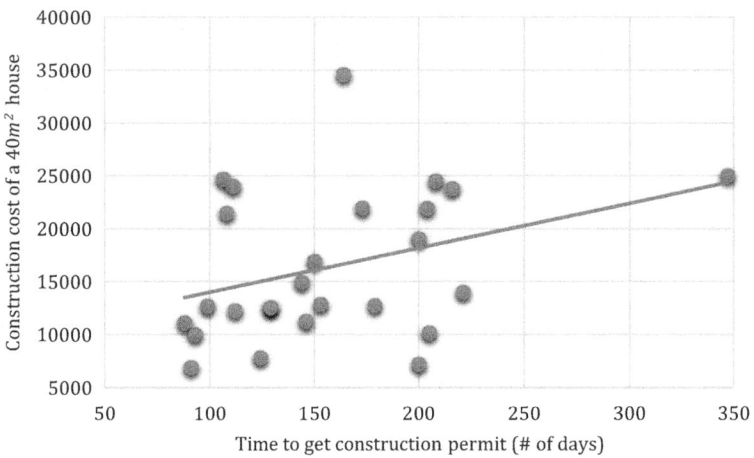

**Fig. 5.8** Association between construction permits and construction costs (*Source*: World Bank Doing Business 2015 and International Comparison Program 2011)

positively correlated, with a correlation coefficient of 0.15, even without including large importers such as Angola and Libya in the calculation. This suggests therefore that import substitution strategies could play a significant role in reducing the costs of construction (Box 5.3).

The rise in local private-sector production of cement in various countries following the opening of the cement market confirms, at some extent, the observation that high imports as well as monopolistic behaviors contribute to high construction costs. For instance, cement prices in Ethiopia have been reduced by more than half as local production increased (Box 5.3). In Zambia, cement prices dropped by 40 percent between 2014 and 2015, following the opening of the Dangote Cement factory. This prompted accusations that Lafarge had been exploiting its monopoly position in the country (CAHF 2015). In Cameroon, the new Dangote plant commissioned in August 2015 led to a swift decline in cement prices of 15 percent in less than a month. Prices were expected to decline further following the opening of another production plant by Ciments d'Afrique, which would increase the firm's installed capacity from 1.6 mtpa in 2014 to 4.2 mtpa. In Tanzania, cement prices were expected to decline by half after the commissioning of a 3 mtpa plant

### Box 5.3 Positive Effects of the Liberalization of the Cement Industry on Costs in Ethiopia

Until the mid-2000s, only government enterprises could supply cement in Ethiopia. These government factories had a combined capacity of 1.89 million tons per year, which have not been sufficient to meet the increasing demand since 2004. During the period of 2004–2006, the price of cement varied between US$249 and US$299 per ton.

In its ongoing efforts to upgrade and expand its infrastructure and housing supply, the government opened the cement market to private investors. As of November 2014, 11 cement factories operated in the country with a combined capacity of over 13 million tons, to supply a total demand estimated at 7 million tons. This excess supply has resulted in a sharp decline in cement prices, by over 50 percent. Today, a ton of cement costs between US$110 and US$124. For instance, Derba-produced cement is 20 percent cheaper than government-produced cement, which reduces the overall cost of construction by about 5 percent, according to Derba's chief executive officer.

The opening of the cement market has also brought in the diversity in the cement grades accessible to customers. Derba recently completed a study of low-cost cement that can be used for flooring, wall plastering, fence construction, and the like. It expects to start producing this grade of cement shortly. The company also plans to sell ready-mix concrete in the future. Today, Derba delivers cement directly to all its retailers in Ethiopia using its fleet of 1000 trucks. Some 80 percent of Derba's customers, about 600 retailers, are located within 400 km of its plant, which facilitates the transportation process. In Addis Ababa, a 50 kg bag of Derba cement costs US$10.40, with transport costs accounting for US$0.62 per bag of cement. Based on this business model, the retailer's profit margin is about US$0.25 per bag of cement.

With an excess supply of about 6 million tons of cement, Ethiopia now exports to neighboring countries such as Kenya, South Sudan, and Djibouti. Derba dominates the northern Kenya cement market, with exports of 500,000 tons of cement per month since January 2014. However, Derba has encountered a few challenges in its Kenya expansion strategy. In October 2014, the Kenyan government eliminated the tax-free regime on imported cement and levied a 5 percent surtax on all imports. Moreover, unlike South Sudan and Djibouti, which allow Derba's trucks to deliver cement to its final destination, Kenya does not permit Ethiopian trucks to enter its territory. Cement trucks are required to unload at the border and load the cement bags on Kenyan trucks. The loading and unloading creates delays, which raises the firm's transportation costs. Factoring in the 5 percent surtax, the price for Derba's imported cement is less competitive in cities such as Nairobi. Derba's CEO expects that the ongoing effort to harmonize and standardize customs regulations in the East African Community will facilitate trade across member countries.

*Source*: Based on an October 2014 meeting with the CEO of Derba Cement.

by Dangote in October 2015. This evidence supports the argument according to which African countries can make progress toward lowering construction costs by increasing local production of building materials.

Ethiopia and Rwanda are two countries that are undertaking import substitution strategies in the construction materials sector. As discussed earlier, Ethiopia increased its cement production more than sixfold and expects to increase its installed capacity and utilization rates. It is also promoting investments for steel and finishing products. Rwanda, with a growing construction sector worth over US$500 million, is also promoting investments in the manufacturing of building materials. The Rwandan Development Board (RDB), an investment promotion agency, is promoting investments in steel products, construction glass, and clay materials such as tiles and blocks. In 2011, more than 51 percent of the investment in manufacturing was directed toward the construction materials sector. The RDB expects a further US$204 million worth of investments in this sector in the coming years (Fig. 5.9).

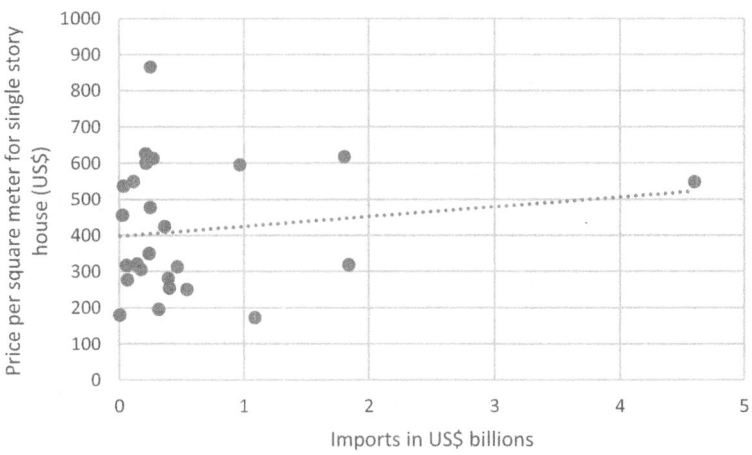

**Fig. 5.9** Imports of building materials versus price per square meter, single-story detached house (*Source*: UNCTAD, World Bank International Comparison Program 2011)

## 5.5.5 Densification for Lower Costs of Urban Infrastructure and Sustainable Cities

Urban sprawl is costly to countries in all stages of development. A report by the Global Commission on the Climate and the Economy estimates that urban sprawl costs the US economy more than US$1 trillion per year (Todd 2015). Two direct consequences of urban sprawl are per capita land development and dispersed activities. The secondary impacts are reduced farmland, reduced natural lands, reduced accessibility, higher costs to provide public infrastructure and services, and longer trip distances. These ultimately lead to economic outcomes such as reduced employment in regional business activity, higher food prices and greater dependence on imported food, less clean air, fewer economic opportunities for those who do not have their own transportation means, more traffic congestion per capita, more accidents and pollution, and higher consumer expenditures on fuel (Todd 2015).

As discussed in Chap. 4, it is noted that in Africa the lack of urban planning, high land costs in urban areas, and household preferences for stand-alone housing have led to outward urban sprawl in most cities. In addition to the economic costs discussed above, a direct consequence of this type of growth is the delayed and costly development of urban infrastructure, and hence an increase in housing prices and in slum development. This calls for more dense cities vertically concentrated around main urban infrastructure and business district.

Building compact cities not only reduces the cost of housing construction and ownership, but also leads to sustainable use of resources. Research has shown that compact cities are environmentally more sustainable because of reduced energy use, greater viability of public infrastructure, preservation of agricultural land, and promotion of cultural diversity (CEC 1990, Kenworthy and Labe 1996). A study by PBL Netherlands Environmental Assessment Agency found that densification increases economic productivity and the creation of regional jobs reduces car usage (Nabilek 2011).

Beyond these benefits, densification of African cities will reduce self-built infrastructure, and hence construction costs, and encourage formal development of infrastructure. Indeed, the construction of high-rise apartments by housing developers often requires a formal process with adherence to urban plans and building codes. It is, however, noted that in some cities such as Kenya, private individuals in the informal sector are developing five- to seven-story rental apartments. These tenements are creating modern slums, where modern buildings with poor quality of construction lack basic infrastructure and promote overcrowding (Huchzermeyer 2007).

### 5.5.6 Alternative Building Technologies

Most of the building systems in Africa follow building methods used in developed countries, which are largely based on cement and steel construction. UN-Habitat (2013) notes that many of the building codes inherited from the colonial era favor the use of conventional building materials and technologies, consisting mainly of bricks and mortar. However, there are other types of materials, locally available and more environmentally friendly, that can be used for the construction of superstructures. Some of these technologies such as expanded polystyrene panels or cement reinforced mud blocks can speed up the construction process, reduce costs, and mobilize a larger number of workers.

Several factors explain the limited use of alternative building materials. The first is related to cultural biases that make customers reluctant to change. Acquiring or owning a house built with conventional materials is perceived as a symbol of status and wealth, as opposed to acquiring or owning a house built with local materials. For example, despite the superior energy efficiency and lower costs of earth blocks, customers still prefer cement blocks. This misleading perception is shared by architects and engineers, who prefer to use materials they are familiar with. Concerted efforts by governments and the private sector are needed to overcome this barrier and sensitize all stakeholders, starting with the architects, designers, engineers, and customers. In addition to this cognitive behavioral aspect, it is noted that government's regulation can act as a barrier to adopting alternative building technologies. In such cases, appropriate policy reforms should be considered if authorities are concerned with promoting alternative building techniques. Building codes should be adapted to local realities (urban vs. rural), promote housing affordability, and favor local production of building materials. A third barrier is technological, as some materials are not adapted to some types of construction. For instance, areas with sandy soils are not appropriate when using earth-stabilized blocks. There is also an issue of quality, given the lack of standards. The final barrier is related to costs, which are high, given the low production capacity of those alternative technologies across the continent. During our fact-finding mission to Cameroon, it was noted that although earth-stabilized blocks are cheaper for a few housing units, the limited production capacity makes them uncompetitive for large-scale housing development. And the lack of access to finance is a key constraint for SMEs involved in production of such technologies.

Recognizing the issues of production capacity and standards, some governments have created agencies to oversee local building technologies. In Cameroon, the Local Material Promotion Authority (commonly known by its French acronym, Mission pour la Promotion des Matériaux Locaux—MIPROMALO) is the government entity tasked with promoting the use of local materials in construction. Its activities are focused on conducting applied research and product development, as well as providing technical assistance to SMEs in the production of local materials. MIPROMALO has identified compressed earth blocks as a viable alternative to cement blocks in many regions of Cameroon. As a result, it built a production plant with the capacity to produce 20,000 compressed earth blocks per day, although its utilization rate is 50 percent because it lacks dryers. Financial and administrative bottlenecks have also inhibited the effectiveness of the institution. Nigeria has an institution with similar objectives called the Raw Materials Research and Development Council. However, this institution has not been effective in fulfilling its mandate as local materials are not widely used.

### 5.5.6.1 Compressed Stabilized Earth Blocks

One of the most available building materials, used for centuries throughout the world, is soil. Earth construction has been the most effective means for building homes for people in developing countries and has shown promising results for an economical solution of the affordable housing problem, reducing costs by at least 25 percent in African countries. In addition, the thermic properties of soil blocks lead to lower internal room temperatures, making air conditioning unnecessary even in hot areas. In some countries such as Sudan, soil is the primary material used for the construction of traditional low-cost dwellings and is well suited to local weather conditions and occupancy patterns. Soil construction is used in 80 percent of urban buildings and over 90 percent in rural areas in Sudan. In other countries, however, there is a cultural stigma surrounding the use of earth blocks as they are associated with poverty. Moreover, poorly constructed and maintained soil buildings can easily discourage the adoption of this technology. Modern knowledge of soil construction techniques such as compressed stabilized earth blocks (CSEB) have been developed but not widely disseminated.

Many housing programs, led by either NGOs or the private sector, have aimed at promoting the use of CSEB. In Angola, Development Workshop (DW) trained clients of Kixi Credito, a housing microfinance institution, on the techniques of CSEB production used in its housing projects.[6] The results have been a gradual acceptance of the use of CSEB. CSEB is also available in Kenya and promoted by the Kenyan government. The Ministry of Housing established the Appropriate Building Materials and Technology Programme in 2006 to address the high building costs by facilitating the provision of improved and affordable housing in both urban and rural areas. The program purchased CSEB machines from the South African manufacturer, Hydraform, and trained individuals and community-based organizations to make interlocking CSEB. However, poor training and supervision from the government led to the failure of the program as the quality of houses built with the CSEB was poor.

Hydraform produces interlocking blocks using a mixture of soil (90 percent) and cement (10 percent), making the building process faster as well as simpler and more efficient. Moreover, the machines used do not require any specialized skills. These bulletproof and earthquake-resilient blocks have a low carbon footprint and can also be produced on-site. Hydraform's biggest clients are the governments of Nigeria, Rwanda, and Uganda and their technology is present almost everywhere on the continent.

The company also sells its blocks and machinery to private individuals, NGOs, and other private sector bodies. In Tanzania, the technology is reported to lead to a 30 percent cost saving over conventional brick-and-mortar technologies. Hydraform noted the reluctance of some builders to adopt the technology because of their familiarity and dependence on regular bricks-and-mortar systems. Lack of access to funding for budding entrepreneurs and limited capacity among small real estate developers were mentioned as additional challenges in scaling up this technology.

Lafarge has developed a technology of stabilized soil blocks consisting of 5–8 percent cement. This technology is currently being used in Malawi. Lafarge's block manufacturing plant, DuraBric, assists in the design of homes and offers technical assistance. It reports savings of 40 percent over conventional technologies with the use of stabilized soil blocks.

### 5.5.6.2 Expanded Polystyrene Panels

Expanded polystyrene (EPS) is a lightweight plastic material used in various sectors including construction, packaging, and insulation. EPS panels are constructed by inserting EPS between two metal sheets. The panels are then assembled to form walls or roofs. The technology can reduce construction time and is energy efficient. It is the most common prefabricated building system proposed in Africa. Although ownership costs are estimated to be lower with EPS than with conventional technologies, construction costs depend on how the design is optimized and how much the panels cost. The Expanded Polystyrene Association of South Africa reports construction cost savings of about 30 percent. An additional advantage cited by the industry is the need for only a small crew for installation.

EPS panels are not widely used in Africa, given the limited local production capacity, low performance in noise reduction, and low consumer acceptance of alternative building materials in general. Notwithstanding these drawbacks, the government of Kenya is promoting the use of EPS panels in construction. In 2012, the National Housing Corporation built a factory to manufacture EPS panels based on the expectation that the EPS technology would reduce the costs of construction by up to 30 percent.

However, the Kenya Federation of Master Builders estimates that the prices of imported panels amount to about half of the prices of the panels produced by National Housing Corporation's EPS plant. Given their anticipated cost saving, EPS panels may be perceived as a solution to building affordable houses in Africa. However, there are a number of reasons to think the contrary. As discussed previously, technology choices should be consistent with the development imperatives of countries, which include job creation among others, and EPS technology is rather capital intensive. For instance, the factory in Kenya employs only 20 people and EPS panel installation is not labor intensive. Moreover, the cost savings do not materialize at project completion, but only after including ownership costs. Another disadvantage is that the production technology uses oil, a nonrenewable fossil fuel, as raw material, which is costly in some countries.

### 5.5.6.3 Other Alternative Building Technologies

Various other building technologies have been studied and found to be cost-effective and energy efficient. These include cross-laminated timber, bamboo panels, and materials such as composite panels made of elephant grass, coconut husk, and the like. Although these materials are widely available in Africa, the long-term sustainability of its production is not certain. For instance, the continent is experiencing a rapid rate of deforestation so it may not be possible to make sufficient timber panels to meet the affordable housing gap. In addition, manufacturing units are required in order to transform the raw materials into construction panels. Thus, many technologies are still in their laboratory phases and are unlikely to be the solution in the near future.

## 5.5.7 Capacity Building and Skills Training

The discussion earlier highlighted the importance of having the right skills mix throughout the housing supply chain as it entails faster construction with less rework and, hence, results in lower construction costs. Therefore, as African countries seek to scale up housing delivery, capacity building should be an integral part of their programs, as in

Ethiopia (see Box 5.1). Education programs need to be overhauled in order to give greater importance to TVET. In this process, multilateral organizations such as the AfDB and UNESCO can play an important role. The AfDB should place greater importance on the availability of practical skills in key economic sectors, including construction. This will help solve the problem of high unemployment rates as well as the issue of skills shortage. During our fact-finding missions in different African countries, a number of stakeholders cited skills development and trainings as areas that need support from development partners.

Besides, another potential area that needs support is capacity building for SMEs involved in housing construction. As noted above, SMEs in the sector have limited access to capital, but they also have poor project management skills. Technical assistance programs combined with increased financial access, through either equity or debt, can help improve their capacity to deliver affordable housing. One of the major findings from this book is that by contrast to the general belief, financial assistance alone may not solve the problems of SMEs in the construction sector. Shelter Afrique's experience working with developers has revealed that defaults from SME housing developers in various countries are often driven by poor capacity in project management and marketing. In the same vein, while the economic literature has shown that in developed countries, provision of financial assistance to SMEs improves their probability of survival and growth, evidence has shown that this may not be the case for developing and transition countries (for a review of the literature, see Bah et al. 2011). Housing developers interviewed in various countries across the continent recognized the lack of managerial skills as a key constraint, pointing to the importance of capacity building and skills development.

## 5.6 Financing Housing Developers

A key impediment to the supply of affordable housing in Africa is the lack of finance for developers. Lack of equity to finance for construction and housing development is a major barrier faced by developers, particularly small and medium-size property developers. The financial crisis of 2008 also had a significant impact on the construction industry. In South

Africa, for instance, the crisis led to the demise of many small-scale developers—most of which lacked the technical and financial strength to weather the economic avalanche. The capacity constraints of developers were further compounded by construction cost overruns and high operation risks. The losses incurred by banks during the crisis spurred them to further tighten their lending requirements, to the detriment of access to finance for many developers. Only a handful of countries—such as Ghana, Morocco, Nigeria, and South Africa—have a well-established class of developers that can develop large-scale housing projects. It is clear from our fact-finding discussions and regional consultation workshops that banks will not provide financing to developers without the necessary risk capital. As discussed in Chap. 3, the lack of market knowledge, including adequate customer credit information systems, by banks may also be a factor contributing to their reluctance to finance developers.

### 5.6.1 Presales as a Financing Mechanism for Developers

According to our discussions with stakeholders, the lack of developer equity accounts for about 20 percent of all project failures. The weak balance sheet of developers further limits their ability to raise risk capital from private investors. In order to cope with this situation, presales or sales on plan, play a significant role in current practice of housing development project financing. Still, even though some financial institutions are willing to provide equity financing for up to 60 percent of the development costs, many developers still cannot bridge the 30 percent equity gap, assuming they can raise 10 percent from presales.

Although presales are an attractive source of finance for developers, they also come with their own challenges, which turn out to be clear limitations for this financing option. First, they reduce the effective demand for affordable housing as they exclude many creditworthy buyers who may not have the resources required in order to pay the upfront house costs. Second, prepurchasers tend to shoulder the credit risks of developers in addition to the risk of not receiving the house as stipulated in the contractual documents. Actually, cases of developer fraud are rampant in many African countries. As a result, countries such as Cameroon and

Sénégal have enacted condominium laws that secure presales payments and facilitate the mortgaging of housing units prior to construction. However, the effectiveness of such frameworks remains limited, given the lack of buyer awareness and weak enforcement. In Algeria, the Real Estate Guarantee Fund (Fonds de Garantie et de Caution Mutuelle de la Promotion Immobilière—FGCMPI) provides safeguards to buyers that make presales payments for houses (Box 5.4).

A robust regulatory framework and the adoption of legal provisions for registering units in uncompleted development projects are vital for the efficient functioning of pre-sales contracts. The package of securities provided under a prepurchase agreement can include escrow accounts,

---

**Box 5.4 A Guarantee Fund For Real Estate Developers**

The Fonds de Garantie et de Caution Mutuelle de la Promotion Immobilière (FGCMPI) is a real estate guarantee fund established in 1997 under the tutelage of Algeria's Ministry of Housing. The FGCMPI guarantees advance payments made by buyers for both residential and commercial real estate in the event a developer defaults on its contractual commitment. In other words, the guarantee provided by the FGCMPI is a mandatory insurance taken by the developer for the benefit of the property buyer. The fund reimburses advance payments made by buyers in the case of death, fraud, or insolvency of the developer. In the event a private developer abandons an outstanding housing development, the Ministry of Housing through the FGCMPI has the power to form a cooperative to complete the project. In 2013, the fund provided guarantees to 11,350 Logement Social Participatif (LSP) and 10,990 Logement Promotionnel Aidé (LPA) units (assisted housing programs targeting moderate- and middle-income households), as well as 7882 low-income housing units. As of March 2015, 1450 real estate development projects and 135,000 housing units had been guaranteed by the fund, which amounts to approximately DA 450 billion (US$4.5 billion).

Before issuing a Certificate of Guarantee to promoters, the fund performs due diligence on the developer examining items such as title, building permits, and the like. Participation in the FGCMPI is mandatory for all developers, who are also required to register in the national database of real estate developers (Tableau National des Promoteurs Immobiliers—TNPI). However, developers have complained about the cumbersome and lengthy application and certification process. In 2013, the fund issued 379 Certificates of Guarantees to developers. However, about 3000 property developers had not registered in the national database as of January 2015, according to government officials.

> FGCMPI membership entails payment of a nominal membership fee, an annual fee that varies according to the size and record of the developer, and a risk-based premium for each insured program—typically 1 percent in the subsidized housing sector and 2 percent for market-based programs. In addition to its role as a guarantee agency, the FGCMPI adds value by (1) screening developers eligible for its coverage, (2) building a rating system, and (3) being the only real estate market observer that gathers information about real estate prices, transaction volumes, and sales trends.
> *Source:* Based on Algerian Ministry of Housing documents.

bank guarantees, insurance, or guarantee funds. Vietnam's residential housing development legislation, which was revised in 2010, provides a good example. The Vietnamese legislation specifically provides requirements for timing and capital mobilization for the development of residential projects. For instance, presales can only start after the house foundation is completed. All in all, managing construction risks is key for attracting private capital to housing development projects in Africa.

### 5.6.2 DFI Financing to Support Developers

Promoting alternative sources of developer finance is crucial for increasing the stock of affordable housing supply in Africa. In Africa, development finance institutions (DFIs) continue to play an important role as market facilitators and a conduit for sustainable private sector financing. Given the development-oriented agenda of DFIs, these institutions are well equipped to assume greater risks such as piloting innovative housing finance instruments on the demand side or mobilizing alternative sources of long-term financing for housing supply. DFIs active in Africa's housing market include Shelter Afrique, the IFC, the National Housing Finance Corporation (NHFC; a wholly owned South African government DFI), and the Overseas Private Investment Corporation (OPIC; a US government DFI). Box 5.5 provides some details on a DFI-sponsored facility to finance developers. Shelter Afrique was established as the AfDB arm in the Housing development sector. As such, the AfDB contributed to the development of the housing sector through its equity participation in Shelter Afrique and equity funds under its management. The huge housing backlogs and the

## Box 5.5 A Construction Finance Facility for Small-Scale Developers and Contractors

Launched in 1995, the National Urban Reconstruction and Housing Agency (NURCHA) is a construction finance institution that finances developers that are undertaking subsidized and middle-income housing, credit-linked housing, and infrastructure projects in South Africa. Over 85 percent of NURCHA clients are small-scale developers, most of which struggle to access affordable financing. NURCHA finances developers that have little capital and experience to the stage where they become economically sustainable. NURCHA lends directly to experienced developers that have at least three years of experience and audited financial statements. It also finances developers through local financial intermediaries. The credit provided by NURCHA accounts for an estimated 70 percent to 95 percent of the working capital requirements of developers. All credit facilities are short term, no more than 24 months. NURCHA manages several facilities dedicated to affordable housing projects.

The Affordable Housing Facility accounts for 78 percent of NURCHA's total loan book for 2014/2015. This facility provides development finance loans to private-sector developers undertaking affordable housing projects with unit selling prices not exceeding R 500,000 (US$41,000). The average loans granted under this facility over the last 10 years stand at R 126 million (US$10.3 million). In 2014, there was a significant increase in the amount of loans signed, to R 230.7 million (US$18.9 million). Altogether, 1619 affordable housing units were developed with NURCHA financing in 2014, compared with 1195 in the previous year. Between 2010 and 2014, this facility has delivered 2300 affordable housing units and sites. By contrast, the Infrastructure and Communities Facility is being redesigned after experiencing significant losses. All in all, only eight projects have been financed under this facility.

NURCHA is currently seeking funding to continue its Subsidy Housing Facility, which ended in 2014 after 10 years of support from OPIC, the Soros Economic Development Fund (SEDF), and First National Bank (FNB), one of South Africa's big four commercial banks. This facility provided bridging finance to small- and medium-scale developers, which ensured their active participation in the housing market. The facility was funded directly through NURCHA or a ring-fenced SPV in partnership with OPIC, the SEDF, and FNB. These partners mobilized over R 1336 billion (US$110 million) in loans for small-scale developers and financed 944 housing projects. The success of this facility was made possible by OPIC's local currency guarantee of R 180 million (US$14.8 million), which provided loan default guarantees to an equivalent FNB facility for contractors. NURCHA continues to play a vital role in supporting small-scale developers in South Africa.

*Source:* Based on NURCHA documents.

pressing needs for housing witnessed by the proliferation of slums and informal settlements, compounded by underdeveloped financial markets, suggest that the possible scope of intervention of DFIs in affordable housing is very large and that more direct players are needed. This explains why AfDB has recently started its direct interventions in the housing sector by supporting mortgage lenders and mortgage refinancing companies. In addition, the failure of Shelter Afrique to meet its promises leaves a large gap for other DFIs to intervene.

In South Africa, the NHFC's pioneering role in using risk enhancement mechanisms has attracted private capital and broadened the range of players involved in the affordable housing market. This has helped spearhead the financing of South Africa's social rental housing market by providing both capacity-building loans to emerging social housing institutions and top-up project finance for social housing delivery.[7] It also provides both long-term and bridging finance to housing development projects in South Africa. As of December 2016 the NHFC has disbursed R 7 billion (US$534.5 million) and has successfully leveraged R 18.6 billion (US$1.4 billion), a 1:3 leveraging factor.

### 5.6.3 Private Equity Funds as an Alternative Financing Mechanism for Developers

Private equity funds could be another source of patient capital for the continent's developers. It is well known that they play an important role in improving access to long-term finance for African enterprises, especially SMEs. In 2015, Africa-focused private equity funds raised US$4.3 billion. As the appetite for Africa-focused private equity funds increases, investment activity across the continent has also been on the rise. According to data from the African Private Equity and Venture Capital Association (AVCA), the total deal value in 2015 was US$2.5 billion, which is a sharp decline from the US$8.1 billion worth of deals in 2014. As the industry continues to grow, private equity can be an important source of patient capital for the continent's housing market (see Box 5.6 for an example of private equity funds involved in housing development).

Notwithstanding the attractive opportunities for affordable housing investment, private equity has been a historically overlooked asset class in

### Box 5.6 Using Private Equity Funds to Build Platforms That Allow Citizens to Get a Foothold on the Property Ladder

South Africa, the continent's second largest economy, currently has a housing deficit estimated at 2.3 million housing units, with over 1 million households living in informal settlements, usually with little or no access to water, electricity, sanitation, education, or health facilities. The hardest-hit market segments are the poor and middle-income populations, for which the supply of affordable housing is very limited. As in other African countries, banks and developers in South Africa have historically focused on the upper-end market.

Recognizing the acute housing shortage, International Housing Solutions (IHS) was the first private equity investor to fund the development of residential property in South Africa through its South Africa Workforce Housing Fund. IHS primarily makes equity investments in residential properties—new development, conversion, and straight acquisition—that are targeted at filling the gap between the demand for and supply of affordable housing for the "missing middle" market segment.

The major innovation of IHS has been its market-making capacity and its ability to reduce the risk of the construction process in South Africa. IHS identifies developers that are sufficiently strong to warrant its investment and provides them with equity capital to build their capacity. Armed with equity financing from IHS, developers are better equipped to access debt financing from banks, which enables them to be able to withstand challenges in the housing delivery process such as municipal delays in regulatory approvals, issues surrounding the provision and financing of bulk infrastructure, land acquisition, and client over-indebtedness.

The Fleurhof housing project is a classic example of how IHS supports affordable housing and community development. The fund committed R 105.8 million (US$8.8 million) to this infill housing development located between Roodepoort and Soweto, two large suburbs close to Johannesburg. Fleurhof is a fully integrated and secure housing project, with one-third of the residential development consisting of Reconstruction and Development Program (RDP) units (i.e., 100 percent government-subsidized housing), while another third consists of affordable houses, and the final third is composed of rental units. Upon completion, the Fleurhof project will have over 9500 housing units, including 8 kindergartens, 4 industrial sites, 5 schools, 14 business centers, and numerous community gardens and play areas (including a skateboard park). This project will accommodate over 30,000 low- and middle-income individuals and help narrow the housing gap in South Africa. Due to the broad base of its residents and the services it provides, Fleurhof won the 2013 Integrated Housing Project of the Year award from the Southern African Housing Foundation.

> What is important is that the Fund has delivered middle-class housing to areas normally associated with poverty, which has supported the cities' socioeconomic integration. The Fleurhof development is a demonstrative case on how private equity can contribute in the delivery of middle-income housing. IHS is contributing to improving property market dynamics in South Africa as it plays a role in changing the housing landscape of the low-middle-income property market.
>
> As of December 2014, the fund has fully exited four projects and has returned R 498 million (US$35.2 million) in cash to investors, or reinvested it in new projects. IHS has also provided opportunities for the finance sector in South Africa by attracting R 2.8 billion (US$228.6 million) of project debt financing for its investments. The fund has also contributed in unlocking an estimated R 2 billion (US$163.7 million) in public-sector funding through infrastructure, subsidies, and government guarantee schemes.
>
> *Source:* Based on discussions, IHS documents, and interviews with IHS management team.

Africa. According to data from Preqin's real estate online service, eight Africa-focused real estate private equity funds are being raised, with a combined target size of US$1.8 billion. This is in sharp contrast to the US$19 billion of aggregate capital targeted by 58 Asia-focused real estate private equity funds. The Pan African Housing Fund, Housing Impact Fund South Africa, and Signature Africa Housing Fund are examples of private real estate funds primarily targeting the lower end of the middle-income housing segment in Africa. Affordable housing not only provides private equity investors with an opportunity to generate market returns, it also presents an opportunity to have a significant social impact in Africa. In order to encourage these investors to go further down market, it would be important, for DFIs in particular, to revisit the hurdle rate, or the minimum rate of return on investment required to compensate for the risk involved in low-income housing projects.

## 5.7 Conclusion

This chapter analyzed in detail the housing construction sector in Africa. The emphasis has been on the causes of high construction costs and ways to increase housing affordability. Although comparable data on housing construction costs are available for only a few countries, they show large variations in costs across countries. The cost per square meter for a single-story detached house in the most expensive country (Republic of Congo) is five times the cost in the cheapest country (Morocco). The main causes of high construction costs are the high costs of building materials, at about 50 percent of the construction costs in several countries, and inefficiencies in the building process.

The chapter emphasizes the need to take into consideration the broader development objectives in the choice of solutions aimed at lowering construction costs. Any choice of building technology should consider the challenge of high youth unemployment in the continent. Considering this, along with large housing deficits in most countries, the analysis suggests a labor-intensive industrialized construction approach. This requires the use of precast concrete panels, optimized design, standardized sizes of building components, and a value chain approach. Import substitution and regional integration through the adoption of common standards can lower the costs of building materials. In addition, construction processes need to be improved and wastage of building materials should be reduced in order to improve productivity. Given the financial constraints of housing developers in general and SMEs in particular, alternative financing mechanisms providing equity and loan guarantees are needed to enable the sector the delivery of large-scale housing. Finally, technical and financial assistance to SMEs involved in housing construction and skills training through TVET are recommended in order for the sector to be able to deliver affordable and good-quality housing.

## Notes

1. There is conflicting information about installed capacity in Ethiopia. An article in *Global Cement* ("Derba Cement Plans US$300M Expansion," 4 April 2016) quoted the Minister of Industry saying that the country had 18 producers with an installed capacity of 11.2 mtpa as of April 2015. During the scoping mission in November 2014, a number of actors estimated the installed capacity at 13 mtpa.
2. We considered the following subsectors: iron and steel bars, rods, angles, shapes, and sections (SITC code 676); wire of iron or steel (SITC code 678); and tubes, pipes, and hollow profiles, fittings, iron, steel (SITC code 679).

3. Interview with Marina Yoveva, program development manager for Europe, the Middle East, and Africa, Nairobi, 9 October 2014.
4. The "home purchase affordability gap" is defined as the difference between the price that the average household can afford to pay for a home and the median price of housing on the market.
5. Interview with Ayani for Habitat for Humanity, 2013, by the AfDB and UN-Habitat scoping mission team in Kenya.
6. Angola's first and largest microfinance institution, KixiCasa, offers housing microloans. KixiCredito, which is regulated by the central bank, has 15 branches in nine provinces. DW is KixiCredito's principal shareholder. KixiCasa has about 25,000 clients and provides over US$30 million in microloans each year.
7. In South Africa, social housing is defined as a rental or cooperative housing unit for low-income persons built by an accredited social housing institution.

# Bibliography

Adekoya, Femi. 2015. Dangote Cement Stakes $600 Million on Tanzania Plant. *The Guardian News*, October 12. http://www.ngrguardiannews.com/2015/10/dangote-cement-stakes-600m-on-tanzanian-plant/

Adewuji, T.O., and M. Otali. 2013. Evaluation of Causes of Construction Material Waste – Case of Rivers State, Nigeria. *Ethiopian Journal of Environmental Studies and Management* 6 (6). https://doi.org/10.4314/ejesm.v6i6.5S.

AfDB (African Development Bank). 2012. *Informal Survey of Developers*. Shelter Afrique. Tunis, Tunisia: AfDB

———. 2015. *Back to Office Report: Scoping Mission for Study on Africa's Housing Market Dynamics*. Addis Ababa. Research Division, Development Research Department, 2014 November 1–7.

AfDB, OECD, World Bank, and WEF (African Development Bank, Organization for Economic Cooperation and Development, World Bank, and World Economic Forum). 2015. *The Africa Competitiveness Report 2015*. Geneva: World Economic Forum.

AfDB, OECD, and UNDP (African Development Bank, Organization for Economic Co-operation and Development, and United Nations Development Programme). 2015. *African Economic Outlook. Regional Development and Spatial Inclusion*. https://doi.org/10.1787/aeo-2015-en.

African Business Magazine. 2012. *Massive Boost for Building Material Manufacturers*, April 23.

Alwi, S., K. Hampson, and S. Mohammed. 2002. Waste in the Indonesian Construction Projects. In *Proceedings of the CIB W107 1st International Conference: Creating a Sustainable Construction Industry in Developing Countries*, 11–13 November, Stellenbosch.

Ameh Oko, J., and D.E. Itodo. 2013. Professionals' Views of Material Wastage on Construction Sites and Cost Overruns. *Organization, Technology, and Management in Construction* 5 (1): 747.

Bah, El-hadj. 2011. Structural Transformation Paths Across Countries. *Emerging Markets Finance and Trade* 47 (2): 5–19.

Bah, El-hadj M., Josef C. Brada, and Taner Yigit. 2011. With a Little Help from our Friends: The Effect of USAID Assistance on SME Growth in a Transition Economy. *Journal of Comparative Economics* 39 (2): 205–220. https://doi.org/10.1016/j.jce.2011.03.001.

Bailey, Martin N., and Robert M. Solow. 2001. International Productivity Comparisons Built from the Firm Level. *Journal of Economic Perspectives* 15 (3): 151–172.

Bossink, B.A.G., and H.J.H. Brouwers. 1996. Construction Waste Quantification and Source Evaluation. *ASCE Journal of Construction Engineering and Management* 122 (1): 55–60.

Business Day. 2015. *Africa in Focus as Lafarge Holcim Launch Globally*. Nigeria: Business Day Online.

CAHF (Center for Affordable Housing Finance in Africa). 2015. *2015 Yearbook – Housing Finance in Africa. A Review of Some of Africa's Housing Finance Markets*. Parkview: CAHF.

CEC (Commission of the European Communities). 1990. *Green Paper on the Urban Environment*. European Commission: Brussels.

Chan, T.K. 2011. Comparison of Precast Construction Costs—Case Studies in Australia and Malaysia. In *Proceedings of the 27th Annual ARCOM Conference*, ed. C. Egbu and E. C. W. Lou. Bristol, September 5–7.

Chen, C., A. Goldstein, and R.J. Orr. 2009. Local Operations of Chinese Construction Firms in Africa: An Empirical Survey. *The International Journal of Construction Management* 11 (1): 75–89.

Collier, Paul and Anthony J. Venables. 2013. *Housing and Urbanization in Africa: Unleashing a Formal Market Process*, CSAE Working Paper Series 2013–01. Oxford: Centre for the Study of African Economies, University of Oxford.

Construction Task Force. 1998. *Rethinking Construction*, Report to the Deputy Prime Minister, UK.

Deloitte. 2014. *Deloitte on Africa: African Construction Trends Report 2014*. Johannesburg.

Ecobank. 2014. *Commodities, Cement*, Middle Africa Insight Series, July 24.
———. 2015. *Commodities, Cement*, Middle Africa Insight Series, June 29.
Egan, J. 1998. *Rethinking Construction: Report from the Construction Task Force*. London: Department of the Environment, Transport and the Regions.
Ermed, M.W. 2015. *Addis Ababa Integrated Housing Development Program: A Strategy for Urban Poverty Reduction and Sustainable Socio-Economic Transformation*, Urban Planning Presentation, Addis Ababa.
Expanded Polystyrene Association of South Africa (EPSASA). n.d. *EPS Housing with Social and Economic Benefits*. http://expandedpolystyrene.co.za/wp-content/uploads/2014/08/EPS_Housing_social_and_economic_benefits.pdf.
Habitat for Humanity in Kenya. 2014. Interview with Marina Yoveva, Program Development Manager for Europe, Middle East, and Africa, Nairobi, Kenya, October 9.
Hill, Liezel, and Matthew Hill. 2015. Cement Is the New Oil as Africa's Richest Man Takes on Lafarge. *Bloomberg News*, August 24. http://www.bloomberg.com/news/articles/2015-08-24/cement-is-the-new-oil-as-africa-s-richest-man-takes-on-lafarge
Huchzermeyer, Marie. 2007. Tenement City: The Emergence of Multi-Storey Districts through Large-Scale Private Landlordism in Nairobi. *International Journal of Urban and Regional Research* 31 (4): 714–732.
IMF (International Monetary Fund). 2008. *The World Economic Outlook. Financial Stress, Downturns, and Recoveries*. Washington, DC: IMF.
Josephson, P.-E., and L. Saukkoriipi. 2007. *Waste in Construction Projects, Call for a New Approach*. Goteborg: The Centre for Management of the Built Environment, Building Economics and Management Chalmers University of Technology.
Kenworthy, Jeffrey R., and Felix B. Laube. 1996. Automobile Dependence in Cities: An International Comparison of Urban Transport and Land Use Patterns with Implications for Sustainability. *Environmental Impact Assessment Review* 16: 279–308.
Kora Housing. n.d. *Company Overview of Concepts and Work Methods*. Luanda, Angola: Kora Angola.
Litman, Todd. 2015. *Analysis of Public Policies That Unintentionally Encourage and Subsidize Urban Sprawl*. Victoria Transport Policy Institute, Supporting Paper Commissioned by LSE Cities at the London School of Economics and Political Science, on Behalf of the Global Commission on the Economy and Climate (www.newclimateeconomy.net) for the New Climate Economy Cities Program.
Malgrem, L. 2014. *Industrialized Construction: Exploration of Current Practice and Opportunities*, Thesis dissertation, Lund University, Lund.
Mathew, Haggai. 2015. Africa in Focus as Lafarge Holcim Launch Globally. *Footprint to Africa*, July 7.

McMillan, Margaret S., and Rodrik Dani. 2011. *Globalization, Structural Change and Productivity Growth*, NBER Working Papers 17143. Cambridge, MA: National Bureau of Economic Research.

Mekuria, T. 2015. *Housing Development. The Ethiopian Experience*, Paper Presented at the Ministry of Urban Development, Housing, and Construction Regional Consultation Workshop on Housing Market Dynamics in Africa, Addis Ababa, February 17–18.

Nabilek, Kersten. 2011. *Urban Densification in the Netherlands: National Spatial Policy and Empirical Research of Recent Developments*, Paper Presented at the 5th International Conference of the International Forum on Urbanism, Singapore, February 24–26.

Polat, G. 2008. Factors Affecting the Use of Precast Concrete Systems in the United States. *Journal of Construction Engineering and Management* 134 (3): 169–178.

Rwanda Development Board. n.d. *Steel Product Manufacturing in Rwanda*. http://www.rdb.rw/fileadmin/user_upload/Documents/Manufacturing/2_Steel_construction_materials_profile.pdf

Sugiharto, A., H. Keith, and M. Sherif. 2002. Waste in the Indonesian Construction Projects. In *Proceedings of the First International Conference of CIB W107*, "Creating a Sustainable Construction Industry in Developing Countries," South Africa, November 11–13, pp. 305–315.

UNCTAD (United Nations Conference on Trade and Development). *Trade Statistics*. Online.

UNECA (United Nations Economic Commission for Africa). 2013. *Economic Report on Africa 2013: Making the Most of Africa's Commodities: Industrializing for Growth, Jobs and Economic Transformation*. Addis Ababa: UNECA.

UNECA (United Nations Economic Commission for Africa). 2015. *Economic Report on Africa 2015: Industrializing Through Trade*. Addis Ababa: UNECA.

UNESCO (United Nations Educational, Scientific, and Cultural Organization). n.d. *Technical and Vocational Education and Training (TVET). Equipping Schooled Young People to Succeed in the Workplace*. http://www.unesco.org/new/fileadmin/MULTIMEDIA/FIELD/Dakar/pdf/Info%20sheet%20TVET%202011.pdf

UN-Habitat. 2013. *Affordable Land and Housing in Africa*, Adequate Housing Series 076/11E. UN Human Settlements Program, Nairobi.

UN-Habitat and Cities Alliance. 2011. *Housing Finance: Ways to Help the Poor Pay for Housing*, Quick Guides for Policy Makers 5, UN Human Settlements Program, Nairobi.

Uttam, K. R., R. Madhumita, and S. Subir. 2008. *Mass-Industrialized Housing to Combat Consistent Housing Shortage in Developing Countries: Towards an*

*Appropriate System for India*, In The Proceedings of the World Congress on Housing, "National Housing Programs, New Visions," Kolkata, November 3–7.

Von Hoffman, A. 2000. A Study in Contradictions: The Origins and Legacy of the Housing Act of 1949. *Housing Policy Debate* 11 (2): 299–326.

Ware, Gemma. 2014. *Infrastructure: Dangote's Cement Rivals*, The Africa Report, September 19.

Woetzel, Jonathan, Ram Sangeeth, Mischke Jan, Garemo Nicklas, Sankhe Shirish. 2014. *A blueprint for addressing the global affordable housing challenge*, McKinsey Global Institute, available at http://www.mckinsey.com/insights/urbanization/tackling_the_worlds_affordable_housing_challenge.

World Bank. n.d. *International Comparison Program 2011*. http://siteresources.worldbank.org/ICPEXT/Resources/ICP_2011.html.

———. 2013. *Measuring the Real Size of the World Economy: The Framework, Methodology, and Results of the International Comparison Program—ICP*. Washington, DC. doi:https://doi.org/10.1596/978-0-8213-9728-2.

World Steel Association. 2013. *Steel Statistical Yearbook 2013*. Brussels: World Steel Committee on Economic Studies.

Zabihi, H., F. Habib, and L. Mirseedie. 2012. Definition, Concepts, and New Direction of Industrialized Building Systems. *KSCE Journal of Civil Engineering* 17 (6): 1199–1205.

**Open Access** This chapter is licensed under the terms of the Creative Commons Attribution 4.0 International License (http://creativecommons.org/licenses/by/4.0/), which permits use, sharing, adaptation, distribution and reproduction in any medium or format, as long as you give appropriate credit to the original author(s) and the source, provide a link to the Creative Commons license and indicate if changes were made.

The images or other third party material in this chapter are included in the chapter's Creative Commons license, unless indicated otherwise in a credit line to the material. If material is not included in the chapter's Creative Commons license and your intended use is not permitted by statutory regulation or exceeds the permitted use, you will need to obtain permission directly from the copyright holder.

# 6

# Slum Upgrading and Housing Alternatives for the Poor

## 6.1 Introduction

In Africa today, in a majority of cities and towns, a twin development process is occurring wherein formal and informal cities are developing in parallel. In a majority of countries, informal cities, which are multidimensional in structure and scope, are predominating and transforming the urban landscape and environment. Cities are essentially being built back to front, with development taking place before the formulation of planning strategies and the implementation of control and management systems—building structures first and services afterward. This reversed development approach is also reflected in the housing development process, with the poor playing a leading role as the construction project manager, laborer, and finance provider.

Moreover, most African cities and towns today are characterized by a dual economy of formal and informal sectors, with the vast majority of the urban population operating within the informal economy, outside existing regulatory frameworks. The development, expansion, and proliferation of slums and informal settlements, in which the majority of urban poor households live and work, are the most conspicuous manifestation of this reality.

This multidimensional informality (in land tenure, housing, servicing, and employment) has given rise to a prevailing urban condition that is evident in cities and towns across the continent, which Pieterse (2013) describes as the challenge of "slum urbanism." According to Pieterse, slum urbanism is driven by a self-fulfilling cycle that drives urban development patterns in most sub-Saharan African cities, as illustrated in Fig. 6.1. Hence, as the continent's urban population doubles in one generation, it can be expected that slum dwellers will continue to develop their own cities because the state and the formal market do not yet have the capacity to address the escalating demand for land, housing, and services. As discussed in Chap. 2, slums are generally the result of a combination of rapid urbanization and demographic growth, bad policies, and inappropriate incentive systems including poor governance, inappropriate

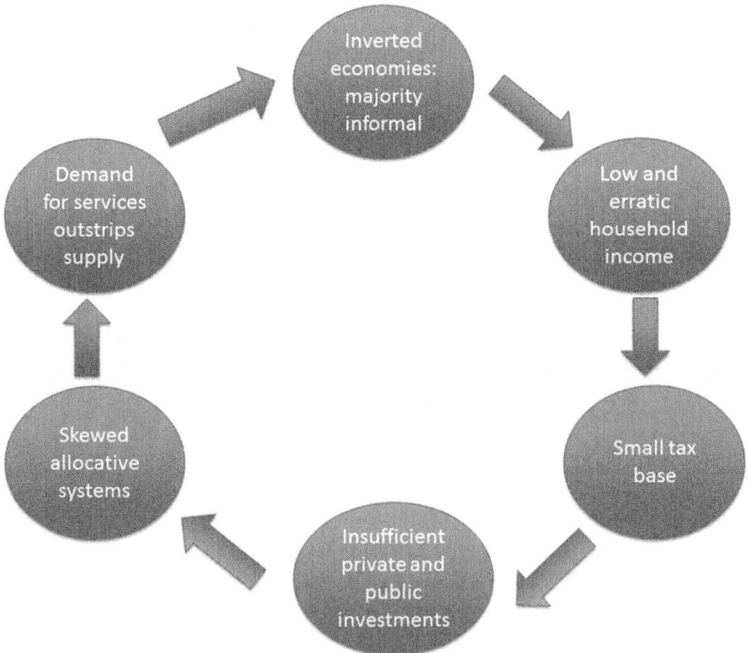

**Fig. 6.1** Urban development cycle in Sub-Saharan Africa: "Slum Urbanism" (Source: Pieterse (2013))

regulatory frameworks, dysfunctional housing markets, and a lack of political will.

With the pace of urbanization and the scale of the urban housing challenge increasing at a rate never experienced before in almost all countries across Africa, the need for effective measures to improve affordable housing supply is becoming increasingly critical. If governments and local authorities are to deal effectively with this challenge, they must have up-to-date knowledge and understanding of housing market dynamics and housing policies; this will enable them to develop and implement effective interventions. Pieterse (2013) maintains that slum urbanism can only be "interrupted, disassembled, and remade" by the "articulation of an effective package of economic, governance, and political-cultural reforms, by civil society organizations rooted in the interest of the urban poor." While civil society organizations can take a leading role in that process, it remains that the role of governments and development partners should not be overlooked, if one is concerned with the implementation of such reforms.

It is noted that UN-Habitat and Cities Alliance have a vast literature on slum upgrading. The main findings are summarized in the discussions below. This chapter discusses the key issues related to slum upgrading and how one should ensure slum-upgrading programs are successful. It also highlights alternative methods for providing housing for low-income households to prevent the proliferation of slums.

## 6.1.1 The Slum Challenge

In 2012, an estimated 863 million urban residents worldwide lived in slum conditions, compared with 760 million in 2000 and 650 million in 1990. The proportion of the urban population living in slum conditions in urban areas was particularly high in sub-Saharan Africa (62 percent) and, to a lesser extent, in Southern Asia (35 percent), compared with 24 percent in Latin America and the Caribbean, and 13 percent in North Africa (UN-Habitat 2014b).

However, the incidence of slums varies widely across countries, as Table 6.1 shows. Cities in East Africa, for instance, have high levels of

**Table 6.1** Variations in the prevalence of slums among African Countries

| Very High (>80%) | High (60–79%) | Moderate (40–59%) | Low (<40%) |
|---|---|---|---|
| Angola | Botswana | Democratic Republic of Congo | Algeria |
| Benin | Burkina Faso | Lesotho | Egypt |
| Central African Republic | Burundi | Liberia | Libya |
| Chad | Cameroon | | Morocco |
| Congo | Comoros | | Namibia |
| Equatorial Guinea | Cape Verde | | South Africa |
| Ethiopia | Côte d'Ivoire | | Tunisia |
| Guinea-Bissau | Eritrea | | Zimbabwe |
| Madagascar | Gabon | | |
| Malawi | Gambia | | |
| Mali | Ghana | | |
| Mauritania | Guinea | | |
| Mozambique | Kenya | | |
| Niger | Nigeria | | |
| Rwanda | Sénégal | | |
| Sierra Leone | Zambia | | |
| Sudan | | | |
| Tanzania | | | |
| Togo | | | |
| Uganda | | | |

Source: Arimah (2010)

poverty and inequality, with the majority of growth occurring in slums and informal settlements. A high proportion of the population in countries in West Africa lives on less than US$1.25 per day, and with poverty and inequality intensifying, densely populated slums and informal settlements exist in most cities. Despite being generally rich in oil, minerals, forests, and biodiversity, Central Africa has a high number of slums and informal settlements as a consequence of deep poverty and inequality, compounded by pervasive poor governance systems. Countries in Southern Africa, with the exception of Angola, Mozambique, and Zambia, generally have a lower proportion of their urban populations living in slums and informal settlements than do countries in the rest of the continent but still face the same major challenges of poverty and inequality, substantial housing backlogs, inadequate infrastructure and service provision, urban sprawl, and the proliferation of slums and informal settlements (UN-Habitat 2014b).

Countries with a low incidence of slums include South Africa and the Northern African countries of Algeria, Egypt, Libya, Morocco, and Tunisia. Within this group of countries, fewer than 40 percent of urban dwellers live in slums, with Tunisia and Algeria having slum proportions of 3.7 percent and 11.8 percent, respectively. When compared with countries in the other regions, these countries have moderate to low urban growth rates, more stable economies, high levels of income, and low rates of poverty, all of which mitigate the proliferation of slums. The low prevalence of slums, especially in Egypt, Morocco, and Tunisia, reflects their "long-term political commitment to slum upgrading, slum prevention, and service provision for the urban poor" (Arimah 2010).

The number of slum dwellers in Africa continues to increase, in large part due to the accelerated pace of urbanization that the continent is experiencing (see Chap. 1). Indeed, more than 25 of the 100 most rapidly growing cities worldwide are in Africa (UN-Habitat 2014b). If these growth rates coupled with the rapidly expanding urban populations continue, it is doubtful that cities will have the institutional, infrastructural, and financial capacity to satisfactorily accommodate urban dwellers. The majority of new urban dwellers will therefore likely reside in slums and informal settlements. Hence, urban poverty and slum proliferation, which already characterize major cities continent-wide, will likely become even more ubiquitous under current urban development trajectories.

## 6.1.2 The Bottom-of-the-Pyramid Housing Market Opportunity

As elaborated in preceding chapters, housing markets in most African countries are characterized by input-side failures, such as the limited availability of residential land, inadequate basic infrastructure, lack of finance, and the high cost of building materials. These market dynamics have a bearing on the affordability of housing (see Chap. 5), particularly for bottom-of-the-pyramid (BOP) households. Today, BOP urban households in most African countries are trapped in a distorted and dysfunctional housing market wherein, "affordable housing is inadequate and adequate housing is unaffordable" (UN-Habitat 2005).

However, most developers and investors overlook the business opportunity at the BOP because of their perception that this is not a viable market due to the high risk involved (see Chap. 3). Yet, the BOP consists of 4 billion people, the majority of the world's population. With a total annual income of US$5 trillion, BOP households represent a potentially important global market, but one that varies substantially across regions, countries, and sectors in size and other characteristics. In general, BOP markets are very poorly served, are dominated by the informal economy, and are relatively inefficient and uncompetitive (Hammond et al. 2007). Africa is not an exception.

Housing is one of the bigger BOP markets, larger than transportation but smaller than energy sectors. It encompasses major spending items such as rent, mortgage payments (or imputed rents), maintenance and repairs, and other services. BOP households worldwide spend more than US$700 billion on housing annually. This varies from 8 percent of total BOP spending in Eastern and South-Eastern Asia to 23 percent in Central America and Caribbean (BOP Learning Lab, and Dalberg Research 2014). In Africa, the measured BOP housing market is worth US$19.3 billion (258 million people), and the estimated total BOP market is worth US$42.9 billion (486 million people) (Hammond et al. 2007).

However, low-income housing provision has proven challenging, owing to the many peculiarities of the BOP market: people's needs and preferences, legal and regulatory frameworks, and the difficulty of reconciling the interests of the different players in the housing market as discussed in Chap. 2. BOP housing markets are not simply a homogenous block whose housing needs can be addressed through a standard solution. Instead, the households that constitute these markets differ significantly and can be disaggregated and classified according to a range of criteria, such as current living conditions, income levels and sources, and future needs and aspirations (Stickney 2014).

The BOP housing market in Africa presents unprecedented and growing levels of demand, which should be seen as a major opportunity, particularly in light of the spreading economic uncertainty in the developed world. However, the high perceived and real risks inherent to the informality that characterizes the BOP housing market, in particular in Africa, presents an exceptional challenge. Furthermore, in most African countries, the political will to develop and promote BOP housing does not exist.

## 6.2 The Twin-Track Approach to Address the Challenge

This section explores ways to address the failure of the housing market to provide an adequate supply of well-located and decent affordable housing, in particular for BOP households, which has been a contributory factor in the growth of slums. Such failures could be packaged under two main challenges. First is the need to improve the living conditions of the BOP majority households living in slums and informal settlements. Second is the equally urgent need to create housing markets in which all urban households, especially the poorest and most vulnerable, are able to access legal, appropriate, and affordable housing so as to prevent the proliferation of slums and informal settlements in the future.

The fact that these challenges are intertwined and of equal level of importance calls for a solution that addresses both issues simultaneously or in parallel. In other words, there is a need for a twin-track approach which focuses on slum prevention by improving the supply and affordability of new housing to reduce the growth of new slums, alongside implementing citywide and national slum-upgrading programs that can improve housing conditions and the quality of life in existing slums. Slum prevention requires comprehensive and forward-looking urban planning, appropriate and effective legal and regulatory frameworks, timely provision of affordable serviceable land, and the availability of affordable finance. It also requires demand-responsive mechanisms for the introduction of infrastructure and basic services, and the availability of adequate and affordable construction materials and components (Payne 2005).

Brazil's social housing program, Minha Casa, Minha Vida (My House, My Life), in combination with the Growth Acceleration Program for Slum Upgrading, is a notable example of the twin-track approach. Under this approach, curative and preventive programs are implemented concurrently to improve prevailing poor housing conditions in slums and curtail both the expansion of existing ones and the development of new ones (UN-Habitat 2013).

## 6.2.1 Slum Upgrading

Slum upgrading is widely recognized as the most proactive and effective way of improving the housing conditions and lives of the millions of low-income and BOP households living in slums in African cities and towns, and thereby contributing to the achievement of Sustainable Development Goal 11: ensuring access for all urban households to adequate, safe, and affordable housing and basic services, as well as upgrading slums, by 2030.

In order to provide a comprehensive understanding of slum-upgrading dynamics on the continent, the following analysis in this section provides a review of the housing and slum-upgrading policies implemented in African countries. It also uses examples of slum-upgrading initiatives in Africa to dissect its key facets and components and then explores ways of crowding in private sector and more capital in slum-upgrading activities.

### 6.2.1.1 Housing and Slum Policies

As already discussed above, in recent decades, formal housing has rarely exceeded 10–15 percent of all urban housing production in sub-Saharan Africa, implying slums and informal settlements' expansion in most cities. This is partly due to the absence of effective policy implementation. Indeed, although several countries in sub-Saharan Africa may claim to have formal housing policies and strategies, and in some cases, relevant institutions and financing instruments, they are unable to offer a significant number of housing units for those in need.

Over the past five decades, authorities in African countries have adopted different attitudes toward the development of slums and informal settlements, and implemented various policies and strategies to address the challenges they present. These include benign neglect, laissez-faire, forced eviction and demolition, resettlement or relocation, slum-upgrading programs, and the adoption of enabling strategies (Arimah 2010). Policies have evolved and are now formulated with recognition of the right to the city of slum dwellers.

Broadly speaking, the "Right to the City" included in the United Nations Rights to Housing seeks to promote equal access to the potential benefits of the city for all urban dwellers and encourages the democratic participation of all urban dwellers in decision-making processes, notably at the municipal level, so that they may fully realize their fundamental rights and liberties. This has significant implications for both slum upgrading and relocation and redevelopment initiatives, as well as rental and social housing. Brazil, for instance, has rebuilt its whole urban governance policy around the concept of the right to the city. A 2001 federal law, "City Statute," which regulates urban policy specifically recognizes the "right to the city" and mandates the inclusion of the dwellers in the urban planning process. However, the effective application of the "City Statute" depends on the political will of public officials at the local and state levels. Magalhães and di Villarosa (2013) provide useful recommendations for the design of public policies for slum upgrading and urban development. They specifically highlight the importance of key factors such as the following: (1) legitimacy based on social demand; (2) political will with involvement of key public actors; (3) a holistic approach with complementary policies addressing urban poverty and sustainability of programs; (4) attention to quality despite cost constraints. They also emphasized the need for flexible design; and proper geographical and social targeting of programs.

## 6.2.1.2 Key Elements for Successful Slums Upgrading

Slum upgrading is widely recognized as the most effective way to improve the housing and living conditions of the millions of low-income and BOP households for whom slums and informal settlements provide the only affordable housing option. Moreover, doing so will contribute to the progressive realization of their right to an adequate standard of living, and more specifically their right to adequate housing. Indeed, slum upgrading is the principal component of the UN-Habitat Global Housing Strategy addressing housing conditions in cities. The five key dimensions of improving slums are summarized in Box 6.1.

---

**Box 6.1 Five Key Dimensions of Improving Slums**

| | |
|---|---|
| **Access to safe water** | A household is considered to have access to improved water supply if it has sufficient amounts of water for family use, at an affordable price, available to household members without being subject to extreme effort, especially for women and children. |
| **Access to sanitation** | A household is considered to have adequate access to sanitation if an excreta disposal system, in the form of either a private toilet or a public toilet shared with a reasonable number of people, is available to household members. |
| **Secure tenure** | Secure tenure is the right of all individuals and groups to effective protection by the state against forced evictions. People have secure tenure when there is documentation that can be used as proof of secure tenure status, or there is either de facto or perceived protection from forced evictions. |
| **Durability of housing** | A house is considered durable if it is built on a nonhazardous location and has a structure that is permanent and adequate enough to protect its inhabitants from the extremes of climatic conditions such as rain, heat, cold, and humidity. |
| **Sufficient living area** | A house is considered to provide a sufficient living area for the household members if not more than two people share the same bedroom. |

Source: UN-Habitat (2006).

---

Slum upgrading consists of "physical, social, economic, organizational, and environmental improvements undertaken cooperatively and locally among citizens, community groups, businesses, and local authorities" (UN-Habitat 2003: 165). Although there can be wide variation in the actual components in different projects, slum-upgrading interventions typically address the five key dimensions in Box 6.1 and include the fol-

## Slum Upgrading and Housing Alternatives for the Poor

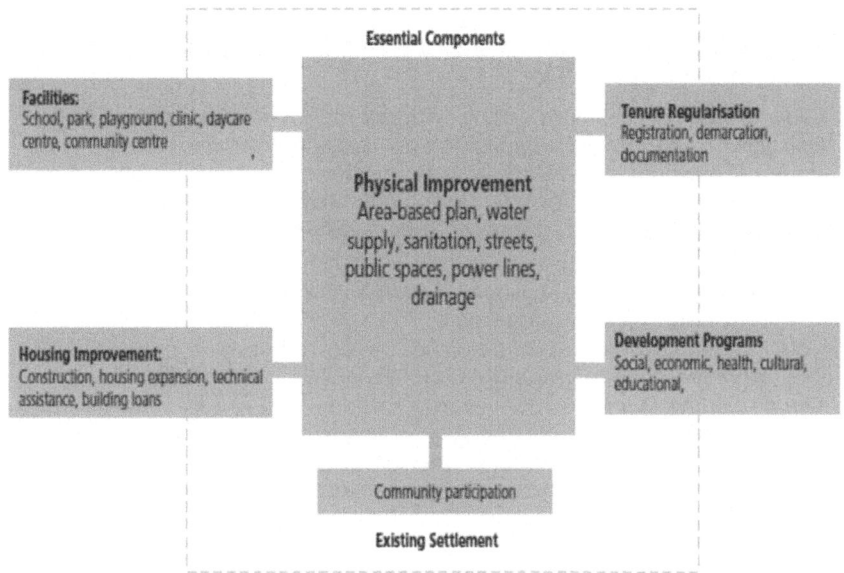

**Fig. 6.2** Components of slum upgrading (Source: UN-Habitat (2012a))

lowing components: physical improvement (water, sanitation, power, etc.), tenure regularization, housing improvement, social facilities, and social development (Fig. 6.2). However, in the context of the commercialization of basic services within slums and a distorted wider housing market, conventional slum-upgrading interventions are not always successful in providing adequate housing to slum dwellers.

As the physical accessibility and habitability of housing units and their access to infrastructure and services are improved through upgrading interventions, tenure security is compromised by the market competition for these improvements. The market thus undermines affordability and tenure security while displacing poorer existing residents and denying them the benefit of convenient location. Cultural adequacy, which is closely associated with habitability, can play an important role in defining slum-upgrading interventions that do not undermine tenure security, affordability, and location (Majale 2013).

The way in which slum upgrading is implemented is hence critical to the success of such programs (Box 6.2). In this respect, gentrification and

> **Box 6.2 Factors Underpinning Successful Slum-Upgrading Strategies and Measures**
>
> Many countries have improved the living conditions and lives of slum dwellers through pro-growth urbanization policies and economic reforms, with targeted pro-poor dimensions, and by making urban poverty alleviation and slum improvement important components of their urban development policies. They have done so through four specific strategies:
>
> (i) Enhancing the productivity of the urban poor by developing skills and providing access to microcredit
> (ii) Improving the living conditions of the poor through the provision of basic services and in situ development of slum settlements
> (iii) Providing security of tenure to poor families living in unauthorized settlements and improving their access to serviced low-cost housing and to subsidized housing finance
> (iv) Empowering the urban poor through community development and encouraging their participation in decision-making
>
> Other success factors include economic and social policies that have improved urban poor household incomes; the development of affordable housing policies that provide for land tenure regularization and slum upgrading, sites and services, and subsidized building material; urban infrastructure and social housing projects; and constitutional amendments that safeguard the right to adequate housing.
> Source: UNDG 2010.

the displacement of tenants are potential adverse effects of slum upgrading if rents and housing costs become unaffordable as a result of the improvements. However, gentrification, which occurs when middle-income households displace low-income and BOP households, is also a consequence of the failure of housing markets to supply affordable alternatives for the middle-income households. Many governments have failed to recognize and address this problem (see Chap. 2). Hence, the institutional setup of slum-upgrading programs is important. Adequate legal and regulatory framework governing slum upgrading should be in place to avoid gentrification for instance. Slum-upgrading programs should be participatory and involve slum dwellers, which could be assisted by NGOs. The private sector can also play a key role in delivering infrastructure and finance. National governments and development finance institutions could play a facilitator role in support of slum-upgrading programs.

### 6.2.1.3 Slum-Upgrading Initiatives

Several countries in Africa have implemented or are implementing slum-upgrading programs and projects. Some have been carried out under the auspices of one or more of the three generations of World Bank urban projects; others have been central or local government initiatives.

A pioneering international best practice, which is often forgotten, derives from the Hai El Salam slum-upgrading and sites-and-services project in Ismailia, Egypt, which began in 1978. The strategy that was used in this context included limited land adjustment interventions, infrastructure installation, and an efficient and transparent financial support scheme. Slum dwellers upgraded their houses incrementally, and over time, as the area became more established, completely replaced the original poor-quality dwellings with good-quality, well-designed housing structures. Today, Hai El Salam stands as a formal residential area in the heart of Ismailia (AUC 2014). This example of self-redevelopment of a slum with minimal intervention from government or other external actors is worth exploring, especially in light of the limited resources available for dealing with slums in most African countries.

Another project with limited government intervention that was successful is the Mathare 4A Development Program in Kenya. This joint project between the government of Kenya and the German development agency, KfW, provided infrastructure, housing, and social facilities. It offers important lessons on how the standard of infrastructure provided in slum upgrading can mitigate the displacement of existing tenant households. However, although governments can quite easily review their regulatory frameworks to allow for lower, more affordable standards for infrastructure and building, most still have outdated and inefficient standards held over from colonial times (see Chap. 5).

Two major World Bank–funded slum-upgrading initiatives have been implemented in Douala, Cameroon, to improve the housing and living conditions of low-income and BOP urban households. The first urban project (PDU1) focused on the worst slum areas of Douala, offering shelter to 250,000 people. The project included the provision of water and sanitation, as well as the construction of primary infrastructure such as transit roads and central market stalls. The second phase of the project involved continued work in the upgraded areas and the extension of infrastructure to other areas of Douala. Although the two projects succeeded in upgrading infrastructure, challenges to land titling remain in 7 of the 22 areas initially improved (World Bank 1996).

Another major World Bank project—an unsuccessful one—is the slum-upgrading component of the Lagos Metropolitan Development and Governance Project. This citywide slum-upgrading program was implemented between 2006 and 2013 in 9 of 42 slum communities through a US$200 million credit facility from the International Development Association. The program included the following components: (1) installation of water supply and public toilets; (2) improvement of roads and footpaths; (3) construction and rehabilitation of education and health facilities; and (4) skills-based training for youth. The World Bank rated the overall project outcome as *moderately unsatisfactory* and the risks to maintaining the development outcome as *high* (World Bank 2014).

Citywide upgrading programs were also undertaken in 2004 by the government of Morocco. The aim of the program, Villes sans Bidonvilles (Cities without Slums, or VSB) was to eradicate all slums, which at that time accommodated approximately 362,327 households in 85 cities and urban areas. The program includes three types of slum-upgrading and prevention programs: rehousing, resiting, and restructuring. The rehousing program involves the demolition of shacks and resettlement into new housing units, typically in four- to five-story apartment blocks, assigned to the former inhabitants at affordable prices. In contrast, resiting involves the demolition of shacks and relocation of residents to another site with newly serviced plots assigned to slum dwellers. The restructuring component refers to in situ upgrading, which involves improving the infrastructure while allowing the residents to remain on their plots. It includes the provision of services (water, sanitation, electricity, and roads) and a reduction of density in the most populated areas. Concurrently, the country adopted a large-scale affordable housing program under a public-private partnership (PPP) model. The VSB program provides important lessons that can be adopted by other countries. As of February 2015, 52 cities had been declared free of slums.

Currently, 24 African countries are implementing various programs under the Participatory Slum-Upgrading Program, launched in 2008. This is an initiative of the Africa, Caribbean, and Pacific Secretariat, funded by the European Commission and implemented by UN-Habitat. The program incorporates lessons learned from past slum-upgrading programs and addresses both key political economy issues and poor implementation capacity. The program's purpose is to strengthen the capacity of local, central, and regional institutions and key stakeholders in settlement and slum improvement through the use of good governance and management approaches and of pilot projects, where necessary.

### 6.2.1.4 Relocation and Slum Redevelopment

Oftentimes, the only safe and effective option is to relocate residents of existing slums and informal settlements from hazardous sites, encroached infrastructure, or proposed redevelopment sites. Relocation is also pragmatic when slums are located in high-risk or environmentally hazardous areas such as flood- and landslide-prone areas.

In contrast to in situ upgrading, slum redevelopment is a more complex strategy. It involves the demolition of existing slums and development of new housing, usually in the form of higher-density, multistory apartment blocks. In most cases, the new housing is subsidized in order to make it affordable for the original slum dwellers for whom it was targeted. But in too many cases, experience shows that even heavily subsidized housing is unaffordable for the originally targeted slum dwellers and ends up being occupied by middle-income households (see Chap. 2).

In the Integrated Urban Housing Program in Addis Ababa, Ethiopia, one of the predominantly implemented redevelopment approaches is relocation, which has multidimensional impacts on the people who are relocated. On the positive side, relocating slum dwellers from Addis Ababa's inner cities to other locations enables them to access better-quality housing with secure tenure, adequate water supply, and sanitation. But on the negative side: "Relocation erodes communities' access to all elements needed for their well-being—economic activity, social ties, and urban services" (Atlaw 2014). It thus compromises their right to the city.

In Kenya, the Kenya Slum-Upgrading Program involves the temporary relocation of slum dwellers of Kibera, the largest slum in Nairobi, to nearby "decanting sites" to enable redevelopment and the construction of new, five-story, walk-up apartment blocks into which they are expected to move. In our discussions with officials at the Ministry of Land, Housing, and Urban Development, they noted that the government recognizes that in order to be affordable to the target group, the apartment blocks will have to be very heavily subsidized and that the government is committed to doing that.

### 6.2.1.5 Cost and Financing of Slum Upgrading

Slum upgrading comprises a range of components, with very different financial implications. The most common investments are those for water, sanitation, drainage, roads, and land regularization. The most frequently observed add-ons are social amenities such as basic education and health facilities, and income-related interventions. Estimates of the distribution of infrastructure costs in slum-upgrading programs cited by Flood (2004) appear in Table 6.2. From these estimates, it can be seen that water supply and sanitation, which usually receives the most attention in slum upgrading, constitutes only about 9 percent of local infrastructure development costs. Integrated slum-upgrading programs can include even more components. The per capita or per household cost of slum-upgrading programs can thus rise drastically to unsustainable levels as more components are added. Hence, from a financial perspective, the first step in sustainable slum upgrading is to establish the cost limits

Table 6.2 Cost estimates for infrastructure provision in slum upgrading

| Activity | Share of total costs (%) |
|---|---|
| Water supply | 5 |
| Sanitation | 4 |
| Drainage | 11 |
| Paved roads | 40 |
| Footpaths and lighting | 19 |
| Solid waste disposal | 1 |
| Schools and clinics | 20 |

Source: Ferguson and Navarette (2003)

(Fergusson and Navarrete 2003). The high costs involved in slum upgrading call for sustainable financing mechanisms involving, beyond governments, several other actors such as financial institutions.

The costs of upgrading slums can be recovered in several ways. They include charging for land title regularization, basic services, and property taxes. However, it is difficult to collect for these charges as many households operate in the informal sector in order to avoid paying such costs. Indeed, they are able to connect to water and electricity lines illegally and access these services for free. This tension is especially acute when private companies operate such basic services.

Governments can also recoup the cost of regularizing land tenure by levying land rates or charging households for outright purchase of the land. Although the prices charged are often well below the market cost, the amounts raised can be significant and represent substantial cash inflows. McLeod (2004) provides a summary of some of the mechanisms that have been or could be used by governments, development partners, and NGOs to finance slum upgrading. The list includes municipal development funds, social investment funds, local development funds, multilateral development banks, cities alliance, slum-upgrading facility, and so on. Many of these mechanisms have also been used for other purposes while financing, to some degree, slum upgrading.

Nevertheless, as mentioned above, the major challenge that African cities face in implementing slum-upgrading initiatives is about financing the necessary infrastructure and services. The trend toward decentralization in many countries suggests that the provision of infrastructure and services is increasingly becoming the responsibility of city and municipal governments. There are various ways in which municipalities can access credit for infrastructure. A relatively new approach that is showing positive results in several developing countries is the use of municipal bonds. This financial instrument enables municipalities to access long-term investments directly from their country's capital markets. They can thus potentially mobilize private investment to supplement local and central government funding, as well as international development aid for slum upgrading (see Chap. 3). However, the effective use of municipal bonds in slum upgrading in African cities will require well-resourced, creditworthy and well-governed local institutions. This may prove to be quite challenging in many countries in sub-Saharan Africa.

Housing microfinance (see Chap. 3 ) is a potential source of affordable funding for low-income households for housing construction and improvement. However, its utility in slum upgrading is limited by three main factors: (1) it cannot be optimally effective unless it is operating in a broader context that includes solutions to land availability, tenure security, and infrastructure provision; (2) in cases where multifamily construction is required, there is a separate need for construction finance; microfinance serves only as the take-out finance; and (3) in many instances, slum households cannot afford a housing microfinance loan adequate to finance a complete new dwelling; subsidies or planned incremental development must be part of the planning for upgrading (Merrill and Suri 2007).

### 6.2.1.6 Private-Sector Involvement

While working in low-income areas, the private sector faces a number of challenges and opportunities. Key issues involve the business environment which is not always conducive for private-sector activity. There are, for instance, some serious constraints related to the legal and regulatory framework facing the private sector. However, there are opportunities for both the private-sector and slum dwellers to benefit from the engagement of private entities (Baker and McClain 2008). The private sector has played a variety of roles in slum upgrading, and many innovative mechanisms have been piloted to encourage its involvement. The following discusses a few options through which the private sector can be involved in slum upgrading.

An interesting, albeit small-scale, example of private-sector involvement in slum upgrading is that of Entreprises de Construction et Aménagement Divers (ECAD) in Kigali, Rwanda. ECAD's approach involved buying rundown, owner-occupied, or rental housing structures in a slum; repairing and refurbishing them; and then selling or renting them at a profit, with an expectation of progressively upgrading the quality of housing in the slum. For example, ECAD would buy a housing structure from a low-income owner for RF 8 million (about US$11,500), repair and refurbish it, and then sell it to a middle-income buyer at RF 15 million (US$26,582). Another example is Trust for Urban Housing Finance (TUHF) Limited in South Africa, which provides loans to entrepreneurs willing to invest in rental accommodation in inner cities. They can, for example, provide financing to renovate rundown buildings or transform old factory buildings into rental accommodation.

Despite the informality inherent to slums, private-sector companies can be involved in slum upgrading through the provision of basic infrastructure and services. In fact, in many cases, where upgrading interventions are implemented in the poorest and hence least attractive areas for private companies, governments can finance the capital cost of the services and then transfer responsibility for operation and maintenance to private companies. In some cases, especially for water provision, the government can offer subsidies to private companies to serve upgraded areas. Another approach is to cross-subsidize the cost of providing service to upgraded areas with that of providing service to business and higher-income consumers (Ferguson and Navarrete 2003).

### 6.2.2 Affordable and Decent Housing Alternatives for the Most Poor

One of the reasons why slums continue to exist and new ones are forming is because they provide the only affordable housing for low-income and BOP households in Africa's growing cities and towns, owing to the failure of the housing market. There are two key ways in which the expansion of existing slums and development of new ones can be prevented. The first is to effectively and sustainably address the failures of the housing market, and, more specifically, the failures on the supply side. Doing so will require lowering the cost and increase the efficiency of housing production. The second is to provide affordable housing alternatives, in particular for the most poor, but bearing in mind that there is also a dearth of affordable housing alternatives for middle-income households. Previous chapters have discussed in detail how to increase land supply and security for affordable housing, reduce construction costs, and provide housing finance including to the poorest. In the next subsection, we discuss alternative mechanisms for providing affordable and decent housing to BOP households. It is emphasized that the drive to lower costs of affordable housing should not be at the expense of quality and adequacy to needs of families. Doing so will lower uptakes and drive up overall costs as infrastructure costs will be spread over fewer households.

### 6.2.2.1 Incremental Housing Development

In many African cities and towns, an estimated 75–90 percent of all new housing is built outside the official process for land development and housing construction. Most of this construction is done through an informal, incremental process. Indeed, self-built or auto-construction is the predominant method of incremental housing development for many low- and middle-income households in many sub-Saharan Africa countries today.

Incremental self-construction is also a pragmatic approach to homeownership for many low-income and BOP households, given their limited and often irregular income streams. Incremental construction enables households to enlarge and improve their housing progressively as their needs dictate and their financial circumstances allow. As a result, such houses vary considerably in size and quality. In most cases, only a small proportion of this housing conforms fully with formal legal, regulatory, and approval requirements and procedures.

Such construction typically involves households acquiring semi-urban plots, individually or in groups, and building their houses incrementally, over a long period of time (typically 10–15 years), through gradual investment according to their financial capacities. The building process may involve hiring skilled or semiskilled labor. Only a small proportion of this housing conforms fully with such formal legal and regulatory requirements as possession of a land title deed, payment of value-added taxes (VAT) on materials and construction, approval of building plans, and possession of building permits. At the bottom end of the scale are rudimentary dwellings built at a minimal cost on unserviced land with uncertain tenure, sometimes in hazardous marshy and hilly areas. At the top end are modern, high-standard, expensive houses constructed on large plots, which are informal by virtue of the fact that they have not fully complied with formal housing development procedures and requirements.

In many African countries, self-build housing developers face numerous constraints. In addition to the challenges faced by formal developers detailed in preceding chapters, self-builders and owner-builders often lack the technical knowledge, skills, and resources needed for constructing houses. While the self-built option is conceivable in terms of affordability, it may induce significant security and well-being implications for slum dwellers in the long run, if appropriate policies and measures are not implemented. More specifically, self-built construction should comply with a minimum set of standards that ensure safety but do not increase costs unnecessarily. This can be achieved through skills development and capacity building programs on construction standards and norms targeting self-builders and workers involved in self-building processes. In so doing, it is obvious that government's intervention will be required, as well as supports from stakeholders such as NGOs and development partners. Local and central governments as well as NGOs interventions can help address some of these constraints through community involvement and the provision of housing support services, as occurs for self-help housing construction. Self-help housing involves households providing some labor and financing with the community or NGOs assisting them. The extent of community involvement and control varies from project to project. Significant costs savings can be achieved through self-help housing development. The People's Housing Process in South Africa and the Masese Women's Self-Help Project in Uganda are some examples of self-help housing construction methods on a large scale.

### 6.2.2.2 Sites-and-Services Programs

In contrast to the era of slum clearance by national governments in the 1960s, the self-help housing paradigm of the 1970s and 1980s in Africa was based on two approaches: in situ slum upgrading and the provision of sites and services (Gulyani and Connors 2002). Sites-and-services and slum-upgrading projects represented a fundamental shift in policy from total public provision of housing to public assistance in private housing construction (an enabling approach). This shift was based on the realization that, in most developing countries, conventional housing was unaffordable for the majority of urban dwellers. The production of sufficient housing units by the public sector to meet urban demand required massive subsidies that most governments were either unable or unwilling to afford. Besides acknowledging that low-income households were building affordable housing through an incremental self-help process, governments also recognized that providing secure land tenure and basic infrastructure incentivized households to invest in housing construction and improvement. Sites-and-services projects aimed to translate these observations into practical solutions by implementing more affordable building standards and providing basic infrastructure services or core-housing units, instead of completed housing units. They thus provided households with affordable housing without the need for subsidies (World Bank 1993).

During the 1970s and 1980s, many African countries set up institutions to undertake sites-and-services provision, for example La Mission d'Aménagement des Terrains Urbains et Ruraux in Cameroon, la Société d'Equipement des Terrains Urbains in Côte d'Ivoire, and the National Site and Services Scheme in Nigeria. With the SAPs in the 1990s, however, most of the institutions faced financial difficulties and either reduced their programs or were liquidated (see Chap. 4).

Development partners also have been fairly supportive of sites-and-services during the 1970s and 1980s before reversing their position in the 1990s. Between 1972 and 1990, the World Bank, for instance, was involved in 116 sites-and-services and slum-upgrading projects in 55 countries including Botswana, Côte d'Ivoire, Kenya, Senegal, Tanzania, and Zambia. The average cost of the projects was US$26 million (US$42 million, if land acquisition costs are added). Project assessments conducted in the early 1990s found that these projects failed to meet their initial three objectives: affordability, cost recovery, and replicability (World Bank 1993; Davis 2006). This together with the rolling out of the SAPs brought the World Bank to discontinue its sites-and-services programs. However, Buckly and Kalarickal (2006), following a review of

30 years of World Bank lending to the housing sector, acknowledge that the concept of progressive development that underlies sites-and-services provision is sound. Moreover, Wakely and Riley (2011) argue that the aforementioned evaluated World Bank programs were not allowed enough time to fully develop before being evaluated.

The phasing out of the SAPs and recognition of the role that sites and services could play in response to the affordability question, brought some countries to revamp their sites and services programs. Currently, a few countries are still implementing site-and-services schemes. Côte d'Ivoire is implementing the program Lotissement d'Équipement Modéré (see Box 4.1 in Chap. 4). Since 2008, the government of Burundi has initiated a number of programs to promote urban planning and housing development, including a sites-and-services project that resulted in the production of 2443 plots in the capital, Bujumbura, and 2000 plots in four provinces. The government of Djibouti has also implemented sites-and-services projects for planned incremental housing development; and an estimated 6000 serviced plots have been supplied since 2000 (CAHF 2013).

### 6.2.2.3 Rental Housing

Rental housing is an important housing option, especially for the urban poor. With homeownership out of reach for many, rental housing provides a viable alternative. Renting gives people budget flexibility and the spatial mobility to look for better work opportunities. It is also an important option for transitory periods in people's lives. Yet many African governments have done little to support the expansion of affordable rental housing. Similarly, they have not made noticeable efforts to implement measures to improve the existing stock of rental housing units.

It is noted also that rental housing appears to be a promising option, if one is concerned with providing alternative affordable housing for marginalized groups such as women who are, by and large, excluded from land market. More women than men depend on rental housing. Because households headed by women generally have lower incomes than those headed by men, women are usually overrepresented among the tenant population. In some places, this tendency is exacerbated by rules governing inheritance that exclude women from formal ownership. It is also more difficult for women to access homeownership through self-help because they are less likely to have the requisite skills to engage effectively in self-help construction. In addition, in some cities in Southern Africa, women migrants outnumber their male counterparts, resulting in a substantial proportion of tenant households being headed by women (Gilbert 2008).

Rental housing provided by the informal and formal sectors exists in all African countries. However, the sector lacks regulation of construction quality, facility size, and tenants' rights. Moreover, the inability of governments to collect fees and taxes makes rental housing a highly profitable activity (Poulais 2012). In most African cities, a vibrant informal rental market with widely different arrangements can be found in many low-income settlements. At one end of the spectrum are small-scale landlords who rent rooms on land where they also live. At the other end, large-scale, absentee landlords predominate—leading to considerable problems with the quality of accommodation owing to a lack of incentive to invest. In Nairobi, a staggering 92 percent of households in slums and informal settlements rent the dwellings in which they live (UN-Habitat 2011d).

Rents in informal areas vary greatly across the continent, but in general they represent high shares of the income of the poor. In Bomi County in Liberia, tenants pay about L$200–250 (US$2.67–US$3.33) a month for one room in a zinc or mud brick house without latrine, safe drinking water, or electricity while 50 percent of tenant households earn less than US$10 per month (UN-Habitat 2014a). Likewise, in Accra, Ghana, low-income households typically pay between C/4 and C/20 (US$1–US$5) per room (UN-Habitat 2011a). Monthly rents for single rooms (3 m x 3 m) in the high-rise tenements of Nairobi, Kenya, range from K Sh 2500 to K Sh 4000 (US$28–US$45). This is substantially higher than similarly sized rooms in low-rise, high-density tenements in slums and informal settlements, which typically range from K Sh 500 to K Sh 2500 (US$5.50–US$28) (Huschzermeyer 2007). In South Africa, the small-scale private rental sector has been growing, especially in the provision of rental accommodation costing between R300 (US$25) and R500

(US$42), with much of this growth taking place in existing townships. Indeed, of the approximately 2.4 million households in South Africa that rent their dwellings, about one in five (21 percent) rent informal dwellings; and empirical studies have found that rental is increasingly becoming the preferred choice of accommodation for poorer households (Melzer and Moothilal 2008).

Given the high deficit in affordable housing and the growing urban population, the condition of rental housing can be scaled up and be an important source of housing for all segments of the population. Although the private sector should be in essence the main player, the government should signal the importance of rental housing as a viable option and provide an enabling environment and incentives for the development of the sector (Shelter Afrique 2014). Clear policies geared toward setting up the legal and regulatory frameworks in the rental housing sector as well as those providing incentives for private-sector involvement are needed. On the demand side, cultural beliefs and norms related to homeownership (see Chaps. 4 and 5) can potentially prevent the adoption of rental housing. Therefore, policies and awareness programs geared toward promoting rental housing and eliminating cultural resistance should be implemented.

### 6.2.2.4 Social Housing

The concept of social housing is difficult to define accurately, especially because its content varies, to some extent, from one country to another. It is also called "affordable housing" or low-cost housing and generally means housing to satisfy the needs of low-income households (UN-Habitat 2011b: 15). It includes rental housing at below market prices to promote affordability.[1] Social housing is often provided by NGOs or through government interventions.

Several African countries are implementing national social housing programs, in one form or another, as shown in Table 6.3. As discussed in Chap. 2, the plan to provide affordable housing is very often high in politicians' agenda during election time, but very often do not materialize. In many cases, this is due to the fact that these programs have been launched

**Table 6.3** Examples of social housing projects in Africa

| Country | Housing program | Target units | Launch date | Comments |
|---|---|---|---|---|
| Algeria | 2015–2019 Social Housing Program | 1.6 million | 2014 | The housing sector is controlled by the state, resulting in large shortages despite government construction of about 2 million units between 2008 and 2013. |
| Angola | Meu Sonho, Minha Casa (My Dream, My Home) | 1 million | 2008 | Implementation is ongoing, and the timeline has been extended to 2017. However, units are unaffordable for low-income households. Under this program, self-built dwellings are expected to account for 685,000 housing units; the public sector is expected to deliver 115,000 housing units; 120,000 units are to be provided by the private sector; and 80,000 are to be delivered by cooperatives. |
| Benin | Subsidized housing program | 10,000 | 2008 | Under this PPP, an estimated 2500 units have been constructed as of May 2016. |
| Burkina Faso | Subsidized and low-income housing program | 10,000 | 2008 | As of June 2014, 3500 units had been completed. |

(continued)

**Table 6.3** (continued)

| Country | Housing program | Target units | Launch date | Comments |
|---|---|---|---|---|
| Burundi | Subsidized and low-income housing program | 1000–5000 | 2014 | The government signed an MOU with Biz Planners to develop a housing project; however, construction had not started at this writing. |
| Cameroon | Presidential program to build 10,000 units and service 50,000 plots | 10,000 | 2009 | An estimated 6000 houses have been constructed; however, these units are unaffordable for low-income families. |
| Cape Verde | Casa Para Todos (A House for All) | 9400 | 2009 | Implementation is ongoing. The program entails the construction of 8400 housing units across the country, 1000 units in rural areas, and rehabilitation of infrastructure in slums. |
| Chad | Presidential social housing program | 15,000 | 2014 | An agreement has been signed with the Moroccan property developer, ADDOHA, for the construction of social housing units. |
| Côte d'Ivoire | Presidential social housing program | 60,000 | 2012 | About 8000 units had been finished by the end of 2015. |
| Egypt | Social housing program for low-income families | 1 million | 2014 | Implementation is ongoing with an expected completion date in 2020, with 200,000 housing units expected to be constructed each year until then. |

(*continued*)

**Table 6.3** (continued)

| Country | Housing program | Target units | Launch date | Comments |
|---|---|---|---|---|
| Ethiopia | Integrated Housing Development Program | 400,000 annually | 2006 | As of February 2015, over 396,000 housing units have been constructed. |
| Gabon | Program de 35,000 logements | 35,000 | 2009 | As of May 2015, 6370 units had been started. |
| Liberia | Affordable Housing program for low- to middle-income families | 5000 | 2012 | The project is ongoing. |
| Mali | Several programs | 5174 | 2013 | Programs were implemented in Bamako and other cities. |
| Mozambique | Affordable housing program | 35,000 | 2014 | As part of its five-year development plan (2015–2020), the government committed to build 7000 housing units per year. |
| Nigeria | Affordable housing program | 1 million annually | 2006 | The annual target has not been met as of May 2016. Moreover, it falls short of the estimated 2.6 million homes needed each year. |
| Rwanda | Affordable housing program | 7480 | 2015 | The program is ongoing in Kigali and expected to be rolled out to other cities. |
| South Africa | National program | 1.5 million | 2014 | Millions of government-built houses have been given free to low-income households since 1994. |

Source: National sources

as election promise or as a result of a presidential directive; without serious planning taking into account the countries inadequate institutional framework, and lack of financial, human, and technical resources to implement them effectively. This has resulted mainly in low completion rates and selling prices that are not affordable by low- and middle-income households in most cases. It is also common that the housing units end up being acquired by households wealthier than those at the BOP.

Two vivid examples of unaffordable social housing are found in Angola and Cameroon. The initial selling price for social housing constructed in Kilamba, Angola ranged between US$ 150,000 and US$ 300,000. Following a massive public outcry, the government considerably subsidized the homes, driving down prices to USD 60,000. A rent-to-own program was also implemented wherein households could purchase a three-bedroom unit at a substantially subsidized rate: US$350 per month on a 15-year mortgage, an interest rate of 3 percent and a down payment of US$14,000. Even this reduced price of US$60,000 is 14 times the Angola GNI per capita in 2015, which suggests a highly unaffordable price for low- and middle-income households.

In Cameroon, the government launched in 2009 the Programme of Construction of 10,000 Social Housing Units and Development of 50,000 Serviced Plots (*Programme Gouvernemental de Construction de 10,000 Logements Sociaux et d'Aménagement de 50,000 Parcelles Constructibles*). The selling prices for units range from US$38,000 to US$48,000, which is 28–36 times the gross national income per capita of Cameroon in 2015.

The most affordable social housing is the free housing delivered under the Reconstruction and Development Program (RDP) in South Africa. Since 1994, the government has delivered over 2.5 million housing units and created over 1.2 million service plots. While this is a great achievement, it is widely acknowledged that the program is unsustainable and will not be able to fully address the housing issues in the country. This argument is supported by the increase in the housing backlog from 1.5 million units in 1994 to 2.1 million units as at end 2015, and the decline in the completion rates from a peak of 235,600 units in 1998/99 to 106,000 units in 2013/2014.

### 6.2.2.5 Housing Cooperatives

Cooperatives are recognized in the Habitat Agenda and the Global Plan of Action as important actors in promoting sustainable housing. They should be promoted and supported, as they serve three key enabling functions necessary to move toward the goal of adequate and affordable shelter for their members. A housing cooperative is a corporation owned by members through equity shares. They enable households to pool resources to acquire and develop land and housing, enable groups to join forces and reduce construction costs, and facilitate access to finance (UN-Habitat 2011b). Members of the cooperative live in housing provided by the cooperative, and they organize maintenance of housing units and common areas and run social activities. There are various forms of housing cooperatives with varying degree of ownership and selling price. A market rate cooperative sells share at full market value and does not restrict the future sale of units at market value. A limited equity cooperative, on the other hand, puts a limit on the sale price of units in order to maintain housing affordability. There are also leasehold cooperatives where the building are owned by a third party and leased by the cooperative, sometimes with the option to buy in the future.

Cooperatives are active in a number of countries, including developed countries. For instance, it is estimated that over 1.5 million households in the United States live in housing cooperatives. In Africa, housing cooperatives are very active in a number of countries such as Cameroon, Kenya, Senegal, South Africa, and Zimbabwe. For instance, the Zimbabwe National Association of Housing Cooperatives, an apex organization for housing cooperatives, has provided services to more than 20,000 plots and constructed over 10,000 houses in the country over the past decade.

A key challenge for cooperatives in Africa, including housing cooperatives, are the role of the state, the optimal size, and governance issues. Since independence, laws regulating cooperatives and the extent of state involvement in cooperatives have changed along with the dominant political economic environment. Just after independence, the state played a critical role in socioeconomic development and gave strong financial and technical support to cooperatives. With the advent of the SAPs, new cooperatives laws were introduced in a number of countries from the 1990s to guarantee them self-reliance with no or minimal support from the state. This made housing cooperative less effective in view of high costs for land acquisition and bulk infrastructure provision. The second challenge is the optimal size of cooperative. To be effective, housing cooperative need a critical mass of individuals to pool their resources to face high investments required for housing construction. However, in many countries housing cooperatives are small and struggle to deliver housing units in a timely fashion. In addition, some cooperatives lack the governance structure to manage effectively their investments. Corruption cases in a few cooperatives discouraged people from joining cooperatives and prevent them from reaching the critical mass. Finally, the escalation of land prices and construction costs in most African countries make the work of housing cooperatives even more challenging as they require external sources of finance.

### 6.2.2.6 Housing Transformation to Meet the Needs of the Poor

An important mode of providing decent and affordable housing that is not widely recognized is user-initiated transformations of government-built houses. In a number of African countries, there are significant stocks of government-built housing which, for different reasons, are in poor physical condition or do not meet the space and accommodation requirements of the occupants. Many occupants consequently make substantial unauthorized changes and extensions (transformations) to their dwellings so that they are better suited to their needs.

Studies of user-initiated transformations to government-built housing in Bangladesh, Egypt, Ghana, and Zimbabwe found that relatively low-income households are capable of supplying new rooms and services both to improve their own housing conditions and to supply rental rooms or accommodation for family members. The quality of the new construction is often, at the very least, as good as the original structure, and sometimes it envelopes the original in a new skin. It is clear that transformation adds accommodation and services to existing housing, upgrades the housing stock, and creates variety out of uniformity. The literature suggests that user-initiated transformations to government-built houses are a valid and important resource for housing supply both currently and in the future (Tipple 2000; Tipple et al. 2004).

### 6.2.2.7 Housing Support Services

Housing support services are commonly called "construction technical assistance" (CTA), or "nonfinancial services"; the two terms are often used interchangeably. Housing support services, combined with access to housing finance, can provide households with the necessary technical and financial information and resources to minimize the risk and maximize the impact of their housing investments. Two types of housing support services can be distinguished: nonconstruction and construction. Nonconstruction support services enable households and communities to access infrastructure and services, and are often provided in the pre-construction phase or before a new incremental improvement. They can include legal assistance for land tenure and the permitting process, design, training, and information access. Construction support services are directly associated with housing and infrastructure construction. As mentioned above, an estimated 75–90 percent of all affordable housing improvement is attributed to self-help initiatives; therefore, there is considerable scope to significantly affect housing outcomes using housing support services (Weir and Williams 2012). This alternative is quite useful and can go a long way to ensure that construction is affordable to BOP households, but also can help ensuring that quality and design of the housing meet the needs of the poor. While government could face challenges to implement such programs, it is important to put the necessary conditions for the private sector involved in the housing production value chain to offer such support.

LafargeHolcim is developing support services through its cement retailers and through partnerships with microfinance institutions (see Chap. 5). The company provides design assistance and training on construction techniques. Although the objective of the company is to increase the sales of its products, the services can also increase quality and lower construction costs for its clients.

## 6.2.2.8 Public-Private Partnerships

African countries are increasingly adopting the PPP model of affordable housing provision. Under this model, governments use mechanisms such as policy reforms, land and tax incentives, and subsidies to incentivize the private and the not-for-profit sectors to engage in affordable housing development for the poor. The principal reason for adopting a PPP model for the provision of housing and urban development is that, if appropriately and effectively applied, this approach can offer greater value for money than traditional models. In addition, governments lack the financial capacity to directly provide affordable housing and urban infrastructure to a large and growing segment of the population. For these reasons, countries such as Angola, Cameroon, Côte d'Ivoire, Ethiopia, and Nigeria are using the PPP approach in their social housing programs. In the United States, PPPs have become the main delivery mechanism for social and military housing as it has been found to be more cost effective, yielding to savings of 20 percent compared to government projects (Apgar 2011).

However, applying the PPP approach to the urban sector presents a number of challenges. The most common challenges facing governments today, as identified by UN-Habitat, include the following: differing goals between the private actors with profit maximization objectives and government with social objectives; limited public acceptability of the housing constructed if cost-saving motives trump design and quality; limited local government capacity in negotiations, finance, and others skills required to manage complex projects; weak governance for sustainable development as projects' implementation units often do not include ministries of environment that have better knowledge of sustainability issues; and lack of financing due to high perception of risks related to housing projects (UN-Habitat 2011c). Moreover, contracts for PPPs may not be flexible, given that strong guarantees are required to attract private-sector involvement.

## 6.3 Conclusions and Recommendations

The analysis in this chapter revealed that African cities are being built back to front, with housing development taking place before planning. This is the result of the combination of rapid urbanization and demographic growth, bad policies, and inappropriate incentives systems including poor governance, inappropriate regulatory frameworks, dysfunctional housing markets, and a lack of political will. Consequently, slums and informal settlements are continuing to develop, proliferate, and expand in cities and towns across the African continent to accommodate BOP households. This dynamic constitutes a significant challenge for governments and policymakers.

This process has translated into a vicious cycle and kept BOP households in a poverty trap. It is argued in this chapter that if this process is to be halted and reversed, a twin-track approach is required. On the one hand, existing slums located in nonhazardous areas should be upgraded. This process is multifaceted, encompassing provision of basic infrastructure (roads, water and sanitation); improving security of tenure; ensuring decency and quality of housing (durability of housing and sufficient living area); enabling residents to upgrade their houses. These interventions lower public health risks and improve the well-being of slum dwellers. A participatory and community-based approach that includes all key stakeholders and the right institutional framework are key success factors.

The analysis also highlighted that the cost of slum upgrading can turn out to be very onerous, in such a way that microcredit and governments' traditional limited budget and transfers may not suffice to mobilize the required funding. This suggests that there is a need to encourage more sustainable financing schemes including governments' domestic resource mobilization, market-based solutions such as municipality bonds, and increased private-sector engagement through PPPs.

On the other hand, given the high urbanization rates, it is argued in this chapter that the large-scale provision of affordable and decent housing is necessary to prevent new slum formation. Countries need to adopt national urban plans and comprehensive national housing programs, which can make a significant contribution to economic growth and development while providing significant livelihood enhancing opportunities to BOP households. It is therefore advisable that a combination of sites-and-services schemes and incremental auto-construction be considered as a viable way to provide housing for low-income households.

An interesting finding from this chapter is that most of the above-mentioned affordable and decent housing development schemes need government subsidy. The limited resources available to governments undermine the sustainability of government-sponsored schemes as well as the magnitude of their interventions. This suggests that there is a need to go beyond financing and put in place adequate institutional and policy frameworks that are needed to rationalize governments' spending. In addition, governments need to crowd in the private sector while putting in place with the necessary incentives mechanisms. In that respect, rental housing is an important affordable housing solution, especially for the urban poor who cannot be homeowners. Measures to govern and promote rental development should therefore be formulated. Such policies should take into account local dynamics and housing market conditions.

## Notes

1. In South Africa, social housing refers only to rental housing provided by NGOs and community organizations at subsidized rates.

## Bibliography

Apgar, Mahlon (Sandy). 2011. Public Private Partnerships: Lessons From Military Housing. *Real Estate Issues* 36 (2): 63–64.

Arimah, Ben C. 2010. *Slums as Expressions of Social Exclusion: Explaining the Prevalence of Slums in African Countries*. Nairobi: United Nations Human Settlements Program (UN-Habitat).

Atlaw, Habtamu. 2014. Slum Redevelopment in Addis Ababa: How Can It Become Sustainable? *International Journal of Science and Research* 3 (9): 2387–2393.

AUC (American University in Cairo). 2014. *Egypt's Strategy for Dealing with Slums*. Cairo: American University in Cairo.

Baker, Judy L., and Kim McClain. 2008. Private Sector Involvement in Slum Upgrading. *Global Urban Development Magazine* 4 (1).

BoP Learning Lab and Dalberg Research. 2014. *My Home, Your Business: A guide to Affordable Housing Solutions for Low-Income Communities*. German Federal Ministry for Economic Cooperation and Development.

Buckley, Robert M., and Jerry Kalarickal, eds. 2006. *Thirty Years of World Bank Shelter Lending: What Have We Learned?* Washington, DC: World Bank.

CAHF (Centre for Affordable Housing Finance in Africa). 2013. *2013 Yearbook—Housing Finance in Africa: A Review of Some of Africa's Housing Finance Markets*. Parkview: Centre for Affordable Housing Finance in Africa.

Davis, Mike. 2006. *Planet of Slums*. London: Verso.

Ferguson, Bruce, and Jesus Navarrete. 2003. A Financial Framework for Reducing Slums: Lessons from Experience in Latin America. *Environment and Urbanization* 15 (2): 201–215.

Gilbert, Alan. 2008. Slums, Tenants, and Home-Ownership: On Blindness to the Obvious. *International Development Planning Review* 30 (2): i–x.

Gulyani, Sumila, and Genevieve Connors. 2002. *Urban Upgrading in Africa: A Summary of Rapid Assessments in Ten Countries*. Washington, DC: World Bank.

Hammond, Allen L., William J. Kramer, Robert S. Katz, Julia T. Tran, and Courtland Walker. 2007. *The Next 4 Billion: Market Size and Business Strategy at the Base of the Pyramid*. Washington, DC: World Resources Institute and International Finance Corporation.

Huchzermeyer, Marie. 2007. Tenement City: The Emergence of Multi-Storey Districts Through Large-Scale Private Landlordism in Nairobi. *International Journal of Urban and Regional Research* 31 (4): 714–732.

Magalhães, Fernanda, and Francisco di Villarosa, eds. 2013. *Slum Upgrading: Lessons Learned from Brazil*. Washington, DC: Inter-American Development Bank.

Majale, Michael. 2013. *Realising the Right to Total Sanitation in Nakuru's Slums: Study on Tenants' Security of Tenure Following Improvement of Sanitation Facilities*. Unpublished Report.

McLeod, Ruth. 2004. *Financing Community-Led Slum Upgrading: Lessons from the Federation Process*, A Paper Prepared for the ITDG Regulatory Guidelines for Urban Upgrading Research Project, Homeless International, Coventry.

Melzer, Illana, and Ria Moothilal. 2008. *Supply and Demand of Rental Housing in South Africa*. Houthon: Social Housing Foundation.

Merrill, Sally, and Ajay Suri. 2007. *Low-Income Shelter Finance in Slum Upgrading*. Washington, DC: The Urban Institute.

Mutunga, Clive, Eliya Zulu, and Roger-Mark De Souza. 2012. *Population Dynamics, Climate Change, and Sustainable Development in Africa*. Washington, DC: Population Action International.

Paulais, Thierry. 2012. *Financing Africa's Cities: The Imperative of Local Investment*. Washington, DC: World Bank.

Payne, Geoffrey. 2005. Getting Ahead of the Game: A Twin-Track Approach to Improving Existing Slums and Reducing the Need for Future Slums. *Environment and Urbanization* 17 (1): 135–145.

Pieterse, Edgar. 2013. Competing Imaginaries of Empowerment in African Cities. In *Afritecture. Building Social Change*, ed. Andres Lepik, 104–113. Ostfildern: Hatje Cantz Verlag.

Shelter, Afrique. 2014. *The African Rental Housing Conference: Formal Rental Housing in Sub-Sahara Africa: Opportunities for Providing Affordable Housing for All*, A White Paper for Policy-Makers, Practitioners, and Academics, Shelter Afrique, Nairobi.

Stickney, Christy. 2014. *Many Paths to a Home: Emerging Business Models for Latin America and the Caribbean's Base of the Pyramid*. Washington, DC: Inter-American Development Bank.

Tipple, Graham. 2000. *Extending Themselves: User-initiated Transformations of Government-built Housing in Developing Countries*. Liverpool: Liverpool University Press.

Tipple, Graham, Stephen Owusu, and Columbus Pritchard. 2004. User-Initiated Extensions in Government-Built Estates in Ghana and Zimbabwe: Unconventional but Effective Housing Supply. *Africa Today* 51: 79–105.

UNDG (United Nations Development Group). 2010. *Thematic Paper on MDG 7: Environmental Sustainability*. New York: United Nations Development Group.

UN-Habitat (United Nations Human Settlements Program). 2003. *The Challenge of Slums. Global Report on Human Settlements 2003*. Nairobi: United Nations Human Settlements Program.

———. 2005. *Financing Urban Shelter. Global Report on Human Settlements 2005*. Nairobi: United Nations Human Settlements Program.

———. 2006. *Analytical Perspective of Pro-Poor Slum Upgrading Frameworks*. Nairobi: United Nations Human Settlements Program.

———. 2011a. *Ghana Housing Profile*. Nairobi: United Nations Human Settlements Program.

———. 2011b. *Enabling Shelter Strategies: Design and Implementation Guide for Policymakers*, Quick Policy Guides No. 2. Nairobi: United Nations Human Settlements Program.

———. 2011c. *Public-Private Partnership in Housing and Urban Development*. Nairobi: United Nations Human Settlements Program.

———. 2011d. *Rental Housing, a Much Neglected Housing Option for the Poor*, Quick Guides for Policy Makers: Housing the Poor in African Cities, No. 7. Nairobi: United Nations Human Settlements Program.

———. 2012a. *Affordable Land and Housing in Africa*, Adequate Housing Series Volume 3. Nairobi: United Nations Human Settlements Program.

———. 2012b. *Streets as Tools for Urban Transformation in Slums: A Street-Led Approach to Citywide Slum Upgrading*. Nairobi: United Nations Human Settlements Program.

———. 2013. *Scaling Up Affordable Housing Supply in Brazil: The 'My House, My Life' Program*. Nairobi: United Nations Human Settlements Program.

———. 2014a. *Liberia Housing Profile*. Nairobi: United Nations Human Settlements Program.

———. 2014b. *The State of African Cities 2014: Re-Imagining Sustainable Urban Transitions*. Nairobi: United Nations Human Settlements Program.

Wakely, Patrick, and Elizabeth Riley. 2011. *The Case for Incremental Housing*, Cities Alliance Policy Research and Working Papers Series No. 1, Cities Alliance, Washington, DC.

Weir, Steven, and Susana Rojas Williams. 2012. Housing Support Services. In *The Big Idea: Global Spread of Affordable Housing*, ed. Scott Anderson and Rochelle Beck, 54–60. Arlington: Next Billion and Ashoka Full Economic Citizenship.

World Bank. 1993. *Housing: Enabling Markets to Work*. A World Bank Policy Paper. Washington DC: World Bank.

———. 1996. *Implementation Completion Report: Cameroon Second Urban Project*. Washington, DC: World Bank.

———. 2014. *Implementation Completion and Results Report (IDA-42190) on a Credit in the Amount of SDR 138.10 Million (USD200.00 Million Equivalent) to the Federal Republic of Nigeria for the Lagos Metropolitan Development and Governance Project*. Report No: ICR00002968, World Bank, Washington, DC.

# Slum Upgrading and Housing Alternatives for the Poor 253

**Open Access** This chapter is licensed under the terms of the Creative Commons Attribution 4.0 International License (http://creativecommons.org/licenses/by/4.0/), which permits use, sharing, adaptation, distribution and reproduction in any medium or format, as long as you give appropriate credit to the original author(s) and the source, provide a link to the Creative Commons license and indicate if changes were made.

The images or other third party material in this chapter are included in the chapter's Creative Commons license, unless indicated otherwise in a credit line to the material. If material is not included in the chapter's Creative Commons license and your intended use is not permitted by statutory regulation or exceeds the permitted use, you will need to obtain permission directly from the copyright holder.

# 7

# The Way Forward: A Stakeholder Analysis

## 7.1 Introduction

This book presents a comprehensive overview of the housing market dynamics in Africa. It highlights the many facets of the housing market challenges on the continent: rapid urbanization, poor urban planning, dysfunctional land markets, rising construction costs, proliferation of informal settlements, underdeveloped financial systems, and the problem of affordable housing supply. While many of these issues are prevalent in most countries, the extent of these problems varies from one country to the next, and across regions. However, beneath these challenges also lie opportunities. In most economies in other regions of the world, rapid urbanization has been accompanied by structural transformation, characterized by a move of resources first from agriculture into industry and services, and then later from agriculture and industry into services. In developing Asia, as in North America and Europe, urbanization was accompanied by substantial economic growth and development. If properly harnessed, Africa's rapid urbanization could also foster the development of efficient and sustainable cities, as well as accelerate inclusive growth and job creation. We estimate that addressing Africa's housing crisis has the potential to create 288 million full-time-equivalent jobs in

10 years and add US$5.07 trillion to the economy for an investment of US$2.08 trillion during the same period.

Thus far, Africa's housing sector has failed to adequately accommodate the needs of low- and middle-income families. As a result, moving up the property ladder is as challenging as getting a first foot on it. In many countries, house prices are out of reach for a majority of the population. New data in our study revealed that the average cost of an entry-level house of 40 m$^2$ in Africa is US$16,495. At this price, 33 percent, or 76 million, African households cannot even get a foot on the housing ladder. Providing affordable housing options to low- and middle-income families is imperative for the development of Africa's housing market, and for addressing the continent's huge housing backlog. Expanding the supply of affordable housing will require policies and regulations that address the root causes of Africa's dysfunctional housing market. It is also crucial to consider the broader development objectives in the choice of solutions aimed at lowering housing costs.

In Chap. 3, we explored the constraints of access to finance faced by consumers, real estate developers, and financial intermediaries along the housing value chain. In drawing linkages between the formal and informal housing finance markets, the chapter sheds some light on innovations being offered to support low-income households in the informal sector in climbing onto or moving up the housing ladder. Chapter 4 drilled down on three key challenges impeding the supply of affordable land in Africa. The chapter also argues that the provision of basic infrastructure, especially transport infrastructure, not only shapes cities, but is an important determinant of housing affordability, particularly for low-income families. Chapter 5 discussed five key approaches to reducing construction costs in Africa, including industrializing housing construction, promoting densification, and producing and using local building materials, among others. Chapter 6 examined enabling approaches for slum upgrading and housing alternatives for households at the bottom of the housing ladder. The chapter emphasizes the need to develop housing rental markets, given that not everyone can be a homeowner.

In this concluding chapter, we draw on findings in previous chapters and lessons learned from other emerging countries and regions to provide policy suggestions to key stakeholders involved in Africa's housing market. Given the breadth and depth of Africa's housing problem, finding sustainable solutions to the continent's affordable housing crisis will require well-coordinated and concerted efforts from all stakeholders, including the public, private, and nonprofit sectors.

## 7.2 Role of Government

The importance of policy and regulation in shaping housing markets cannot be overemphasized. As Fig. 5.4 shows, the government plays an important crosscutting role in the housing market, intervening in all of the steps of the housing delivery value chain. Building standards, energy-efficiency requirements, competing land usage demands, provision of bulk infrastructure, housing finance, subsidy programs, and the need for sustainability in new housing projects all have an immense impact on the housing market. Besides affecting the quantity of housing supplied, these policies have a significant bearing on housing affordability. Overall, policies and regulation can result in important changes in the functioning and performance of the housing market. Governments have a long history of supporting affordable housing across the globe. The Malaysian national mortgage corporation, Cagamas, the United States' Federal National Mortgage Association (Fannie Mae) and Federal Home Loan Mortgage Corporation (Freddie Mac), South Africa's National Housing Finance Corporation, and Morocco's FOGARIM guarantee program are but a few examples from a long list of institutions and programs created by governments to encourage homeownership and increase housing affordability.

Africa's housing crisis can be solved only by the unwavering commitment and political will of national governments, given the long-term nature of housing assets. Morocco provides a concrete example of how restructuring the relationship between the state, the private sector, and the community can accelerate progress in easing the housing crisis. The strong political will demonstrated by the Ethiopian government in its Integrated Housing Development Program is another notable example. The starting point for government support should focus on creating an enabling environment that induces private agents and nongovernmental organizations to build and finance housing acquisition for all household segments, especially low- and middle-income families. Several governments in Latin America, such as that of Chile, have adopted the enabling approach to successfully reform their housing policies and systems.

In Africa today, an enabling market approach will require an overhaul of government housing policies, institutions, laws, and regulations in order to support a well-functioning and efficient housing market. The enabling approach changes the role of government from a provider of housing, which it had not been effective in fulfilling in most cases, to that of a facilitator. In the context of the housing delivery value chain discussed earlier, the roles of government can be grouped into three categories: regulator, input provider, and facilitator.

### 7.2.1 Government as Regulator

Effective and streamlined regulations with the right institutional setup and implementation are necessary throughout the value chain and will determine the effectiveness of housing markets in Africa. Here, we focus on a few key policy areas.

#### 7.2.1.1 Urban Planning

Perhaps the most important regulatory tool at governments' disposal for guiding urbanization and city growth is urban planning. It is the policy that defines the use of land, the design of urban infrastructure, communication networks and provisions that provides protection of the natural environment. It also provides mechanisms for urban expansion and for making land available for housing development. It is the absence of up-to-date urban plans and/or the effective enforcement of existing plans that have led to urban sprawl and unplanned growth in many African cities. These conditions have led to a scarcity of well-located lands for housing and to cost escalations for land, infrastructure, and housing. Therefore, to improve the efficiency of cities and enable them to fully play their economic role, African governments should regularly update their urban plans and ensure that they are grounded in local realities.

## 7.2.1.2   Housing Policies

Housing policies include governments' regulations and actions that affect the demand and supply of housing. In an enabling environment, regulations should promote the efficient functioning of different segments of housing markets. For instance, very stringent quality standards may well be appropriate for high-rise luxury apartments, but the same standards for less luxurious units may make housing unaffordable for low-income households. Similarly, plot size requirements copied from colonial powers in the 1950s and 1960s push the majority of households into the informal housing sector as the formal one becomes unaffordable. Although the list of possible recommendations for effective housing policies is long, we focus on three key policies that have significant effects on housing access and affordability: property rights, housing finance, and construction efficiency.

*Promoting Property Rights*

Notwithstanding the validity of the continuum of land rights, the large-scale housing provision needed in most countries will be difficult to realize without clear property rights based on secure land titles. Secure property rights are not only important for the supply side, but also crucial for a well-functioning housing finance market. Governments should enact streamlined frameworks that provide for individual property rights and facilitate the ability to transfer these rights. Computerized central information systems and decentralized mechanisms for registration and transfer of property will lower the time and costs involved in the process and improve security. Rwanda's approach in overhauling its property registration system should be considered by other countries' governments.

In addition, governments should enact clear procedures for registering property as collateral and for realizing such collateral when necessary. Building such information systems is particularly important for the development of secondary mortgage markets, wherein the legitimacy of underlying assets and securities needs to be ascertained. Moreover, a system that is accessible to financial institutions, insurers, investors, land registries, and other relevant stakeholders will help eliminate the use of the same collateral for multiple loans and reduce the use of forged documents to obtain loans. However, the protection of property rights and secured collateral systems are effective only if the judicial system is independent and capable of enforcing contracts. Establishing a separate system that deals specifically with property rights and collateral claims related to housing may be an effective way to jump-start the mortgage market.

*Promoting Inclusive Housing Finance Systems*

To deepen housing finance markets, laws regarding securitization, bankruptcy and collateral reforms, sound frameworks for collateral valuation practices, an overhaul of credit registry systems, and housing information systems are needed. Two types of regulations have a large bearing on housing finance systems. The first is regulation of the activities of banks, microfinance institutions (MFIs), and other nonbanking financial institutions (NBFIs) that can broaden and deepen housing finance systems. For instance, regulations limiting the share of holdings of different types of assets can be used to promote inclusive mortgage systems. In Kenya, the simple requirement of having banks report their mortgage assets has pushed some institutions to increase their exposure to the sector.

Given the right regulations, NBFIs can play a vital developmental and complementary role to banks in housing finance systems. Institutions such as pension funds, insurance firms, housing finance companies, mortgage liquidity facilities, and private equity vehicles are risk-pooling institutions that can mobilize long-term finance and address the liquidity needs of the housing market. Financial sector policies and regulations should permit these institutions to invest in the housing sector, including rental housing. Legal and regulatory reforms that strengthen borrower and creditor rights, bolster credit analysis, and promote sound macroeconomic management are essential for expanding housing finance markets. Moreover, prudential requirements and conversion ratios of short-term liabilities have an important effect on housing finance. However, a balance between the promotion of lending and prudent management of systemic risks is necessary.

The second type of regulation with a large impact on housing finance is fiscal policy. Fiscal incentives such as tax exemptions and a housing finance guarantee fund accelerate the construction and uptake of housing for low-income households. Morocco provides vivid examples on how policy reforms accompanied by institutional and fiscal incentives can accelerate the production of affordable housing by private developers. The Finance Law of 2010, which was renewed in 2013, exempts low-income housing developers from paying corporate taxes, value added tax, cement taxes, and land registration fees. In addition to these tax exemptions, the government also offers incentives to homebuyers. For instance, housing for middle-class households is exempt from registration fees for property titles, as well as stamp duty and fees on land. In Senegal, housing cooperatives and social housing developers pay a value added tax rate of 10 percent, as compared with the standard rate of 20 percent. Other tax breaks include a 5 percent tax rate for affordable housing developers and 1 percent for housing cooperatives, whereas the standard construction tax is 15 percent.

### 7.2.1.3 Promoting Efficiency in Housing Construction and the Use of Local Building Materials

As discussed in Chap. 5, cumbersome and poorly targeted regulations lengthen construction times, increase costs, and promote corruption, which inherently lead to an inefficient housing delivery process. Through in-depth analysis and discussions with stakeholders, governments should identify gaps and streamline processes to improve efficiency and lower construction costs. For instance, the government of Kenya was able to reduce considerably the time it takes to obtain a construction permit by adopting an online process. Moreover, regulations related to building standards, plot sizes, and standards for building materials should be flexible and should meet the needs of not only high-income households but also those at the bottom of the housing ladder.

Policy proposals should also promote the use of local building materials such as compressed stabilized earth blocks, bamboo, and laminated wood. In general, despite being cheaper, such local materials are not widely used because of market failures and the poverty stigma associated with the use of these materials. Our analysis has also shown that heavy imports of building materials are contributing to rising construction costs. Therefore, governments should use strategic trade policy to promote local production of building materials, which will contribute to the development objectives of many governments to industrialize and create jobs for their growing labor forces. Ethiopia and Rwanda are moving in this direction, and we recommend other countries to follow suit and work together to create common standards to promote regional trade through economies of scale.

### 7.2.2 Government as Input Provider

Even though the government should mainly focus on its role as regulator, there are inputs that the private sector either cannot provide or provides at higher costs. We recommend that governments focus on two main inputs:

- *Bulk infrastructure*: Because of its public good characteristics and large initial investment requirements, bulk infrastructure (primary roads, electricity, water, and sanitation) is best provided by the public sector. Governments should create mechanisms to ensure that all new housing developments are connected to the bulk infrastructure networks, which will reduce the proliferation of slums, which are characterized by unsanitary living conditions. Urban planning can lower the costs of such infrastructure as good planning anticipates and builds infrastructure before housing settlements, as opposed to the current sequence in most African cities. Given the fiscal pressure on governments, we recommend that policymakers explore the possibility of financing bulk infrastructure through municipal bonds and of recouping investments through land value capture. It is also possible to recoup part of the costs of infrastructure provision in slum-upgrading programs through various levies and cost-sharing arrangements.
- *Land and finance for affordable housing projects*: Given the high land prices and construction costs, formal housing is unaffordable to the

majority of low- and middle-income Africans. Governments in various countries have been working with the private sector in affordable housing projects by contributing land as well as finance through various subsidies and tax policies. If well structured, these public-private partnerships (PPPs) can increase the supply of affordable housing with minimal effect on government revenues. On the demand side, we believe that guarantee schemes, such as FOGARIM in Morocco, provide a great opportunity to leverage private-sector funding to reach specific segments of the population. We emphasize the need for strong governance and good targeting of government programs that have input elements. There are various examples of social housing programs that have benefited the rich and well connected, so a systematic approach should include well-designed targeting and monitoring mechanisms that primarily benefit underserved households.

### 7.2.3 Government as Facilitator

Increasing the efficiency of the housing sector in Africa requires a value chain approach with close coordination between various stakeholders. The government can play a pivotal role in facilitating such coordination and ensuring all stakeholders work together. The government can also promote best practices from other countries and provide valuable information to builders and households on various issues. For instance, in many countries, a poverty stigma is preventing the adoption of local materials. The government can help to remove such stigma through information campaigns and through demonstration effects in its public buildings. The government can also facilitate partnerships in slum-upgrading and affordable housing programs.

Another role of the government is to provide training in the needed skills in the construction sector. As discussed in Chap. 5, the shortage of skills in many countries is having a negative impact on the costs and quality of housing. Governments need to increase the technical and vocational training of youth in the various skills needed by the construction and manufacturing sectors, among others. This type of training should be done in close partnership with the private sector to ensure that needs are identified correctly and training is delivered effectively.

## 7.3 Role of the Private Sector

The private sector is a key partner to governments and nonprofits in scaling up the supply of affordable housing. Essentially, the private sector should be at the forefront of developing, innovating, and financing affordable housing solutions. As the government creates a better enabling environment, the private sector needs to improve its processes to increase efficiency and capacity to deliver at scale. The construction sector in many countries is currently dominated by SMEs that lack the capacity to build more than 500 housing units a year. Better linkages between firms of different sizes and capacity-building programs through industry organizations can improve both the capacity and productivity of the sector. Industry organizations also need to promote best practices and combat inertia and resistance to change, which is endemic in the construction sector. Moreover, better industrial organization with a greater role for prefabrication of building systems can boost productivity and lower construction times and costs. However, for this to work, the regulatory environment needs to be supportive as, for example, through standardizing building codes and dimensions of housing components.

On the financing side, the financial sector should develop new and innovative solutions for serving low- and middle-income households. As standard mortgages are not the solution for all housing segments, other products such as incremental building loans should be developed for low-income households. In addition, more work needs to be done to better understand and serve households in the informal sector that may have decent incomes yet are entirely excluded from housing finance.

## 7.4 Role of Development Partners

Given the sobering facts of Africa's housing crisis, and the large economic and employment multiplier effects of housing construction, DFIs such as the AfDB and the World Bank Group have a fundamental role to play in addressing the continent's housing needs (see Table 7.1 below). The housing sector represents an opportunity for these organizations to achieve their larger development goals of industrializing Africa, and improving the life of African people for the AfDB, and reduce poverty for the World Bank.

The intervention of development partners should focus on improving the housing conditions of low-income households, promoting efficiency, and supporting innovative solutions to address the continent's colossal housing shortage. The subsequent paragraphs provide a few priority areas for development partner interventions. Based on these policy recommendations, the AfDB should develop operational guidelines for its housing sector as part of its urban development strategy.

## 7.4.1 Support Government in Its Role as Regulator

The previous discussion emphasized the crucial role of the government to design and implement effective regulations to improve the efficiency of the housing sector in Africa. However, in many instances, governments lack the institutional, human and financial capacity to fulfill this mission. Therefore, development partners should assist governments in fulfilling this role. Specifically, DFIs should assist governments in training urban planners and should provide financial assistance, if necessary, for updating urban plans. Given the importance of effective land governance systems, DFIs should assist governments in setting up appropriate institutions for land management. Given their large cross-country focus, DFIs are in a good position to assist in the transfer of lessons learned from other countries in Africa and globally. A key reform with great potential benefits is the use of computerized land registry and transfer systems. Assistance from DFIs in designing and implementing such systems can improve the functioning of land and housing markets. Similarly, a computerized approval process for building permits has shown great effect in reducing time and cost, as well as in improving transparency.

Our research has also shown that most African governments have an acute shortage of building inspectors. This often leads to delays and corruption, resulting in the lack of application of building codes, which has led to deadly accidents in some countries. Improved capacity and governance in this area is urgently needed.

Table 7.1 The role of development finance institutions

| Lending Activities | Urban Planning/Infrastructure | Land | Finance | Construction | Slums |
|---|---|---|---|---|---|
| | Urban Development and Housing policy-based operations to reform urban planning and services delivery<br><br>Investments in Sites-and-Services Projects in satellite cities to stimulate housing development<br><br>Investments in urban infrastructure projects (transport networks, electricity, etc.)<br><br>Institutional support (cadaster, local governments) | Policy-based operations focusing on land reforms (improving land governance and security of tenure)<br><br>Institutional support (modernize cadaster systems, land records, strengthen land administration)<br><br>Institutional support to promote fiscal decentralization and resource mobilization at central and local level to finance infrastructure and urbanization (tax administration systems) | Policy-based operations for housing finance reforms (putting housing at the heart of financial inclusion policies and strategies)<br><br>Credit enhancement/guarantee schemes to derisk housing finance transactions<br><br>Equity and long-term debt to support the development of the mortgage market Banks, HFCs, HMFs, Refinancing facilities)<br><br>Equity for SME developers as well as local construction and building materials sector<br><br>Debt to microfinance institutions to provide housing micro-loans and micro-mortgages<br><br>Long-term debt to mortgage originators to increase mortgage penetration<br><br>Guarantees for housing bonds and municipality bond issuances<br><br>Promote local currency bond issuance<br><br>Debt for rental housing | Investment in production of building materials<br><br>Investments in alternative building materials (cost-efficient and environmentally friendly) | Policy-based operations to reverse slum urbanism (curative and preventive policy reforms)<br><br>Investments in well-targeted Social Housing Programs |

(continued)

Table 7.1 (continued)

| | Urban Planning/ Infrastructure | Land | Finance | Construction | Slums |
|---|---|---|---|---|---|
| Non-lending Activities | Policy dialogue on how to put housing, land, service delivery and decentralization at the center of the urban planning and strategies<br><br>Technical assistance and advisory services (drafting urban planning/ strategies, capacity building for administration in charge of urbanization) | Policy dialogue and advisory services (land valuation, land formalization, property rights, modern land management techniques)<br><br>Policy dialogue (encourage the development of housing policies and the development of national land use master plans)<br><br>Technical assistance (computerizing land registries, land information system, modern land valuation techniques, resource mobilization, and land value capture, etc.)<br><br>Technical assistance (guided land development policies) | Policy dialogue and advisory services (housing finance and affordability)<br><br>Technical assistance (Financial literacy programs, prudent lending practices, revisiting banks, underwriting processes to meet the need of the unbanked and informal)<br><br>Technical assistance (establishing credit bureaus and credit information registries, adapting the financial infrastructure and engineering to respond to a risky environment, legal, and regulatory frameworks) | Policy dialogue and advisory services (reforming building codes, harmonization of legal and regulatory frameworks, standardization of building codes, norms and systems, regional dimension of industrialization, promote uptake of alternative building techniques)<br><br>Technical assistance (amending building codes, drafting legal and regulatory frameworks, new and alternative building techniques) | Policy dialogue and advisory services (technical assistance for self-builders, local artisans, and incremental house builders housing support services, construction processes, building codes and standards, housing transformation) |

On the demand side, designing and implementing institutional, legal, and regulatory frameworks to promote access to long-term finance is critical for the development of housing finance. DFIs should assist governments in putting in place the right instruments for inclusive housing finance systems.

### 7.4.2 Support Government in Its Role as an Input Provider

Providing bulk infrastructure for new housing developments or slum-upgrading programs requires large amounts of funding that may be hard to recover fully from land value capture, taxes, and the like. Hence, DFIs may need to assist by providing concessional funding to governments directly or by contributing to private sector stakeholders in PPPs. DFIs can also support governments by providing guarantee schemes for fundraising instruments such as municipal or infrastructure bonds.

### 7.4.3 Support Affordable Housing Developers

Initiatives such as the US$300 million IFC-CITIC platform that works with local housing companies to develop affordable housing projects should be supported. Technical assistance and capacity-building initiatives that strengthen the core skills of local developers to raise capital for affordable housing and facilitate knowledge sharing are ways to ensure that high-quality housing is produced at lower cost. Providing developers with equity finance will help alleviate their financial constraints, which will inherently increase private-sector investment in the production of affordable housing for all income segments.

### 7.4.4 Promote the Broadening and Deepening of Housing Finance in Africa

In addition to effective institutional, legal, and regulatory frameworks, the development of housing finance requires not only long-term financing but also adequate financial instruments to mobilize and deploy funding.

### 7.4.4.1 Assist in the Development of Secondary Mortgage Markets

The scarcity of long-term financing is one of the biggest constraints cited by banks in explaining their limited financing of the housing sector. Institutions with long-term funds, such as pension funds and insurance companies, are often prevented from investing in housing or lack proper instruments for investing. DFIs need to work with financial sectors and governments to develop those instruments. This effort should include the development of secondary mortgage markets.

In recent years, a number of countries—for instance, Egypt, Nigeria, Tanzania, and those in the West African Economic and Monetary Union—have set up mortgage refinancing companies with the help of the World Bank Group. Although this is a welcome development, the companies are limited by the deployment of shareholders' capital subscriptions or funds raised through bonds issuance, in some cases at high costs. The secondary mortgage market should be further developed to include securitization and listing in financial markets. This will allow greater participation by financial actors and will improve liquidity. DFIs should assist countries or regional markets in putting in place the necessary regulations and instruments. Guarantee schemes can also be provided to reduce the risks for a nascent market.

Real estate investment trusts (REITs) and mortgage-covered bonds are other cost-efficient instruments that provide the housing market with long-term funding, as well as open up investment opportunities for long-term institutional investors such as pension fund and insurance companies.

### 7.4.4.2 Provide Funding to Financial Intermediaries

Before supporting the full development of housing finance with a well-functioning and liquid secondary market, DFIs should provide long-term funding to financial intermediaries for on-lending to households. DFIs can also provide risk mitigation products to enable financial intermediaries to raise long-term funding. Such support can lower funding costs and hence lending rates for borrowers, which is important in making housing affordable. However, DFIs must be vigilant to ensure that households benefit from the preferential lending rates given to financial intermediaries.

Only high-income households are fully served by the current housing finance market. As such, the bulk of direct support by DFIs should be aimed at improving access and lowering financing costs for low-income and underserved markets. Credit enhancement facilities for the low-income and underserved markets will promote a more inclusive housing finance market.

DFIs should also support MFIs, which can offer products more suitable to the building process and livelihoods of low-income households. Today, microfinance housing products are not well developed within the continent as they are limited by the scarcity of funding and by high interest rates. However, there are interesting models, which were discussed in Chap. 2. Beyond financial support to MFIs, DFIs should provide technical assistance and encourage partnerships models. Bank-MFI partnerships will contribute to eliminating the financing constraint faced by MFIs, thereby enabling them to serve a swath of low-income customers while opening new markets for banks. Other partnerships could include the self-help group-bank linkage model and partnerships between NBFIs and MFIs. However, the focus should be on building sustainable and scalable systems.

## 7.5 Conclusion

In recent years, many governments have announced measures to tackle the housing crisis in their countries. However, tangible action steps have not accompanied most of these public pronouncements. The role of the government in creating an enabling environment for the housing sector is extremely critical. As demonstrated in Morocco and Ethiopia, governments cannot reach their goals of affordable housing provision with partial solutions. The provision of affordable housing depends in particular on the strong and unwavering political will of governments, as well as the development and implementation of effective housing policies. Achieving this and these policies will require strengthening the coordination among public institutions and government ministries that play a role in housing, including ministries of finance.

In view of the housing challenges catalogued in preceding chapters, it is clear that African governments on their own cannot resolve the continent's housing crisis. There is an urgent and growing need for development partners and the private sector to join government efforts to tackle the crisis. This book has provided an orientation for housing stakeholders to the identification, design, and implementation of housing sector operations. Pursuing some of the policies proposed here can help overcome the policy, regulatory, and structural barriers to addressing Africa's housing crisis.

**Open Access** This chapter is licensed under the terms of the Creative Commons Attribution 4.0 International License (http://creativecommons.org/licenses/by/4.0/), which permits use, sharing, adaptation, distribution and reproduction in any medium or format, as long as you give appropriate credit to the original author(s) and the source, provide a link to the Creative Commons license and indicate if changes were made.

The images or other third party material in this chapter are included in the chapter's Creative Commons license, unless indicated otherwise in a credit line to the material. If material is not included in the chapter's Creative Commons license and your intended use is not permitted by statutory regulation or exceeds the permitted use, you will need to obtain permission directly from the copyright holder.

# Erratum to: Housing Market Dynamics in Africa

El-hadj M. Bah, Issa Faye, Zekebweliwai F. Geh

**Erratum to:**
El-hadj M. Bah et al., Housing Market Dynamics in Africa, https://doi.org/10.1057/978-1-137-59792-2

The original version did not include the 'Acknowledgements'. These have been added to the front matter of the book.

---

The updated online version of this book can be found at
https://doi.org/10.1057/978-1-137-59792-2

© The Author(s) 2018
El-hadj M. Bah et al., *Housing Market Dynamics in Africa*,
https://doi.org/10.1057/978-1-137-59792-2_8

The manufacturer's authorised representative in the EU is Springer Nature Customer Service Centre GmbH, Europaplatz 3, 69115 Heidelberg, Germany. If you have any concerns regarding our products, please contact ProductSafety@springernature.com

Printed and bound by CPI Group (UK) Ltd, Croydon, CR0 4YY

23/03/2026

02076655-0001